# WHAT'S GOING ON?

Exploring the backstory of contemporary political polarization, *What's Going On?* recognizes that simple stories of blame and uncontested stories of polarization prove themselves to be bad stories that produce bad politics.

This book argues that stories have increasingly become matters of affect rather than meaning—instead of asking what stories mean, we are likely to ask how they make people feel. These stories are cultural tendencies that define the possibilities and limits of political action and behavior, and the book tells its own story about how the stories of America's crises have defined our political culture as they struggle over questions of ideology, identity, and social belonging. It lays out a theoretical position that recognizes the need for complicated stories and rigorous thought, pointing a way forward, out of the chaos, seeking to repair the world and offer better stories and more humane political possibilities.

This work is a vital resource for students and instructors in sociology, political science, cultural studies, media studies, and communication, in such courses as contemporary social theory, contemporary political theory, media, politics and society, and social movements and resistance.

The book will be an important guide for activists, organizers, and community field workers, and for anyone else who wishes to have a better understanding of the contemporary political moment and how to mobilize toward building a better future.

**Lawrence Grossberg** is Distinguished Professor Emeritus of Communication at the University of North Carolina at Chapel Hill and the author and editor of numerous books, including *Cultural Studies in the Future Tense* (2010), *We All Want to Change the World* (2015), *Under the Cover of Chaos* (2018), and *On the Way to Theory* (2024).

# Critical Interventions

Ecology and Revolution: Herbert Marcuse and the Challenge of a New
World System Today
*Charles Reitz*

Anxious Creativity: When Imagination Fails
*David Trend*

Rising Fascism in America: It Can Happen Here
*Anthony R. DiMaggio*

Rethinking Higher Education and the Crisis of Legitimation in Europe
*Ourania Filippakou*

Horizons of the Future: Science Fiction, Utopian Imagination, and the
Politics of Education
*Graham B. Slater*

Surveillance Education: Navigating the Conspicuous Absence of Privacy in
Schools
*Nolan Higdon and Allison Butler*

Culture, Power and Education: Representation, Interpretation, Contestation
*Peter Mayo*

Herbert Marcuse as Social Justice Educator: A Critical Introduction
*Charles Reitz*

What's Going On? The Struggle for Contemporary American Identity
*Lawrence Grossberg*

"Our public culture is composed of the stories we tell ourselves, individually and especially together. And it has become deranged. In *What's Going On?*, Lawrence Grossberg draws on his own life experience and engagements as a public intellectual to narrate America's decades of growing confusion and self-delusion. He goes beyond complaining about media manipulation and promotion of false narratives to probe underlying problems – like how we divide fact from value, affect from thought, music from politics, and academic from public life."

**Craig Calhoun,** *University Professor of Social Sciences, Arizona State University, and author of Degenerations of Democracy*

"Lawrence Grossberg is one of the greatest cultural critics in the English speaking world of the last half century. 55 years after Marvin Gaye shook up the world with *What's Going On*, a pop album teeming with politics and prophecy, Grossberg offers his summum bonum, *What's Going On?* a career defining volume that echoes Gaye's classic grappling with a world in crisis. Grossberg mines the rich world of social meaning and excavates the deep resonance of cultural identity to wrestle with who we are as a nation and how we got here. Charting a path beyond narrow ideology and partisan politics, he asks deeper questions about the stories we tell to explain how we know and think of our lives and the political and social choices we make. Grossberg wields both a mirror and a window as he questions his way – and ours too as we follow him – into more profound insight about what exactly America means, what the West offers, and how we can make meaning out of seeming meaninglessness. This is a tour de force that will leave us clearer about our ambitions and more determined to achieve a common good that seems fugitive and impossible to embrace in our deeply polarized world. Grossberg brings us nearer than most others – that is his great gift to us."

**Michael Eric Dyson,** *University Distinguished Professor of African American and Diaspora Studies and Centennial Chair in African American & Diaspora Studies, Vanderbilt University*

"This book tackles the political meltdown of our moment with staid authority, something Lawrence Grossberg has earned over the course of his career. It is a useful and important contribution to understandings of contemporary politics, culture, economics, affect, epistemology, democracy and more. This is a revealing culmination of 50 years of a cultural studies giant grappling with history as it is being made. Grossberg defends knowledge as worth fighting for and a means to a better world. It could not be more timely or necessary."

**Carolyn Hardin,** *Associate Professor of Media, Film, and Journalism and Associate Director of the Humanities Century, Miami University*

"This is a major intervention in crucial debates about contemporary politics and the sense of failure and despair about left responses to authoritarian and alt-Right movements that permeates contemporary US society. The book is lively, new, and interesting. Lawrence Grossberg is one of the leading figures in contemporary Cultural Studies, and this book is a further advancement of his distinguished contributions to understanding contemporary cultural politics of modernity."

**John Pickles,** *DW Patterson Distinguished Emeritus Professor of Geography and International Studies, University of North Carolina*

# WHAT'S GOING ON?

The Struggle for Contemporary
American Identity

*Lawrence Grossberg*

Routledge
Taylor & Francis Group

NEW YORK AND LONDON

Designed cover image: #1909641286 Shutterstock

First published 2026
by Routledge
605 Third Avenue, New York, NY 10158

and by Routledge
4 Park Square, Milton Park, Abingdon, Oxon, OX14 4RN

*Routledge is an imprint of the Taylor & Francis Group, an informa business*

ISBN: 978-1-041-12002-5 (hbk)
ISBN: 978-1-041-11999-9 (pbk)
ISBN: 978-1-003-66258-7 (ebk)

DOI: 10.4324/9781003662587

Typeset in Sabon
by Newgen Publishing UK

*To Barbara and Zachariah Claypole White, wife and son, novelist and poet, who are the reason I continue to care, hope, struggle, and think.*

*And to my mother, Miriam Grossberg. I never said it enough: Thank you. I am sorry.*

*And to the music makers, who help me find order in the chaos, every day, even when I think it is impossible.*

# CONTENTS

*Invocation: To Repair the World*      *xiii*
*Preface: How Does It Feel?*      *xv*
*Author's Note # 1: Under the Cover of Chaos*      *xxii*
*Acknowledgments*      *xxiii*

1   Tilting at Windmills      1
    *Stories 1*
    *Thinking 7*
    *Author's Note #2 12*
    *Politics 13*
    *The Road Ahead 15*
    *The Humility in Arrogance 17*

**PART I**
**Everybody Knows**      **21**

2   A Question of Affect      23
    *Music and Affect 24*
    *Four Structures of Feeling 25*

3   The Problem of Thinking      31
    *Stories about Knowledge 31*
       Infoglut   31
       Conspiracies   33

Commensuration Crises  36
Valorizing Experience  38
*Media Anti-Intellectualism 38*
*The Threat of Relativism 41*

4   On the Way to Thinking                                             45
*Conceptual Thinking 46*
*Critical/Theoretical Thinking 48*
*A Brief Detour: Anti-Intellectualism on the Left 49*
*Critique 52*

5   Contextual Thinking                                                56
*Contexts and Compositions 56*
*Doing Contextuality 59*

6   The Discipline of the Conjuncture                                  63
*Conjunctural Thinking 64*
*Constructing Problem Spaces (Problematization) 67*
*Conjunctural Analysis 68*

**PART II**
**You Want It Darker**                                                  **71**

7   The Problem Space of Affect                                        73
*Affect and Discourse 74*
*Problematizing Affect 77*
*Living in an Affective Landscape 79*
*Revisiting Structures of Feeling 80*
*Conclusion 86*

8   The Problem Space of the Modern                                    89

**PART III**
**In the Dreams That We Dream, We Ask What Have We**
**Done?**                                                              **95**

9   We're on a Marathon (Prelude)                                      97

10  We Stumble and Fall: The Liberal and Hegemonic
    Tendencies                                                        103
*The First Moment 103*

*The Second Moment and the New Right 105*
*The Second Moment and an Uncertain Left 113*
*Conclusion 116*

11  We Find We're Alone: Stories of Polarization                    118
*The Third Conjunctural Moment 119*
*Affective Polarization 122*
*Polarization and Identity Stories 126*
*Conclusion 131*

12  We Beg Warmth from the Sun: The Speculative
    Tendency                                                       134
*The Enlightenment versus the Pluriverse 135*
*The Enlightenment versus Ontology 137*
*The Modern versus the Other 141*

13  We Stand for What's Right: The Pseudo-Revolutionary
    Tendency                                                       146
*Politics as Fanaticism 148*
*Overturning Truth 153*
*A Necessary Detour 155*
*Politics as Chaos 159*
*The PRT Right 160*
*The PRT Left 164*
*Conclusion 166*


**PART IV**
**We Would Build a New World if We Only Knew How**            **169**


14  There Is a Crack in Everything (Politics)                      171
*A Popular Politics 171*
*Higher Education 174*
*The Popular 179*
*A Movement of movements 181*
*Conclusion 188*

15  That's How the Light Gets in (Stories)                         190
*Engaging with Stories 192*
*Everyday Stories 195*
*Understanding 200*
*The Pragmatics of Climate Change Stories 201*

16  I Wish There Was a Treaty We Could Sign
    (Difference and Belonging)                                   206
    *A Story of Differences 208*
    *A Story of Belonging 210*
    *Conclusion 212*

17  Dance Me to the End of Love                                  214
    *Communication Fail 215*
    *Hope and Care 216*
    *You Don't Need a Secret Chord to Love Music 218*

*Appendix: The Academy and the Crises of Knowledge*             220
*Not Quite a Glossary of Key Terms (and Not*
    *Quite a Summary)*                                           229
*Index*                                                         234

# INVOCATION: TO REPAIR THE WORLD

The Jewish principle of *Tikkun Olam* calls for a different kind of politics: Neither a war nor a revolution; neither the fatigue of inevitability nor the pretense of change. It seeks an ordinary politics, bound up with the everyday lives of people. A politics for an always imperfect, fragile, and changing world. A politics for people willing to embrace their fallibility and uncertainty. It offers the hope that our sacrifice to ameliorate the suffering of others, without distinguishing neighbors and strangers, opens the greatest possibilities of joy and love. It asks us to bring order out of chaos, to bring new harmonies out of the many competing voices of the world. It implores us, simply, to leave the world better than we found it.

| | |
|---|---|
| עולם תיקון | (Hebrew) |
| العالم إصلاح | (Arabic) |
| исправление мира | (Russian) |
| 世界修复 | (Simplistic Chinese) |
| दुनिया की मरमत | (Hindi) |
| Rekebisha dunia | (Swahili) |
| Reparar el mundo | (Spanish) |

# PREFACE: HOW DOES IT FEEL?

America is facing more crises and threats than anyone can deal with. And in these precarious times, there is no system in place to help, and the rules you thought governed life no longer seem to apply. The political-economic game is rigged, and people's actions have little or no effect. Everyone is frightened, desperate, distrustful, cynical, nihilistic, angry, hopeless, numb, exhausted, enraged, and stuck. They feel deeply threatened by the uncertainty and chaos and seek solace wherever it becomes available. They are certain that everyone else is becoming mean, closed off, selfish, callous, entitled, etc.

No one agrees who is to blame—the left or the right, capitalism or socialism, culture or technology, religion or secularism, fascism or liberalism, social movements or the state—but whoever it is, they are betraying America and western civilization and destroying everything precious. It is obvious that society has become so polarized that there is no way forward, no way out of the quagmire. People have abandoned any hope of understanding (to say nothing of empathizing with) the other side. That has become the limit of their political imagination.

There are at least three ways these experiences are understood: First, we are stuck in a moment of transition, facing an impasse that we cannot escape. Second, we are witnessing the intentional destruction of the democratic liberal nation-state that has flourished since the postwar period and this is bad. And third, we are witnessing the intentional destruction of the democratic liberal nation-state that has flourished since the postwar period and this is good.

The difference between the latter two depends upon how different populations lived through the bubble of prosperity and freedom that characterized the postwar decades, and the stories they came to believe. Lots of people felt that they were excluded from the bubble, or perhaps that they were, at some point, banished from sharing in its benefits. Consequently, while many people find these feelings obvious in the present moment, I am sure that there are many others for whom they have always been obvious. Their world has always been crazy, always been coming to an end, always been the place where power was quite happy to fail as long as it could ensure its own survival.

Just as importantly, the country has been going to hell in a handbasket for some time. Despite the feeling that we are living through a uniquely dangerous moment, many of the frightening, insane, and inane things that are happening, many of the things that lead us to think that this could only be happening in some deranged movie or some impossibly distorted reality, have been observed before, both quite recently and in eras past. People have thought everything was falling apart, that the dominant institutions that were supposed to protect them and hold the order of the world in place had failed, that lunatics had taken control. Many generations have been horrified, scared, angered, hopeless, desperate, numb, or oblivious in the face of the end of everything, or the possibility of humanity's self-annihilation. Many saw their battle against the monsters as humanity's last chance. This is the seductive romance of the revolutionary story, doomed to failure. Others embrace the failure in the nihilist's tragic void of self-revelation. Maybe we have forgotten because ... we are too caught up in our own melodramas. But you can hear it repeated over and over in the music of the past decades, from Barry McGuire's "Eve of Destruction" (1965), to Marvin Gaye's *What's Going On?* (1971)—the source of my title—and 4 Non Blondes's "What's Up?" (1992).

This matters! Keep reminding yourself of this. There are new things defining the present context, but these feelings are not by themselves new. People will say that no one else has felt these feelings so strongly, or that they were not so reasonable, etc. The feelings are real and there is some truth behind them, but it will only be when we understand them contextually that we will glimpse what is different about the present.

Events may take on new intensities and new meanings as they are located in ever-changing relationships. Like notes in a song, pieces in a puzzle, or characters in a story, you often don't know what's going on until you start putting things together and imagining the possible outcomes. That is the challenge: To account for the feeling of the uniqueness of the present moment by telling better stories.

But perhaps I should start by saying something about this book. It is deeply personal, driven partly by a lifetime of ethical and political passion. It is, therefore, partly autobiographical. My intellectual and political lives have always been inseparable, determined in large measure by where I was inserted into history and how I positioned myself in those contexts. I am an early baby boomer, who grew up in some of the most exhilarating (and what seemed to be, at the time, the most frightening) times in recent U.S. history. The baby boomers are almost always identified with the various social movements, protests, countercultures, celebratory practices, spiritual regimes, and popular musics of the 1960s and early 70s. I was an active participant and sometimes minor leader in this "Movement of movements." Eventually, partly out of desperation, I was also among those who returned to the academy because I believed that knowledge and ideas were the soil from which effective and creative oppositional strategies might emerge. I needed time to understand the many differences condensed into the Movement. I needed time to consider what it had done, where it had changed things, and where it had failed to do so. I needed time to make sense of the cultural-political landscape. I needed time to examine the intersection of my political activism, my cultural pleasures, and my intellectual struggles. 60 years on, I ask myself, what have we done? And the answers are still unclear. My optimism is all but gone. The best I can say, looking back, is that my despair has moved on from where it began, all those decades ago.

The truth is, to put it simply, that like many others, I feel deeply conflicted. Did we baby boomers fuck it up? Not exactly. We made some progress on some problems but not enough; perhaps just enough to continue the efforts. But we also ignored some problems, we were unaware of some problems (and perhaps could not have been aware of some), and, no doubt, we made some problems worse without realizing it. We opened up possibilities, but we did not see all the ways those openings could be taken up. We never found a politics that was comfortable "on the far side of vengeance," to borrow the words of Seamus Heaney; we never found a way to live in a different relation to the future. I no longer know to which world I am answerable—to that which shaped me in both opposition and sustenance for so many decades, or that which now confronts me? I no longer know what my responsibilities are.

In ways too numerous to list, we have been living in the shadows of the 60s and its various political and cultural movements. It transformed mainstream culture as well as left and progressive politics, and it helped birth a new conservative movement. Equally important, it brought culture—and, in particular, a landscape of feelings—to the main stage of politics. It gave expression, especially in its music, to feelings of absurdity and despair and of pain and sacrifice (but also of hope and joy) that sound extraordinarily familiar today. And it experimented with political tactics that blurred the line between enjoyment and power. I sometimes think that the 60s have come back to haunt us, but in ways we had never imagined. The bottom line: I feel angry, guilty, and depressed about unfulfilled dreams. And horrified by what those dreams have become. I wonder what sort of responsibility I have to the present.

I am fighting back the feeling that my life's work has been a failure. I never thought that I would change the world, but I did think I was part of an intellectual movement attempting to repair the world, to intervene into and help shape the tides of change, the directions of history. But given what has happened in the U.S. at least, over the past seventy-five years (the time span I have studied), it sounds rather absurd today. As Springsteen put it: is a dream a lie if it doesn't come true or is it something worse? I guess I was living in an intellectual fantasy; I had a dream and I was hoping that my work would make a small contribution to realizing that dream. Talk about arrogance and delusion.

The questions that have driven my work have been shaped by my sense that my life, the life of my generation, has run parallel to America's steady drift away from the progressive values of the stories I hold dearest. These developments have been interrupted and contradicted along the way by victories and many moments of joy, but the overall trends haven't looked good. I have been scared since I began studying American politics and culture. And like so many others, I am terrified by what is happening after Trump's second victory—by the ravaging of the country and by the numbers who have surrendered to its politics or given up and withdrawn from politics completely. And however much I am happy to see the rapid growth of protests and alternative communications, I worry that they are reproducing old, short-term tactics and old simple stories.

Speaking from my own position on the left, we need to be brutally honest with ourselves. Demonstrations and protests are not going to stop Trump/MAGA/DOGE; they are important to keep our spirits up, to tell us we are not alone, and to tell Trump we will not go gently into ... The courts may or may not help us. But we have to ask, what might actually work: Money will not save us. They will always have more than we do, unless we can convince some billionaires to think differently. The Democratic Party seems to assume that even those who support it are idiots, sending out messages like this, from Nany Pelosi: "The New York Times just reported that our resistance to Trump's extremism is 'TIRED.' I know that couldn't be farther from the truth – and I'm asking you to help prove it with just $1." Really? That's all you've got?

I don't mean to insult anybody, but it doesn't seem like there's a lot of useful thinking going on in this moment of crisis or maybe is it better to say that a lot of the thinking that's going on is about what we already know and often what is and has been obvious for some time: as if we were discovering that Trump is producing chaos or that we're facing "conspiracies" or that the wealthy are trying to grab the more of the wealth of America or that we're still fighting racism. But there's very little discussion about how we got here and how we're going to get out of here. And almost none about the left's role in that history, not as blame but as lessons for how we might think about formulating better strategies and better stories.

People tell me now is not the time to criticize ourselves or our allies, but it is a question of how and why we are criticizing. It is not the time to criticize them because they do not meet our standards of perfection. It is the time to criticize them because they are not considering their own role in the story of how we got to where we are, and in the responses to the exigencies and demands of the moment.

We should start by accepting the unacceptable: They won, we lost. It is not only the Electoral College. Republicans won the popular vote even if it was only a fraction of the population. The left started the culture wars, but the right is winning them. Did they break the law? I don't know. Did they cheat and break all sorts of rules and norms, undermining democracy? Yes. Do they work through forms of intimidation? Yes. Did we know what they were going to do when they took power? Yes. Did they tell us they were doing it? Yes. Did we do anything about it? Apparently not. Did we know that people resented the left's arrogance and what they understood to be its self-righteousness? Yes. Did we do anything about it? Apparently not. Did we have strategies? No. Have we mounted a cultural campaign? Only one that assumes we are right and ignores or attacks those who disagree with us.

The dilemma is that you cannot predict what will work, or even how it will work. You cannot predict what stories might speak to which fractions of MAGA or of Trump supporters. The right has reconfigured what can be thought, what can be imagined. But you can put yourself in a better starting point by thinking, analyzing, criticizing, and strategizing. It will demand a willingness to experiment, to fail, to understand why you failed, and to try again. Of course, it will demand resources, including money, but that is what the right has been doing for decades.

I always believed I had work to do and something to contribute. I do not know if anyone is listening. Increasingly, it feels like you put out a message in a proverbial bottle and you don't know what will happen to it, whether anyone's taking it seriously, or even reading it. Most likely, you don't know if anyone is sending the same message out in their own bottles. I think my work has given me some useful and interesting things to say, as arrogant as that might sound. I still do. So, I keep asking, "what's going on?" and how do we "get outta this place?" I assumed that the best way to answer these questions was to ask, how did we get here? Why do we keep repeating such horrors? We need a different kind of story because the story we tell matters! I wanted to tell a better story than those that were generally available, one that looked back from the present and forward from the past.

I sometimes think I have been writing the same book for 50 years: A political history of the present of the U.S. since the 1950s, through the lens of the relations between culture and politics. I started with the mysteries of the relations between popular music and the 60s movements and moved on to the broader relations of postmodern culture and politics. But I got caught up in the success of the new right (and the victory of Ronald Reagan). That was quickly followed by how the changing conditions of kids in the U.S. were connected to the "compassionate conservatism" of the younger Bush. Questions continued to appear: The failures of the left during the Obama years and, finally, the rise of Trump and new, more reactionary, formations of the right (Grossberg, 1992, 2005, 2015, 2018). I had trouble keeping up. I had to constantly adjust my own thinking to the task at hand. And as the context changed, as my own thinking changed, the questions themselves changed as well.

This book is as close as I have come to an answer to my questions. While it marks the end of my long academic career, it is not academic (although I am sure some people will still find it too academic). It does not present a traditionally empirical argument; it does not attempt to persuade you with evidence and data. There is simply too much evidence, an overwhelming amount of evidence, providing too many contradictory examples, which are open to too many interpretations. Since you are always having to choose your examples, it is hard to avoid the appearance of selecting those that prove your point.

Even when you can identify patterns in the evidence, they do not seem capable, on their own, of resolving our uncertainties. But such observed patterns or relations, whether the wisdom of pundits or recent additions to what is obvious to everyone, often serve as my starting points (the end of stories we have forgotten). Nor does this book present a scholarly argument. I do not delve into the rich—and often contradictory scholarship—on almost every topic I touch upon. There is always more to be read, and there are always people who know more than the people I have read. Scholarship is an exhausting but exhilarating task. But it is not my task here.

Its argument is compositional: It tries to compose a story out of the stories we tell ourselves by distilling over 50 years of research, thought, publications, and public arguments. You might think of it like trying to orchestrate a musical piece, always defined by a balance of possibilities and constraints. My task is pragmatic: I am not reaching for some final and indisputable truth but for a possible contribution to a larger conversation. This book proposes a number of interconnected stories to help us better understand where we are, how we got here, and how we might get out of this place. It is an attempt to go on thinking, and a call to find ways of repairing the world, together.

Let me leave you with a quotation from Bertolt Brecht:

The truth must be spoken with a view to the results it will produce in the sphere of action... Nowadays, anyone who wishes to combat lies and ignorance and to write the truth must overcome at least five difficulties. He must have the courage to write the truth when truth is everywhere opposed; the keenness to recognize it, although it is everywhere concealed;

the skill to manipulate it as a weapon; the judgment to select those in whose hands it will be effective; and the cunning to spread the truth among such persons.

*(Brecht, 1935)*

## References

Brecht, Bertolt. "Writing the Truth Five difficulties." https://autonomies.org/2024/06/bertolt-brecht-writing-the-truth-five-difficulties-1935/

Grossberg, Lawrence. *We Gotta Get out of This Place: Popular Conservatism and Postmodern Culture*. New York and London: Routledge, 1992.

Grossberg, Lawrence. *Caught in the Crossfire: Kids, Politics and America's Future*. Boulder: Paradigm Books, 2005.

Grossberg, Lawrence. *We All Want to Change the World: The Paradox of the U.S. Left (A Polemic)*. 2015. www.academia.edu/13048909/We_all_want_to_change_the_world_The_paradox_of_the_U_S_left_A_polemic_

Grossberg, Lawrence. *Under the Cover of Chaos: Trump and the Battle for the American Right*. London: Pluto Press, 2018.

# AUTHOR'S NOTE # 1: UNDER THE COVER OF CHAOS

This book was completed well before the election of 2024. I have resisted the temptation to rewrite it in the light of Trump's second electoral victory and the early days of his administration. But I have continuously revised it as every conversation presents new thoughts. I think Trump/Musk etc. are best understood in the light of the larger and longer story that I have begun to tell here. I will only observe that Trump seems set on letting loose the dogs of chaos, scoring points with various MAGA demands and even more with spectacular promises of wealth. Chaos dissipates and drains energy and causes panic. (I recommend you read my 2018 take on the rise of Trump and MAGA, *Under the Cover of Chaos*.)

What is happening "under the cover of chaos" is still unclear. It may be a simple story about a con job to steal America's information/wealth or the establishment of a new kind of fascism—and some people will stand opposed while others retreat into fear and silence. Or it may be an equally simple story about a strongman restoring American greatness and a new American empire—and some people may think profit is the American way and accept that there is always great pain. But it may be much more complicated. The present chaos may call for more than scattered opposition and the repetition of past accusations or acquiescence; the present chaos may implode, taking the attempts at order with it, for any number of reasons. We may need to help it along. We certainly need to ask: What happens after? Will we have better stories that don't suggest simply rebuilding old failures? Will we be able to identify people who, for reasons unknown to us, supported positions we found despicable, but who now seek new stories? Will we be able to talk to them? Whatever happens, we will need some serious thinking and better stories. We cannot know, in advance, what stories might open possibilities for repairing the nation and the world.

# ACKNOWLEDGMENTS

This book is a temporary rest-stop in a life of conversations—some in the real world of people, some in the strangely real worlds of technology, and some in the eccentrically real worlds of my head. Some have been going on for quite some time, and some lasted only for a moment. Some have been with friends and people I know well, some with professional acquaintances, and some with relative strangers. Some involve ancestral voices and some the shared voices of public and popular cultures.

I cannot separate myself from these conversations. They have their own agency; at different times, they demand to be heard, often challenging each other. Which voices get to speak and which speak the loudest is never guaranteed. Some of the voices have grown weak or remain only as echoes. Some of the conversations have faded; some of the sources been lost to the failures of memory, leaving only traces without an inventory. To those who recognize their ideas here, thank you for your generosity. I am sorry if I failed to sufficiently acknowledge my debt.

Each conversation has its own textures and tones; they range from enthusiastic agreement to enjoyable difference, from pleasurable engagement to horrified avoidance, and from playful banter to contemptuous dismissal, but they almost always involve mutual questioning and learning. The conversations continue, and as they do, I continue to revise my thinking—and up until the last minute, this book has continued to evolve. I cannot capture all the pathways, nor all the passions and demands, so I offer a snapshot, akin to the monologue you overhear of someone talking on their mobile phone. For this, I apologize. Because I am not a better writer, I have to ask you to be better readers.

Every voice has its own backstory; in my head, each has a beginning but never ends. Some were my teachers: Stuart Hall, Jim Carey, Richard Hoggart, Richard Taylor, Hayden White, and Jarold Ramsey. Others nurtured me in my studies: Jim Kaufmann, Lewis Beck, Loren Baritz, N. O. Brown, and Calvin Schrag. So many friends continue my education: John Clarke, John Pickles, Meaghan Morris, Paul Gilroy, Dick Hebdige, Chris Lundberg, Ken Wissoker, Cathy Davidson, Ellen Wartella, Chuck Whitney, Chris Clemens, Della Pollock, Catherine Hall, David Sontag, Henry Giroux, and Janet Newman. And there are still more voices: Roman Horak, Christina Lutter, Stefan Erdei, Andre Frankovits, Chen Kuan-Hsing, Anne Allison, Michael Hardt, Wang Xiaoming, Arturo Escobar, Tony Bennett, Simon Frith, Dilip Gaonkar, Ghassan Hage, Mikko Lehtonen, Juan Ricardo Aparicio, and Eduardo Restrepo. And along the way, I met so many people who supported me, who enriched and enlivened the conversation. Many of them became dear friends. I thank you all.

Some of the most cherished voices belong to the graduate students who have allowed me to teach them and to learn with them. I will have to be satisfied with acknowledging those who have helped me directly with this book: Jennifer Slack, Gil Rodman, Greg Seigworth, Ted Striphas, Bryan Behrenshausen, Carolyn Hardin, Andrew Davis, Megan Wood, Nick Gerstner, Preston Adcock, and Victoria Le Sweatman. The rest of you know who you are; please know that I am grateful for our conversations.

And there are the voices of the undergraduates, too many to name, who made my academic career more interesting and fun than I had any right to expect. I have often been in awe of your possibilities. You provided the testing ground for the ideas that became the substance of almost everything I published. But I would be remiss not to acknowledge those special moments and relations that have often highlighted my career, including Jon Ginoli and Sally Green) at Illinois, and Sarah Bufkin, Hudson Vincent, Vera Parra, Ben Elkind, and Ariana Lutterman at UNC. This book, however, was written after my retirement, without the benefit of your generous listening. I have missed you. And I fear the book has suffered as a result.

All of you, all the voices, deserve part of the credit for this book. I thank all of you for your friendship, for your willingness to challenge and criticize me when I needed it, and for your love and loyalty even when I didn't deserve it.

The publication of this book owes a special debt to my long-time friend and comrade Henry Giroux, who has always stood with me, and to Michael Gibson, my editor at Routledge, who championed this book against the prevailing academic and commercial wisdom.

# 1

# TILTING AT WINDMILLS

This book tells (part of) a story about contemporary America by looking at
the increasingly important role of political culture, telling a story about the
stories we tell ourselves. It thinks about the relations among stories, feelings,
and politics. Hopefully, doing so will allow us to see the transformative
possibilities of what can easily appear to be something that is merely
happening around us, to us.

## Stories

Stories are expressive (discursive) forms that impose order on chaos; whether
they find it already there or construct it is irrelevant for the moment. Stories
are the organizations in which we live; they specify how we live in the world.

Stories are composed of the relations of various voices, not all of which
need be human; but the human voices are usually the loudest and the most
seductive. You can think of voices as positions that can be taken up or
occupied, each having its own capacities, depending on where and how it
participates in the story. Stories call you into their space-times, their rhythms,
their possibilities, their way of being in the world, and, hence, their reality.
Stories crystallize ways of living, of inhabiting a world.

Stories make sense of the world for us; they tell us what things mean,
how they fit together, and what the whole thing means when taken together.
They tell us who and where we are, how we got here, and where we might be
heading; they tell us how we feel, how to live, how the world is supposed to
be, and how we can get there. They tell us what we can desire and imagine.
They dictate the ways we calculate our choices. Stories are our imaginations
made concrete and livable. They tell us what matters and what does not. They

DOI: 10.4324/9781003662587-1

enable us, even direct us, to see and hear certain experiences, complications, and contradictions while remaining blind and deaf to others. They tell us where we belong, what sorts of relations can or should exist among different groups, and how to live with differences; they simultaneously connect and disconnect people.

There is no prescribed material of a story: It need not be verbal; and there is no prescribed form: It need not be narrative. The tattoos I wear and the music I love are stories that compose my life. Calendars are stories. The arts are stories, and the sciences as well. A story need not have a beginning and an end (although it certainly can); it only needs a middle, a between. In other words, I am not talking about a story as a thing that you can hold on to and reproduce. I am talking about the story that exists in its telling, the story that is alive, that has a truth because it feels alive. A story is greater than the sum of its parts and greater than any single telling.

People need to believe that their place in the world and how they live their lives make sense and are even, in some sense, virtuous. Sometimes, stories enable us to feel that we deserve whatever comfort and dignity we have, and that, in the end, overall, we are the good guy in at least some of our own stories. Our stories can change; they may contradict one another, and each may be full of contradictions. But they are deeply felt, deeply inserted into our very being, and often not entirely within our control.

Everyone's stories are composed of elements drawn from the many stories they have heard and shared, both private and public; from family and friends, from schools, churches, and work, from the media and politicians. Hence, most of their stories, as personal as they may feel, are never entirely their own; they are shared with many others. For the past decades, many of the most powerful stories have been drawn from a highly contested political culture.

Such public stories offer visions of some part of or even the whole of society; they define its identity and our expectations. They tell us what sorts of people populate it, and what sorts of actions and events are common. They tell us what is typical and, as a result, they give us the frameworks we use to understand any particular image or information we may confront. For example, most of us operate with stories that tell us the "truth" of urban, rural, and suburban life, even though we may have not experienced them. Most of us operate with stories that tell us the "truth" about others—immigrants, minorities, religious orthodoxies, etc.—and we often fit our experiences into the frameworks provided by the stories. Even if experiences contradict the stories, or the stories fail us, that does not guarantee that we would seek new stories rather than doubling down on the old ones.

Generally, these are simple stories. Simple stories say: This is what cities are like; this is who southern whites are; this is who immigrants are; this is what universities do; this is liberalism; these are Trump supporters; this is what trans people do; this is what vaccines do; this is what tariffs do; this is who's to blame; and so forth. Usually, simple stories leave out at least half of the story. They tell us how the other side is doing whatever it is doing but write themselves out of that history, as if it was never part of the real action and has no responsibility. There is enjoyment in repeating the same stories, assuming that it will work this time (whether or not it has worked in the past): Basically, it's the same old things, perhaps in disguise. (e.g., it is basically the same capitalism, the same racism, the same dehumanization, the same elitism, the same liberalism, etc.). Browse the many online sites or blogs, read the many publications, listen to the many screeds and manifestos of either political side. You will find too many almost liturgical incantations that we are caught in the throes of the same evil institutions of power that have been operating for some time, and while many generations have thought that these forces had achieved the height of success in their lifetimes, eradicating both opposition and the imagination of other possibilities, today it is finally true.

How stories shape our lives, and our places in the world, is a more complicated matter. A story offers people a position they can inhabit or imagine inhabiting and, hence, it contributes something to their sense of themselves and a viable way of living. It captures people, speaks to them, and pulls them into their spaces. It may even tell people how they are going to get somewhere else and pull others along with them. What you might think of as the most ludicrous conspiracy theory speaks to someone, resonates with them, and fits in with the other stories in which they live. It is not a matter of truth, and saying that such stories are crazy or false is making what logicians call a category mistake: Comparing apples and automobiles. You may not like how they work or what their effects are; you may not think that they offer "reasonable" accounts of what's going on, but that is not what is at stake.

I am concerned with the difference between bad and better stories (an admittedly odd scale, since I don't talk about good stories). For the most part, simple stories are bad stories, and as I will constantly repeat, bad stories make bad politics. The problem with simple stories is not that they are not true; they often contain some truth. They problem is that they are arrogant; they speak, whether intentionally or not, as if their partial truths were the whole truth. They see the world in a grain of sand.

They claim to have mined down past the complications, past the chaos, and identified the Truth of what's going on. Sometimes it is found in a single domain (e.g., finance, white supremacism, revolutionary religious movements); sometimes it is explained by forces that have taken advantage of a single experience (e.g., "obscurantism" as opposed to reason, social isolation as opposed to community); sometimes it involves a specific contradiction (e.g., between wealth and competition). So many stories end up filling in the details of our depression, offering particular conspiracies. They offer micro-stories as if they could stand by themselves and make sense of everything going on. It is easy to be overwhelmed and confused. It is easy to see everything as a threatening monstrosity. (I hope I do not end up doing the same thing.)

It is too easy to allow the complexities to disappear into moral certainties and political condemnation and embrace a glib anti-intellectualism. Public discourse is reduced to normative sermons followed by an indictment of the perpetrators, be they individuals, institutions, or a broad swatch of the population, usually known in advance. And once you know who is to blame, and who is complicitous (even if they did not know it), the story can have a happy ending. But of course, it rarely does. It is not sufficient to identify, indict, and judge (especially without much possibility of punishment or redress).[1]

As you will see, I think the left (my use of the term will become clear shortly but whatever it is, I am a part of it) has not successfully pushed back against the increasing rightward turn of the nation, or against the rise to power of a reactionary right political force. In 2025, people are looking for signs of hope and for explanations of why they are so hard to find. They are asking how could this (Trump-Musk) happen? How did this happen? How did the right win the support of significant and diverse segments of the population? How does it continue unchecked?

The left has often found comfort in telling itself a number of bad, simple stories that always locate the blame elsewhere, and it continues to do so. It blames, e.g., a small cadre of evil and greedy conspiracists who have overwhelmed us with lies and misinformation while fueling the flames of hatred. It blames social media, elite wealth, anti-rationalism, the press (for acting like this was business and politics as usual), etc. And when necessary, it blames a significant number of its fellow citizens, who are stupid, gullible, self-absorbed, poorly educated, and irrational; or perhaps they are evil, fascists, and filled will hatred (racists, misogynists, etc.). Sometimes, it seems that anyone who opposes any of the central pillars of the left agenda or thinks it may have gone too far—be it affirmative action (DEI), or trans rights, or unions—can be called out as either ignorant or bigoted. They can become the enemy.

The not so hidden message of such stories—I see no reason not to call them conspiracy stories—is that it is not the left's fault. The left can tell itself: We tried to stop it. We did all we could. In 2024, we warned the country. We told them Trump, Inc. were fascists, racists, sexists (even rapists), liars, conspiracy mongers, greedy, and corrupt. We protested, signed petitions, and registered voters. We threatened catastrophe if Trump won and promised wonderful changes if he didn't. Apparently, lots of people didn't believe us or did not care. Still, it's not on us; we're not to blame. After all, we were right. The result is that the left has, for all practical purposes, written itself out of the history of the rightward movement of the country and the recent victory of the reactionary right. The left's conspiracy stories only make defeat palatable.

History is never that simple, and political struggles are never defined solely by the unthwarted advance of one movement, however rocky it may be. Struggles are struggles precisely because they involve competing forces, movements, and tendencies. We need to write the left back into the story but not as another locus of blame. We need to ask what part the left has played in the story.

History is not about conspiracies, which doesn't mean they are not real. It is rarely made by any single conspiracy if only because there are always so many competing conspiracies. But if conspiracies suggest secrecy, the so-called conspiracies of the right have been surprisingly public. We should probably call them strategies instead. Plotting to achieve your goals is not a conspiracy or, if it is, it is the conspiracy woven into the heart of representative democracy. Strategies are the politics of the long term (at least of decades). They are built on shared knowledge of what's going on and of the possibilities for intervention and change. The most successful strategies will also prepare for contingencies: Particular tactics may not have the desired effects, or they may be taken up in unforeseen ways; they may have to be reconsidered, or tweaked, or repeated but somewhere else; they may have to be reconceived and even possibly renounced.

Let me offer one small example of what it means to be strategically prepared. In my home state of North Carolina, Republicans are challenging 65,000+ votes in the state Supreme Court election. I doubt that they picked those voters at random the day after the election. There is a reason—however ludicrous—for each challenge. My wife met one person on the list at a rally; the challenge to her ballot came from a slight discrepancy 20 years ago, which had been fixed 20 years ago. Think of the labor invested in this effort, on the off chance that they would need it. Five months after the election, the matter has yet to be settled. This is likely a test for a strategy that can be replicated in other elections.

Much of what has happened over the past 50 years has been the result of strategic politics. It has not proceeded as a single smooth line but as a learning curve of trial and error, fueled by serious wealth. That doesn't mean that there weren't conspiracies behind the scenes, which often played vital roles. But it has been driven as well by shared understandings of the possibilities of American politics. Despite what the left often thinks, there is serious intellectual work, often competing ideas and intelligent stories, behind the right.

The result of absenting itself is that the left has never taken up a strategic politics, either in response to the right's attacks or to forge an alternative affirmative project. It has rarely prepared itself for what it knew had a reasonable chance of happening. It knew what might be coming because the right was surprisingly public about its long-term strategic politics—its goals, operations, and tactics. It literally announced that cultural politics would play a central role, and its use of simple stories was there for all to see. For example, its plans for overturning Roe v Wade, its attacks on DEI, its anti-immigration politics, etc. were never part of a secret conspiracy; enough was shaped, debated, and storied online for the left to be aware of the playbook, and to have had counterstrategies and better stories in place. Unfortunately, all too often, the left simply ignored the challenges and, dare I say, opportunities to prepare itself for the coming storm. Its part in history was, in large measure, written by its decision to operate off-stage, in other political scenes. Those scenes are important, but did they preclude the possibility of a strategic politics organized in response to the failures of existing governance and the strategic efforts of the right?

We need better stories and better ways of telling them because the stories we tell matter! The better story (I doubt there is ever, finally, a one and only best story) depends largely on what you expect the story to do, on where it may enable you to move toward. A better story listens to the demands of the world, listens to the problems that the world poses, and allows the world to answer back to its story. But it knows that it can only embrace so much of the world's chaos. A better story listens to the stories of the people it is trying to address, but it does not take their stories for granted or as truth. It is no less empirical than what we commonly think of as the most empirical sciences, but it does not claim some unique power or privilege. Better stories are constantly conversing with other stories. As a result, a better story never claims to encompass all of the messy realities of the present.

Better stories allow for the possibility that they may be wrong or still dangerously oversimplified. Sometimes, stories fall apart, they are criticized, or they end in crisis, and new stories have to emerge. Better stories are concerned with making visible and enabling the possibilities of change; they constitute a context of possibilities. They seek to open up the present to other futures, to other "possible" realities, but insist on remaining firmly anchored in an understanding of the present. Better stories work in the gap between the failed present and the possible future, but there are no guarantees as to how the relation will be worked out.

A better story begins with the stories in which people are already living— the simple stories, the bad stories, and the "good" stories. It does not dismiss them by assuming that those who live in them are stupid or ignorant. They may not be educated according to some pregiven standards; they may be lazy in ways that allow them to stay in their comfort zones, but, then, aren't we all. Nor can they be dismissed so easily on moral grounds. Moral truths have meaning and truth (usually they are assumed to be self-evident) only within a story.

A better story recognizes that people's lives are complicated and even contradictory, and they live in multiple stories. It seeks to understand them, how they have come about, how they have successfully called people into their imagined visions and lived realities, and what work they do on the larger field of political culture. It examines how stories are related and calculates the state of play within and between the stories—the field of possible change. Only with understanding is judgment possible.

Better stories put the pieces together and listen to the symphony of stories, however cacophonous it may seem at first. This book brings together a number of the best stories I can tell about the political culture, knowing that there are other stories that need to be told. I hope that, taken together, they might enable us to see our present moment in a different light and to grasp something more about the stories we are telling. I am not suggesting that culture (stories) is the singular truth of the present. I do think too many of our stories bracket out culture, or at least its complexity. My stories may prove to be wrong, depending on what other stories and subplots I have missed or misread. It is the best I can do for the moment.

One thing I am sure of: Culture matters. The stories we live in are the glue, the rhythm section, that binds together the many aspects of our lives into a song, even if it is not quite so melodious. And those studies might provide some ways to begin to repair the nation.

## Thinking

Better stories demand better thinking about stories. As panic increasingly becomes the default mode of response to the challenges we face, I want to defend the idea that thinking matters, and that how we think matters. It has become more urgent than ever to say this as serious thinking, the kind that seeks out the best knowledge possible, has collapsed into a field of crises: The overwhelming number of claims to the truth; the increasingly common retreat into confirmation biases (where we believe whatever reinforces what we think we already know); the deconstruction of all truth claims (it's all opinion and opinion be damned!) without any answer to the charge of relativism; the political rejection of any hierarchy of value or standard of comparison. Taken together, these crises have challenged the link between thinking and judgment and undermined the possibility of productive conversation (see Chapter 3). The resulting paradox is that we "know" lots of things but we don't know what they mean, and we don't know what we know. We no longer trust thinking and, to some extent, we no longer know how to think.

Yet every human being thinks. They live by thinking. Thinking involves ideas; it is nothing without ideas (and for those who are already nervous, 'concepts' is merely another word for 'ideas'). Thinking uses concepts to define the logics by which the connections or relations among elements are constructed. There are many ways to think, and no single right way. Different ways of thinking offer different logics that strive to find ways of structuring chaos even as they hold onto the joy and beauty that chaos offers. I grew up in New York City. Visitors would always tell me how chaotic the city was, but I knew how to navigate—live in—its chaos. Not that it wasn't still chaotic, but it was an organized, livable chaos. That is unconscious, everyday thinking. Anyone who gets high knows the experience of seeing order in what straight people see as chaos. You see the choreography in people's random movements. You may both see the beauty in chaos, but you see it differently.

And different ways of thinking offer different notions of what counts as reason. Every human being reasons: They have reasons for what they do, even if what counts as a reason is strange to us. It is, at its simplest, about answering questions, addressing problems, and making choices. Most of the time, in big and small ways, thinking has to do with the truths that are the signposts that stories use to organize people's lives.

When people talk about speaking truth to power, they are assuming a particular register of truth. Truth is juxtaposed to misinformation, falsehoods, hypocrisies, lies, etc. and is assumed to be available through empirical observation and thought. In the current moment, knowledge and truth have become matters of political opinion. It has become too easy to stop thinking and lay claim to truth by calling out other claims as lies. Speaking truth to power does not seem capable of altering the directions of social transformation (if it ever was). When listening to someone who disagrees with you, who holds positions that are abhorrent to you, becomes unacceptable, what are we left with? When intolerance becomes a virtue and argument becomes a sin, then the constant to and fro of knowledge becomes impossible and the possibility of unknown futures disappears. When criticism becomes rejection instead of engagement, when people ignore what they need in order to attack what they want, thinking stands still and the future collapses into a fraught present.

Whatever kind of thinking we are thinking about, it is more than a mental activity; it involves bodies and feelings as well (despite what the enlightenments would have us believe). And it is more than a logic. Each offers a unique way of seeing, understanding, and experiencing the world. Ways of thinking are the underpinnings, along with our material sustenance, of our ways of living. Thinking is inseparable from stories. They have a unique—dialectical—relation; each makes the other possible. Thinking enables us to identify, differentiate, and connect elements and provides the directions for composing stories that render reality intelligible and livable. New ways of thinking can deliver insights otherwise unavailable, allowing us to end up somewhere other than where we began and even somewhere other than where we might have expected. They can show us what we might not have seen before and enable other possibilities for change to emerge.[2]

Thinking always involves structuring a body of data or evidence. Actually, it's more complicated (another of my mantras!) because something becomes a structure or a piece of evidence only in the process of thinking. Thinking constructs an archive—a collection and organization of examples or data—in the very selection of whatever it is attempting to think about. The archivist is a collector, perhaps a discoverer, of material, some of which may have been ignored or actively erased. Thinking simultaneously organizes the archive into a structure or story, which in turn determines the archive. There may be many stories that can arise from an archive, and different archives may stand alongside the same story. In the context of thinking, stories serve at least three functions: They can describe, interpret, or theorize the archive. Theories are stories that give us directions for constructing other stories. As the archive or story changes, the other changes as well. Different ways of thinking will understand each of these terms differently.

Each way of thinking will likely have its own "research" practices, its own understanding of what are acceptable elements for an archive, its own logics, and its own measures of rigor or adequacy. Each way of thinking will tell its own kind of story. We need to be able to see where and how different ways of thinking connect with the political-cultural worlds and what they enable us to see, say, and do.

Recognizing that there are different ways of thinking has led me to face a ghost that has haunted my entire academic life. People all too commonly assume an almost impenetrable wall separating academic thinking from the thinking of ordinary people. I cannot count the times I was told: This is too complicated, or too theoretical, for a "popular" audience.[3]

The judgment is usually justified by some combination of three claims: First, ordinary people respond best to simple stories while academics prefer complicated stories. Second, ordinary people only respond to stories they find immediately understandable, while academics use concepts to trouble their stories. Third, academics are more self-reflective about their stories than ordinary people. The result is that little effort is made to bring these different and diverse audiences together. Need I say it: All three claims are false.

This assumed wall is built upon intellectuals' common mystification of their ways of thinking: Not only do they take the "truth" of their own way for granted, but they assume that its truth is visible for all to see.[4] Simply put, academics rarely actually discuss how they think, how it affects what they think they know, and why they think it is useful. Just as importantly, such mystification is often accompanied by an arrogance that assumes that if only other people knew what they know, if only they thought the way academics do, everything would be all right. It is not surprising that many people hear academics saying, "This is so, is it not," and our evidence and arguments as little more than ex post facto justifications for what are basically opinions. And by definition, ordinary people are unqualified to respond.

What if we began by being open about how we construct our stories and how we think about the worlds we live in. If we share how we think with others who think differently, then perhaps we can see the strengths and flaws in different ways of thinking and find points where we can understand each other—or at least understand the differences. And if we have a better sense of how we think, perhaps we can step out of the all too easy voices of the pedagogue, the know-it-all, the demagogue, the preacher, etc.

In fact, when I was a graduate student in the late 1960s, the most compelling cultural critics often explicitly justified their argument with the rhetorical question: This is so, is it not? It was an assertion of authority and expertise that few were willing to challenge. Many young intellectuals, myself included, sought more public ways of demonstrating how we arrived at our conclusions and how we interpreted texts and evidence. We searched for more rigorous, even "objective" methods of analysis. (Everyone at the time was obsessed with methods.) But now that we are overwhelmed by texts, evidence, and theories, methods don't seem up to the task of supporting rigorous arguments and well-constructed stories. I hope that describing my way of thinking will provide a sturdier scaffold, allowing the reader to understand the processes by which I am attempting to reconfigure the political culture into a better story.

To that end, I want to expand briefly upon my own way of thinking and doing research (elaborated in Chapters 4–6). Perhaps the discussion will seem too academic (usually shorthand for theoretical, esoteric, or abstract) to some, and unnecessary to others, but we should not confine any way of thinking to the academy. Instead, we can put our thinking on display, making our story-telling more explicit. There are certainly some ways of thinking that are more complicated and esoteric; they include not only many academic ways, but also the ways of thinking of a devout Catholic, Jew, or Buddhist (and maybe even the intricacies of common sense). These often gather together a number of practices of thinking from different sources to compose a somewhat messy recipe for thought. I am not saying they are not difficult to understand. I will describe mine as a particular version of "slow thinking," which is offered to face the current crises, knowing that it is only one among several possibilities of intellectual work.[5]

Let me explain why I call it slow thinking. It points to a crucial condition of such work. Slow thinking takes time, and it is constrained by the time allowed. How often do we say we need time to think? Admittedly, having the time to think about something in a self-critical and uncompromising way, to examine its complexities, contradictions, and nuances, to expand the archive and the context in unexpected ways, is a luxury. If the academy ever provided it, it has not done so for quite a while; instead, it has been made into an unequally distributed privilege dependent on grants or the unrewarded labor hidden in the cracks between bureaucratic metrics. How sad it is, then, that so few people actually demand the time. How sad it is that the academy rarely understands itself in such terms. And how sad that we have not found ways to gift time to people who passionately want and deserve it.

This time is often dismissed as a waste of time, as irrelevant in the face of the immediate struggles that demand our attention. People too often only see the privilege. But there are intellectuals from many sites—including various workers and activist organizations—that try to nurture such thinking and even to find ways of making time available. We need to find better ways of distributing time to people with the capacities for and commitment to such thinking.

The rigor of slow thinking starts by distancing itself somewhat from our taken-for-granted, common-sense world and sometimes, when necessary, from the languages in which we ordinarily speak. It demands that understanding precedes judgment. It questions what we think we know and asks why we think we know it. It acknowledges that our accounts are always incomplete and may even be wrong. It seeks out criticism and alternative accounts, putting itself to the test, as it were. It looks in unexpected places and traditions.

Slow thinking expects to be surprised, to end up somewhere unexpected. It knows that the world is always changing and that the problems it poses will change as well. You can assert what you know today, as long as you are willing to admit that you were wrong tomorrow. It refuses to choose between the passions of political commitment and the rigors of intellectual work; it understands that the impossibility of ever achieving objectivity does not mean you should not try to be more objective but that the effort is only made more difficult by the claim of disinterest.

It has become easy to refuse the costs of slow thinking in the face of the urgency of suffering. I understand the urgency, but I also understand that by looking further back and further ahead, by seeing the depths of the problems, we might see things that help us engage with the struggles in more profound ways, over longer periods of time, because they did not begin and will not end today. Slow thinking produces the deep stories, visions, and vocabularies that shape a society's sense of itself and define the possibilities of change. It is the basis on which we are able to think about transformation as a more strategic, long-term project, to find the better stories that can speak to different futures and different people; capable of reaching out across passionately held disagreements, which ultimately depends on loosening the ossified relations of trust and truth: People believe the sources they trust, and they trust the sources they believe. It is in slow thinking that arguments and disagreements can be given their due and new distributions of trust negotiated.

While for some people, thinking is the loneliest of endeavors, slow thinking takes place in overcrowded conversations that are always threatening to leave you behind. But its conversations attempt to avoid the Scylla of relativism that results from treating every voice as equal and the Charybdis of certainty that results from the assertion of authority. It attempts to avoid both the rock of particularizing and the hard place of universalizing. Instead, slow thinking grants every voice respect while recognizing that authority is both complicated and unequally distributed. Every conversation is punctuated and differentiated by a distribution of capacities, education, and passion.

Sometimes we do have to act in the face of unbearable suffering and unforgivable evil. But even the more immediate tactical efforts demand to be thought through, for they are rarely enacted in a vacuum. You enter into struggles with opposing forces with their own agendas and tactics. It may be useful to consider whether your actions provide openings for your opponents, for example, to accuse you of obvious hypocrisy (e.g., Do Democrats really want to claim they champion individual freedom over one's body when they demand vaccinations or oppose book banning when some oppose racist or homophobic books?). It may be useful to consider what battles to fight at any moment and not allow opponents to force you into struggles that they have chosen. Politics, however immediate and urgent it may feel, demands thinking. Such conversations will certainly elicit deeply felt, intense feelings, but if we cannot think through them, we will not be able to realize a democratic project.

It is especially important for those who believe that ideas matter to stand up for the time of slow thinking and stand against the claim that urgency must always trump such efforts. I am tired of hearing that these are old notions whose time has passed, that these are the practices of the privileged and the powerful. I am tired of having certain understandings of the relations of thinking and politics being reduced to generational struggles. It feels like I have been through this before, that I've seen this before, that I have fought many of these battles before. I know how the story is going to turn out because we keep repeating the same bad stories. I can only repeat that in a world in which the possibilities of rigorous thinking have been so severely limited if not utterly denied, it can be fruitful to step back, restore thinking to its rightful place, and be as open as we can about how we propose to go on thinking.

## Author's Note #2

Whatever arguments I make, I know that there are people who will not or cannot deal with my presentation of slow thinking because they will find it too abstract. I do not want to exclude you or drive you away from the substance of my story. So, I have provided a glossary of the key terms and concepts you will need to grasp what I am trying to do. I hope that it is sufficient and that you will avail yourself of this resource rather than simply give up in frustration.

## Politics

There are many reasons to think, beyond the pleasures of thinking itself. We think to fulfill tasks necessary to our survival; we think to express ourselves, whether in forms of art or social relations. We think to increase our status, wealth, and power, which may involve us in politics as well. Politics is a field of struggles among competing actors and forces.

I am sometimes told that political struggle is not about success. I do not know what this means. I know that success is a difficult notion to define, and that there are different definitions of success, but sometimes, you have to stop and consider what you have been doing, with what effects, where you have advanced and where you have retreated, what the problems are, and what possible solutions might be considered. Of course, political change and social struggle cannot be reduced to a simple matter of winning or losing, succeeding or failing, as if there were only two possibilities. You have to think about where you are and how you arrived here.

I have (along with many others) tried to account for the successes and limits of various right-wing politics at particular moments. I have also tried to offer an account of the role that progressive and left-wing forces have played in constituting the current political culture. At any moment, there is a struggle to achieve a balance between the right and the left. Since the 1950s, groups in both political currents have gained substantial followings; they have mounted highly visible protests and organized sophisticated campaigns; they have won important victories. And yet, it certainly seems as if the country has been heading in increasingly conservative directions for some time. It does seem that the right has the upper hand in redirecting U.S. politics and political culture, with more liberal and progressive forces fighting largely defensive battles.

How do we account for this apparent disparity of effectiveness? This suggestion has been greeted with hostility, despite the fact that I am clearly not equating the responsibility of the lefts and the rights for the current state of affairs, nor am I suggesting some moral or political equivalence. That would be one way of talking about success, but it is not mine.

I start with the obvious statement that politics is complicated. It is not just that politics is defined by a multitude of problems, issues, positions, interests, and constituencies; those are the easiest aspects to acknowledge. The more difficult—but at the moment, the more important—complication is the many times of politics. Politics is always defined by the confluence of various temporalities or timelines, each with its own extension (into a measurable past and a limited but uncertain future), velocity, tempo, and rhythm. For example, the temporalities of racism and xenophobia are quite distinct, and these both differ significantly from the temporalities of populism and religious awakenings. Political struggles are constructed in part by understanding and negotiating the ways these timelines intersect and interact at particular historical moments, producing particular historical contexts.

As a result, different struggles have to be approached differently. Some have to be faced immediately, using the best tactics available. Others—such as changing the political culture in which stories compete to define our sense of the world—operate in a slower temporal register. The two efforts are not the same, however interconnected they may be. And while our political mood is shaped by the more immediate crises we face—and face them we must—we cannot put off the struggles over political culture for the sake of the frightening challenges we face in the here and now. Recent history suggests that such battles are only becoming more important, and they are increasingly determining both the future possibilities and which immediate battles matter. These longer temporalities demand a strategic rather than a tactical politics.

This suggests a different way of thinking about success. Politics is often assumed to be defined by some imagined future, a utopian ideal toward which we hope we are heading. Without denying the power of such imagined futures, strategic politics is defined by a different futurity, the futurity of the not-yet, a futurity that is of and about the present. Strategic politics recognizes that the present is only defined by the next moment and the next moment, and .... And the next moment is never guaranteed; it is always uncertain, and the uncertainty increases the farther out you go. The present is a moment of becoming—the opening up, opening to, and taking up of possibilities. The work of politics is always just ahead.

For me, success involves advancing in directions that keep open and even expand the field of political possibilities, especially if they seek to repair the world while holding back the chaos. *Tikkun olam*. They may not advance in precisely the ways we expected: they may be hijacked, or closed off, or enclosed. We may unwittingly interfere with other lines of possibilities and, perhaps, have to go back in time, as it were, to repair the damage we have done and further proliferate unperceived or previously unavailable possibilities. But as long as there are possibilities for moving forward, however improbable and however uncertain, there is success. We can continue to try to repair the world as best we can. One of my teachers used to describe it as attempting to navigate—which is more than simply giving yourself over to—the tides of history.

One final comment. I have not tried to hide my own political leanings, although I have worked hard to be conscious of how they have inflected my story-telling. I have always identified myself as a radical progressive, a leftist, but I am no longer comfortable with where that might take me today. That is my personal stake in the story I am telling. I wonder why it is so hard, to find a livable, viable, and effective political position in the contemporary world.

## The Road Ahead

Bad stories make bad politics. I want to contribute to a somewhat discontinuous history of the present. Drawing together a number of often not well-understood, if not entirely ignored, features of our political culture, my story seeks to shed some light on the questions I have already posed: What is the specificity of the current moment? Why does it feel so strange and strangely unique (even while such feelings have been experienced many times over in the past or in other places)? How have we ended up in this present, headed toward a future that we did not choose, a future so threatening, so distant from everything we thought we were fighting for? Why is it so hard to find hope in the contemporary maelstrom?

I start by telling a story about a significant change in how culture operates. Culture has traditionally been characterized by the co-existence of, and in fact, the necessary interactions among, various kinds of structures and effects. The most important of these deeply intertwined ways of relating to the world are meaning and feeling, although it is meaning that has been foregrounded as most highly valued. Beginning in the 1950s and increasingly into the present, there has been a shift in emphasis from what does it mean to how do you feel; feeling has become the most prominent and valued dimension of culture. This has had profound consequences for political culture: Everything becomes a matter of feeling, will, intensity, emotion, etc. "Where there's a will, there's an A." I will describe the result as an "affective landscape" (Chapters 2 and 7). It has established a certain autonomy or independence from any claim of content, substance, or meaning, but it is, as culture has always been, a contentiously structured realm.

Then I introduce a framing historical story of the emergence, over time, of two (organic—sometimes sympathetic and sometimes antagonistic) crises that challenge the country's very identity and status as the ultimate example of a modern nation-state. In the earlier crisis, which dominated the last few decades of the 20th century and continued into the new millennium, the struggle had been over what it means to be modern and the possibilities of alternative versions of the institutions of a modern nation-state. The later crisis, which appeared in the new millennium, has more radically challenged the very possibility and desirability of being modern, seeking to identify alternatives to the modern nation and nation-state.

Dividing U.S. history into roughly three historical moments: 1950s–late 1970s, 1980s–2000, and 2000–present, I present the political culture as a struggle among competing responses to these crises. But I do not repeat the common stories that contrast two starkly competing ideological and moral positions, or even the ethical questions surrounding many current political practices. These are crucial stories and, indeed, I have strong feelings about them, which I will not always try to hide. But I think they are built on a prior story of the political culture that has been told so often, in so many ways and places, that it has become commonsensical and incontestable: America is a polarized nation. Polarization seems to rule the contemporary political culture and organize contemporary political stories and struggles. I don't doubt it is true, but it doesn't have to be true, and it is not the only truth. It is a bad story, and it has resulted in bad politics. The political field is always messier, and our stories should not erase the very richness of political culture.

I am interested in questions about the nature and composition of the political culture itself. I want to construct a story about some less obvious cultural forces, the underlying, active logics that both enable and constrain our political possibilities in the present. I might describe it as a pragmatic and formalist story of the political culture as a struggle among four tendencies: Liberal (LT), hegemonic (HT), speculative (ST), and pseudo-revolutionary (PRT). These tendencies set out the possibilities and limits of political action by defining the acceptability of any achievable balance in the field of cultural and political forces and the parameters for political actions and rhetoric. While these tendencies have longer histories than the story I am telling, the question is what happens to them when they operate at the intersection of the emerging affective landscape and crises of modernity I have described.

There are reasons I have chosen to think in terms of tendencies rather than political groups, movements, ideologies, etc., even though they may be closely related at times. Most importantly, and most controversially, these tendencies are comparable to formal logics. They don't care about ideologies or traditional political categories. They are not more real than them. They are not deep structures that make them possible. But they do determine how ideologies and political differences are manifested. The same tendency can be expressed on both sides of the aisle. Using them allows me to tell a very different, and, I hope, a useful, story about the contemporary political culture.

Additionally, categories that identify specific political groups, movements, ideologies, etc. are, in a sense, too concrete, too detailed, and too complicated and contradictory; simply put, they are too messy. They have already been defined within an already assumed partisan divide. This became most obvious when I began thinking about the current dominance of the pseudo-revolutionary tendency. I found myself referring to what appear to be the most immediate expressions, the woke left and the MAGA right. But these terms are thrown around without careful definition, easily generalized from some worst-case scenario, and often used pejoratively. For example, does MAGA refer to all reactionaries, or anyone supporting Trump, or only those who have made Trump into a messianic figure, or only those who have bought into absurdist conspiracy theories? Does wokeness refer to social justice warriors, or what used to be called PC, or simply more radical leftists, or Marxists, or critical race theorists, or identity politics, or ...? I struggled to find other adjectives, which might capture future manifestations as well, such as extremist, partisan, radical, far, or ultra, but realized that these can be just as vague and are often used relative to some taken-for-granted normative position. Eventually, I decided to avoid using such terms altogether and, instead, simply refer to the PRT right and the PRT left, hoping you will be patient until I am able (in Chapter 13) to fully explain the contours of this tendency.

I suggest, rather pessimistically, that as the PRT has become increasingly dominant in the new millennium across the political culture, disagreements become chasms, and bridges, however fragile, collapse under the slightest pressure. Yet its expression on the right seems to have found stories responding to the second organic crisis. And it has, subsequently, constructed a new practice of politics and won the reins of power, with which it seeks to tear down the modern nation and the nation-state.

If only to keep the doors of optimism open, in the final part, I consider a fifth "popular" logic (PT), which embraces uncertainty—the future is never guaranteed—and the hope of repairing the world.

## The Humility in Arrogance

I know that my story is seriously incomplete, and that even the parts I have begun to compose are themselves incomplete. I do not claim to have done anything more than offer a part of a larger story. I know there are serious absences, some of which I want to acknowledge here. First, I do not seriously consider the place of capitalism. Obviously, the effects of capitalism are frighteningly visible, but we should not assume we know all there is to know about them. Yes, the difference between the rich and the poor is growing, but it is not a simple binary. Yes, there is still an excess of exploitation and suffering at its hands and it is growing, but there is also a good deal of pleasure, however artificial it may be. Yes, corporations seem to have morphed into a new form of power brokers, and to be increasingly driven by fictive valuations, but do we actually understand the vicissitudes of the corporate form? Yes, there are certainly forces pushing toward the marketization and commodification of everything, but there are many places where people still refuse and resist. And yes, capitalism has so deeply infiltrated the fabric of culture and everyday life that it seems impossible to separate them, but do we know what that means? Can we simply assume that capitalism has "colonized" all space, effectively eradicating all exteriorities?

There is a lot of serious work on contemporary economies and capitalism. Some recognize that capitalism is not a single thing, and that it is always multiplying, changing, and reconfiguring itself. The challenge is not to get lost in endless debates about its supposed essence. Capitalism is a historically and geographically complex mix of often competing forces. Understanding how it is inserted into the contemporary field of struggles requires coming to terms with its changing configurations, with the changing power of its various sectors (including tech, finance, logistics, real estate, agribusiness, extraction, and manufacturing) and the various configurations of their relations (including the changing nature of colonialisms and labor markets and the various flows and stases that define a reified economic space and time). The changes in capitalisms (and broader economies) since the mid-20th century have been momentous: The rise of finance (and its relation to real estate) and technology, the changing nature and power of corporations, the return of primitive accumulation and mercantilism, the expansion of the social factory, etc. The ways the various capitalisms relate to other aspects of modernity, to forms of governmentality, and to the affective landscapes are also changing.

Unfortunately, many of the stories of capitalism continue to treat it as an independent force. They do not sufficiently contextualize it, and most ignore questions of culture and lived realities. Politics and culture, political culture, however much they are shaped these days by the forces of capitalism, are never completely determined by them, and they have their own stories that are shaping economies as well. We need better knowledge of realms other than capitalisms if we are to understand how capitalisms are working. That is, whatever changes are happening in the sphere of economic effects and relations, they are not happening in isolation and it may be more strategic at this time to attack various capitalisms or various developments from other, more exterior sites. Whatever horrific damage and suffering capitalisms cause, they are not alone; not all the damage and suffering can be laid at the economies' feet.

Second, I realize that the U.S. is not an isolated space with clear boundaries. Its impact—whether welcomed, grudgingly accepted, contested, or despised—is felt in every part of the world. And the country is impacted as well, entangled in all these relations. Further, I realize that some of the struggles I am describing appear to be similar to those taking place in other parts of the world, but I do not want to be pulled into the all too easy parochialism of the U.S., or the tendency to slide, even if unintentionally, into universalisms. I cannot speak about other countries or regions. Differences matter as much as similarities. At the same time, I realize that part of the struggles over the nation are also struggles over the configuration of the globe; the three-world model (first, second, and third worlds) no longer describes the world, and we seem to be heading to a new organizing principle (*nomos*), perhaps an imperial model of empire or spheres of influence.

Third, I have not given nearly enough attention to two crucial aspects of contemporary political culture: On the one hand, there is the full range of technological architectures, including social media, digital technologies, and the hyper-inflated claims of virtual reality, with their many contradictory effects. I am neither comfortable in these realms, nor have I found many convincing analyses. On the other hand, there are the far-reaching effects of "religion," including both the continuing presence of various countercultural forms of spirituality, mysticism, rituals, mythologies (e.g., Odinism), etc. and the changing roles and contours of Christianity (both Catholicism and the many Protestant denominations, some arising from the prosperity gospel), often taking charismatic and evangelical and apocalyptic and millenialist (messianic) forms. These were first identified with the Christian Identity and Christian Dominion movements, which were thought of as marginal sects, but they have subsequently exploded. Often placing a personal relation to Jesus and an increasingly politicized mission at their center, they have moved into commercial spaces (e.g., coffee shops) and make regular and comfortable use of popular culture (e.g., music). The truth is that I have neither the time nor the expertise to carry out such investigations, although there is a substantial body of useful research on these movements, although, again, only a few treat them contextually.

I know that any claim I can make about the usefulness of my story, about its necessary complexity, will be limited by its very incompleteness, but I also know that there can never be a single, finished, story.

## Notes

1  On the other hand, some others find enjoyment in constantly taking up new stories about themselves and society (e.g., that society has entered a radically new era in which power has taken on entirely new shapes, that new conspiracies or new scientifically and technologically enabled systems of control have emerged). These too are simple stories.
2  See Grossberg, 2024.
3  The exception are those disciplines whose practice depends on highly detailed story-telling, such as history and some anthropology. The media have played a large and harmful role here, increasingly assuming that the "general public" demands simplicity. They do little to raise collective intelligence. I believe people will work to understand if they think it is important and consequential.
4  It may be the case that we all mystify our own ways of thinking,
5  See Grossberg, 1997, 2010. It is what, in other contexts, I call cultural studies.

## References

Grossberg, Lawrence. *Bringing It All back Home: Essays on Cultural Studies.* Durham: Duke University Press, 1997.

Grossberg, Lawrence. *Cultural Studies in the Future Tense.* Durham: Duke University Press, 2010.

Grossberg, Lawrence. *On the Way to Theory.* Durham: Duke University Press, 2024.

# PART I

# Everybody Knows

# 2

# A QUESTION OF AFFECT

It all started with music.[1] As an undergraduate, I was fascinated by the unique relation between popular music and the social movements and countercultures of the 1960s. Interestingly, in ways not well understood, significant numbers of youth seemed to live the music politically, whether it had any explicit political content or not. I wrote an honors thesis on the subject. When I started teaching classes on the cultural history of postwar popular music and youth culture, I had to think about what music does and how it works.

Most understandings of culture focus on matters of meaning and representation (and subjectivity) as the bases of common sense, ideology, and identity. Whatever differences may exist among theorists of culture, most assume that this is what separates humans from brute reality and fully instinctually defined forms of life. But when I tried to use such theories and the tools they provide to understand people's relation to music—when I treated the music as meaningful texts, expressions of ideological and commonsensical beliefs—they did not get me very far. They did not capture the ways music mattered to people, the ways music affected people. I conjectured that the experience of music, its effects, its power, was a matter of feeling. When called upon to explain, I would often point to the story of Phil Spector defending The Ronettes' hit "Da Doo Ron Ron." Phil Spector was a pimply teenager and one of the most successful producers (mainly of so-called girl groups of the early 1960s) and the inventor of the "wall of sound" in the early 1960s. When Steve Allen, a popular mixed-genre show host, condemned the lyrics as verbal nonsense and triviality, Spector responded by dancing across the stage while calling out: "Can't you feel it?" The words didn't matter, or, rather, they mattered only in a specific way, as part of a larger composition

DOI: 10.4324/9781003662587-3

of sounds, resonances, textures, rhythms, timbres, and melodies. I could feel it—on my body and in my head. Clearly Steve Allen could not.

## Music and Affect

As I tried to think about the notion of feeling, I took up the concept of affect from Freud, who argued that desire entails an object and a quantity of energy (libido=affect). I was not interested in his psychoanalysis but in his earliest work, in what Paul Ricoeur called his "energetics."[2] Freud imagined the nervous system to be a hydraulic system through which quantities of energy flow, are interrupted, and are stored. Human relations to the world always involve an investment of quantities of energy; there is a dimension of lived reality defined by measures of intensity.

Almost fortuitously, this solved another problem I had with theories of culture as meaning: They were unable to account for the different relations that different people or groups might have to the same meanings or ideologies. This is partially captured in the ambiguity of significance, which can refer to meaning but also to importance. Some things are more meaningful or differently meaningful than others. Some things matter passionately to some, and not at all to others. Was it a matter of the quantity of the investment?

Adding an energetics—a dimension of intensity with its variable quantities—seemed to take me a step closer to grasping why music, and perhaps culture, more generally, mattered so much. It is the energy that animates life, that makes it feel lived, that makes experience into something more than passive reception. But then, it has to involve more than quantities of energy. There has to be a qualitative side to affect, if only to account for the many forms and expressions that describe the density and vitality of a lived and living reality and the work they are called upon to do: Passions, feelings, emotions, attention, moods, outlooks, sentiments, desires, longings, concerns or matterings, belongings or identifications, states of energy (such as panic and calm), etc. Obviously, each of these has many variations and specifications. Now consider just a few of the many feelings that define our lives today: Helpless, confused, resentful, envious, terrified, bored, desperate, annoyed, baffled, overwhelmed, angry, disenchanted, befuddled, hopeless, sad, worried, discomforted, anxious, afraid, frustrated, cynical, concerned, discombobulated, resigned, ashamed, defensive, disturbed, crazy, bothered, depressed, unbelieving, crazy, vulnerable, incredulous, insecure, and shocked; but also, caring, sympathy, generosity, pride, joy, solidarity, hope, and love.

Affect plays a crucial role in popular culture, everyday life, commerce, and politics. The latter two have long depended on the construction of affect, in particular, of simple emotions such as fear, panic, and, occasionally, sympathy. Create fear and then offer the solution, presumably because someone has already invented the solution. Continue to present an inflated sense of the dangers and violence of everyday life. Show unbearable suffering so people will donate money. Barrage people with inflated claims of the crisis waiting just around the corner (e.g., campaign emails). Such appeals are not new, although the techniques have become increasingly sophisticated.

Returning to the importance of music in the various social movements of the 1960s (and even earlier), I could see that politics itself was being transformed—becoming less ideological and more affective. In retrospect, I saw other things that might be connected to affective changes in the lived realities of postwar America. There was a widespread and passionate search for new ways of thinking and living, of relating to and understanding the world. This was a major aspect of the counterculture, especially in the turn to non-western religions (including their rituals and drugs) and philosophies. But the counterculture also explored a wide range of largely marginalized western theories—often first popularized in media such as the Whole Earth Catalogue. And it had its gurus, including Herbert Marcuse, N.O. Brown, Timothy Leary, R.D. Laing, Wilhelm Reich, Baba Ram Das, etc. To be honest, I am not sure that people sought to understand them, but they were deeply invested in them.

In the academy, there were similar attacks on the Enlightenment's privileging of cognitive meaning and reason, and on various versions of positivism, which asserted that knowledge was to be found in, and only in, the realms of objective and passionless science. These opened the floodgates, especially in the humanities and social sciences, to theories that increasingly emphasized the role of culture, experience, imagination, human agency, and affect, as well as the ongoing historical constructions of experience.

Additionally, there were changes afoot in the broader culture. A powerful "therapeutic culture" emerged in the 1950s and 1960s. Large parts of popular culture were dominated by what were too easily seen as mere naïve sentimentalisms which simple-minded audiences took as ideal-types to define that truth of their lives. But these were more likely complicated, historically specific forms of affect that functioned as the grounds on which the possibilities of life in postwar America were debated.

### Four Structures of Feeling

I want to identify some affective signature keys that shaped the 1950s and 1960s. I will use the concept of "structures of feeling," offered by the Welsh cultural historian Raymond Williams.[3] Structures of feeling are the specific and most important affective organizations. They constitute the distinctive sense of livedness, the felt sense of a lived reality, what it "feels" like to live at a particular time and place, in a particular historical context.[4] Together, they define a specific sense of wholeness (if not completeness), not only of a life but of a way of life, and a lived reality. They hold together the tensions, irritations, and contradictions. Without them, all is chaos and insanity. They structure the experience of a lived reality. For example, in the 1950s, there were structures of feeling that held together terror and boredom, hope and complacency, paranoia and comfort, and despair and convenience. These continue to play important roles in at least some American lives.

Every context is defined by relations among numerous structures of feeling. Some will be dominant; others will resist or even oppose them. Some will be residual, the inheritance, if you will, of the history of prior contexts. And some will be emergent, locating the horizons where changes struggle to become knowable and livable and where habit meets creativity and the as-yet unknown. They are all actively shaping the lived reality of the context. To some extent, they call or sing their contexts into existence. At the same time, they are shaped by and called into existence by their contexts. Structures of feeling do not arise ex nihilo, nor are they naturally or universally occurring events. They are socially organized and historically specific.

I will focus on four structures of feeling, which emerged in the 1950s and have strengthened and evolved to become increasingly dominant in the political culture of the country. Each one has its own history, going through a series of transformations. Some are variations of earlier structures, while others may be relatively new. Moreover, each is necessarily inflected by the others, as well as other forces (e.g., forms of insecurity), making their descriptions tentative at best. While I will keep my examples to a minimum on the assumption that you will have your own, I can tell you that I have derived these structures of feeling largely from extensive observation of popular and commercial culture, including TV commercials, music, TV shows, news, etc.

The 1950s saw the emergence, out of a long history of forms of exaggeration, of **hyper-inflation**. Hyper-inflation dictates that everything not only has to serve its purpose well, but it has to be great, the best; or the worst. Everything has to be amazing, has to excel. Nothing is worse than being average, where average is not even a matter of being mediocre but of not standing out. Every movie is one of the best of the year, every car is rated number one; every brand is the best selling; everyone should feel like a million. Designing the latest model of a car is equated with Einstein's discovery of relativity; purchasing a new commodity recreates the courage of a war hero; and a single act of repression becomes proof of fascism. Offices of human relations present themselves as talent acquisition. Whatever you are suffering is worse than anything anyone has suffered before, and no one can understand your suffering.

Hyper-inflation makes the unimaginable into the normal and mundane (e.g., the overload of shocking tragedies). Everything becomes too emphatic; nothing can matter unless it is followed by an exclamation point, and everything sounds like it is followed by more exclamation points than one can imagine. Hyper-inflation operates according to an endless logic of escalation, always ramping up the claim. When combined with the media's propensity toward sensationalism, the results can be beyond any possible claim to representation. The only response to any bad news is immediate and total panic. And any small joy becomes an occasion for celebration.

What matters is the intensity of your commitment. Hyper-inflation in any realm of life—whether religion, politics, economy, music, philosophy, etc.—can easily slide into fundamentalism. Fundamentalism marks every decision with certainty (as a matter of faith). No longer limited to extreme choices at the frontiers of "normality," there are fundamentalist ways of occupying any position, including the center. Fundamentalism becomes the new expectation. And compromise becomes the new problem: On the one hand, it is a strategy to advance your commitment, and on the other, it is the new treachery.

Anxiety might be said to have a long history but that is only in retrospect. It is only in the 1950s that **anxiety** emerges as an identifiable problem. Psychologists began distinguishing it from other affects such as fear, stress, nervousness, and worry. Nervousness and worry were mental states; fear and stress were more directly visible as conditions of the body. Fear generally has a referent, even if it is invisible, absent, or displaced into the future; moreover, it is generally a temporary state of affairs. While the same may be true of stress, nervousness, and worry, i.e., that they are responses to a particular situation, they may also describe a personality type or a temporary state of existence. Anxiety was becoming a unique diagnosis as a form of individual abnormal or pathological psychology (often linked to depression), to be treated with therapy and drugs.

But it was also becoming something more. Drawing especially on the work of the German philosopher Martin Heidegger, various philosophers and intellectuals ontologized anxiety and made it into an existential condition of human life, in order to rethink the early-20th century concern for alienation and authenticity.

It was also becoming a unique social problem and an object of social investigation. The 1950s began problematizing anxiety, moving it closer to the boundary of psychology and sociology.

Anxiety was increasingly thought of as a more enduring and threatening problem that transcends the division of mind and body, of the temporary and the permanent. While its various forms and expressions (e.g., identity crises, anal compulsiveness) had not quite come together, its presence was felt across many different social spheres. Various social psychologists and historians from the 1950s through the 1970s began to assign it a unique social and historical reality (e.g., a loss of control) that arose from specific postwar challenges. Anxiety was emerging as a powerful structure of feeling.

Every age has its own **narcissism**. Tom Wolfe called the 1970s "the me decade." He wasn't wrong, but he had identified only a particular form of narcissism, organized primarily around greed, consumption, and a lifestyle of hedonism and self-gratification. Narcissism creates a mirror image relation between the individual and the world. When I look out into the world, I (expect to) see myself. Many have, mistakenly, I think, identified narcissism with a sense of social isolation or anomie, which was the major argument of the mass society debates at the turn of the 20th century. Communities—in which people had intimate knowledge of their neighbors and those they interacted with on a regular basis—were being replaced by more formal and contractual relations. In the 1950s, this was taken up as the experience of being alone in the crowd.

But narcissism as a structure of feeling suggests that this involved the emergence of a different and increasing investment in individualism, a hyper-individualism if you will. It was at first expressed in a desperate search, especially but not only among youth, for authenticity against anonymity and conformity. Not coincidentally, this was one of the themes of the mass culture debates at the time (which often measured the difference through cultural taste and consumption).

But as I shall observe, it was not long before authenticity became a problem and was called into question. It no longer served as a viable way of living and expressing narcissism. If any vestige of authenticity remained, it was increasingly fractured and disposable. Instead of seeing yourself in the world, you expected to see, and were supposed to see, the world in yourself.

The fourth structure of feeling, the **time warp**, is the most difficult to describe and to locate historically. In the 1950s and 1960s, most people thought of time as a continuous and linear unfolding of progress. The relations of past (memory), present (experience), and future (anticipation) are defined by the sliding of the future into the present and the present into the past. The present or "now" is an isolatable, yet fleeting and ever-changing, moment that is privileged because it is the moment of immediate experience, the moment in which "I" as the subject of my own experience lives. I know my experiences are real (and true?) because they are my present.

But time itself was becoming a problem and the ways we understand and think about time were changing, making it less stable and certain. Science was rendering time as infinitesimally small and infinitely large. It was relativizing time. The strange consequences of these changes were beginning to appear in popular culture.

More immediately, our understanding of history began to change. History was handed over to entertainment and capitalism, to technological possibilities and creative profit making, to what makes people feel good, or guilty, or .... And this had consequences which were only dimly visible (and become visible only in retrospect). The past itself becomes a chaotic collection of images and affects to be taken up and arranged at will and, as a result, the past becomes little more than fodder for reinventing the present. We feel nostalgia for some imagined memory of what was supposed to be. The past has been both emptied and supersaturated; we simultaneously remember everything and nothing.

At the same time, political discontents were raising questions and debates about the politics of culture and history. There were suggestions, soon to become common sense, that history was often written from some partisan perspective, usually that of the victor. People would even proudly declare that the past matters only as a contrivance to explain their suffering or their victorious arrival at the present.

Meanwhile, the future was beginning to slip away. Any reference to a future that was both connected to and significantly different from the present, other than as measured by economic growth and technological enhancement, began to recede from people's presence. The future was to become no longer unknown and unknowable but simply an extension of the present. This present was on its way to becoming the best or the worst of all possible worlds. Both of these were imagined in the 1950s, in the fantastic utopias and terrifying dystopias that filled postwar dreams and nightmares.

History was beginning to be transformed so as to forget the future and imagine the past. Everything was collapsed into the present; the present was all that mattered or, better, the present defined how everything else mattered. This reification of the present was expressed as well in the various movements and countercultures of the 1960s and 1970s, It found a home in the naivete of the pseudo-revolutionary demand: We want the world and we want it now! Or in the popularity of Bertolt Brecht's retelling of a Buddhist sutra: Buddha is asked about the nature of the nothingness that is Nirvana—whether it is pleasant or repulsive. He refuses to answer. Later, he offers a parable: He sees a burning house with people still inside; he calls upon them to leave, but they ask him questions ... about the weather outside, about their needs tomorrow, etc. To them, Gautama says, "I have nothing to say," and he leaves them.

These were not the only structures of feeling that shaped life during the 1950s and 1960s. I simply want to emphasize that they emerged! My descriptions point well beyond the point of their emergence in order to make them visible. Further, I cannot even be sure that these four were the most important. But I am relatively confident that they were to become so as they continued to shape people's lives in the following decades.

But I still have to think more carefully about the concept of affect. This will require a detour into slow thinking; but, first, a detour into why it has become so hard.

### Notes

1   Grossberg, 1992, 1997.
2   Ricoeur, 1970.
3   Williams, 1961, 1977.
4   Williams, 1960, 1961; Hoggart, 1957.

# References

Grossberg, Lawrence. *We Gotta Get out of This Place: Popular Conservatism and Postmodern Culture*. New York and London: Routledge, 1992.

Grossberg, Lawrence. *Dancing in Spite of Myself: Essays on Popular Culture*. Durham: Duke University Press, 1997.

Hoggart, Richard. *The Uses of Literacy*. London: Chatto & Windus, 1957.

Ricoeur, Paul. *Freud and Philosophy*. Trans. Denis Savage. New Haven: Yale University Press, 1970.

Williams, Raymond. *Culture and Society: 1780–1950*. New York: Columbia University Press, 1960.

Williams, Raymond. *The Long Revolution*. New York: Columbia University Press, 1961.

Williams, Raymond. *Marxism and Literature*. Oxford: Oxford University Press, 1977.

# 3
# THE PROBLEM OF THINKING

Let me begin with a rather brazen statement: The current state of knowledge of our social world is, to say the least, not good. The very idea of careful thought and the authority of knowledge have been deeply troubled. And despite their proclamations of innocence, intellectuals have, perhaps unknowingly and unwillingly, contributed to this in numerous ways. I want to offer a partial portrait of the conditions of knowledge. Many of the problems facing knowledge production resemble those that have been facing other cultural sectors (e.g., entertainment, information, news, arts, cuisine, fashion, etc.) over the past 50 years or so. Some are unique. Perhaps Nietzsche was right that the search for truth leads to nihilism, but I cannot see why it is inevitable.

## Stories about Knowledge

There are lots of simple stories offered to explain this state of affairs, lots of targets to blame: The ignorance of the masses; the proliferation of media which, either for economic profit or for political ideology, present whatever they think audiences "want" to hear or what they want audiences to believe; anti-intellectualism; the failure of public education; the increasing power of fundamentalist faith; tenured radicals; growing political and economic interference with cultural institutions; etc.

### Infoglut

There are a number of more elaborated stories; each probably contains some truth. The first and most common is an empiricist account that claims that there is quantitatively too much—often inconsistent and constantly

DOI: 10.4324/9781003662587-4

changing—information (facts, data) out there. The "truth" seems to get lost in the forest, or to change from one moment to the next, or to contradict itself. What was true yesterday is not true today. One source says one thing that is contradicted by another. People can be forgiven for feeling confused and skeptical, incapable of deciding what is actually true or whom to trust, whatever the topic.

This explosion is often laid at the doorsteps of the new media conduits made available by new technologies (and capitalist greed). There are too many places to look and too many places claiming your attention. Whatever the topic, whatever your own comfortable media orbit, you are likely to be overwhelmed. How can anyone keep up with it—and who can risk missing what may turn out to be that one crucial piece, the one example, the latest development, the newest meme? We are faced with little more than a huge data bank with no filters.

But our confusion and skepticism do not stop there. Someone has to provide the filters in the form of stories that select and organize the information and then interpret it so that it makes sense, so that the story works for us. These stories, sometimes in the form of theories, tell us what the facts mean and what counts as valid knowledge. But there are too many stories and too many theories out there as well. And once again, we don't seem to have filters and we don't know how to choose. You might think we could go back to the facts, but there are so many facts out there that you can find examples, evidence, of almost anything.

These experiences of overload drive people to find ways to protect themselves and limit the possibility of being overwhelmed. In both cases, the only criterion seems to be that it "feels" true (hence, truth becomes "truthiness") or that we already agreed with it. And as for those claims we confidently reject, we are amazed at how easily some people can embrace unproven, disproven, or even outrageous claims, even when they are exposed. This has been called the Amazon effect: Increasingly insular and isolated bubbles devoted only to reproducing themselves and their audiences, circumscribing the boundaries of the acceptable.

The capacity to insulate yourself is magnified, perhaps exponentially, by algorithms that analyze and correlate your tastes and feed the results back to you. We do not yet understand its effects. After all, this experience of being overwhelmed by information and stories is not new. It has happened time and time again, usually with the introduction of every new media technology that expands human perception into ever smaller and larger scales. With every new cultural technology (the printing press, the phonograph), people eventually wonder how they are supposed to choose from the overwhelming number of possibilities. New secondary media arise to tell stories and help people locate themselves on some organizational chart (e.g., of genres) they (or, more likely, the industry) have constructed.

The more product there is, the less likely it is that any product will make a difference; it may just be adding to the chaos. Some think there is more repetition, or a decline in creativity. They will say that there seems to be no quality control. Others will say that it has become impossible to find anything. There is wonderful product out there if you know where to look. But how do you know where to look? There are so many places and no map, no single story. For example, one website I happened upon listed over 500 progressive websites, podcasts, etc., and I quickly discovered that at least a dozen of my favorite sites were absent.

Stories of being overwhelmed take a bypass around a deeper problem. They ignore the way bits of information seem to inevitably slide into facts. Facts are thought of as what is given, what is self-evident; they provide the evidence on which disputes can be resolved; they cannot be false unless someone has either lied or made a mistake. As I said, we need stories or theories to make sense of facts. But that is not the end of the story. Facts do not pre-exist stories; they are not waiting around to be picked up by one story or another. Stories make (data into) facts. Stories tell us which are facts, what is allowed to be a fact, what facts matter, and how they matter. This question of the status of facts is nudging us toward questions of relativism, which I will take up later in the chapter.

### Conspiracies

A second story of the current state of knowledge says that we are swimming in misinformation, which it generally attributes to a conspiracy from whatever the other side is. It describes an intentional explosion of fake news and manipulated quotes, photos, and videos. Each side argues that the leaders and media of the other side lie, and their followers irrationally refuse all appeals to real evidence; they are ignorant of the basic principles of reason, and they are slaves to the power of political and religious prejudices. In the end, they are either devils or idiots. And since our side knows the truth, it is simply a matter of education and, sometimes, censorship.

But if we do not assume that they were born stupid or evil, then we have to accept that devils and idiots have to be made; people have to be schooled into ignorance or immorality. We have to invent a conspiracy behind the conspiracies. It sees a conscious effort to muddy the waters of knowledge and education.[1] For example, some critics on the left claim that the right is constantly injecting a sense of irreconcilable controversy (even when none actually exists) and attacking every claim to expertise.

While the left is very good at pointing to the conspiratorial logics of the right, it is equally good at denying its own conspiratorial logics (e.g., it's all being controlled by capitalists, or racists, and so on). All too often, certain tendencies of the left are to be happy to believe what they are already committed to believing, even against compelling evidence. Recently, a close friend asked me how I felt about the protests around diversity initiatives at my own university, about which he assumed he had reliable information. I was surprised—I should not have been—to realize how wrong he was, and that everything he thought he knew came from a narrow set of media sources that had selectively reported—and distorted—what was happening on the ground.

The descriptions of conspiracies of misinformation are also inadequate, if partially correct. This is not to deny that both sides do engage in conspiracies and do ignore evidence that argues against their assumed truths. For example, both sides have more complicated relations to science—attacking it at one moment over here and defending it over there as it fits their agenda—than is generally recognized. Neither side is above constructing nightmarish scenarios that simply ignore or selectively appropriate the evidence.

While both sides have committed followers who speak only what they already know, both sides also have rigorous and responsible intellectuals. The right, however much it does muddy the possibilities of knowledge, has invested enormous sums of money, talent, and energy into intellectual and scholarly work and into institutions such as think tanks, publications, strategic planning, etc. And despite the left's naïve assumption that everyone on the right is an anti-intellectual, it is clear that many people (perhaps not all the actors on the streets) are listening and taking this work seriously. If they are rewriting history, or simply lying, how do you know? The left assumes there are trustworthy outlets (e.g., reporters, pundits, blogs, news media), but sometimes, not so long ago, it was attacking them for ... you guessed it, spreading lies and fabricating evidence. So, when the left attacks the other side for misinformation, it is asserting its faith in ... what? Facts? Objectivity? Science? Legacy media? Academia? Those who agree with it?

The claim of conspiracies is also not new. Conspiracies are one of the contemporary forms of propaganda. Propaganda always uses whatever techniques are available. And lies have always played a significant role in politics. What are the differences? What does it mean to claim that we are inundated with misinformation? Does it mean anything beyond the statement that there are contradictory claims to knowledge on offer and, depending on where you locate your own sense of truth—in science, experience, faith—you will take some claims as truth and others as lies?

Again, I am on the threshold of relativism, and I do not mean to simply claim that everyone has a right to their own truth. But the (epistemic) logic of true and false has not always been a very effective political tool. It does feel hard to confidently grab hold of the truth. And not all falsehoods are lies. There have been moments when scientists were convinced of some truth that later turned out to be not so true. And there are moments when even experts make mistakes. This does not mean that the problem of truth has always been the same; for many reasons, the problem has become a crisis, and our ability to think and discriminate among claims has been suffocated by the toxicity of the culture wars.

In yet another version of a conspiracy theory, digital media are often held responsible for the demise of our ability to make critical judgments, of our communication skills, and even of our attention and concentration. Literacy is often used as an example. This seems to assume that, previously, people read important works in intelligent and self-conscious ways, and made acute and accurate judgments of quality, validity, and worthiness. I seriously doubt this. Literacy, like so many other capacities, changes over time. If the new media have pushed certain forms of literacy to the side, they have done so to make space for new capacities. It is possible that they are creating new forms of attention and making people capable of extraordinary feats of multi-tasking (of holding multiple foci of attention). They also create spaces of freedom in which people, especially young people, can escape the regimen of rules and norms they see as an imposition of control. We don't know yet if this is true, or, if true, where this will lead society, any more than we knew where the literacy enabled by the printing press would lead society.

Once again, this is an old story. Every new technology and every new medium (as well as the genres to which they gave birth) have been greeted by apocalyptic warnings that they would destroy all that is good in the world. And, at the same time, they have been celebrated as the coming salvation of the world's problems. John Phillip Sousa, the composer of many marching band songs, claimed the record player would destroy the family. Others claimed it would make the pleasures of music available to all and educate the aesthetic palate of the masses. There is no doubt some truth to both sides of the endlessly repeated stories. Every significant cultural/technological change poses new problems and amplifies old ones, but it also presents new capacities and possibilities, many of which had not been foreseen. We are only beginning to understand the longer-term consequences of the emergent digital technologies—computers, internet, surveillance and tracking, smart phones, social media, AI, etc.

The recent introduction of AI (and of "deep fakes") makes these concerns all the more palpable. In a recent episode of *Law and Order*, the verdict is decided because of what we are led to believe is a deep fake video. The heroic district attorney walks away musing on what happens to justice when you can't tell the difference between true and fake evidence. But this seems to put the burden, once again, back onto technology. That has it backwards. The problem is not AI. The problem is not even that we have lost our faith in truth. The problem is that we don't care enough about truth to defend it. We have not asked how we might protect truth, at least in the courts. How might we decide to control a technology, perhaps even refuse it? When do the costs outweigh the benefits? What are we willing to give up to protect truth? If we no longer believe in the possibility of better truths, what difference do deep fakes make? It is not social media or AI that is to blame.

### Commensuration Crises

There is a third description of the troubled state of knowledge, beyond infoglut and conspiracies: The crisis of knowledge lies in a crisis (or crises) of commensuration, a loss of the capacity to critically evaluate competing claims to knowledge, of the ability to make judgments of comparative worth based on some kind of logic of distinction and discrimination. Commensuration is not merely a question for knowledge; it operates wherever something claims to have some value.

Modern societies distinguish between the fact that something is worthy and the measurement of that worthiness. Generally, that measurement involves comparisons: This song is more beautiful than that one; this painting is worth more money (where money is a neutral term) than that. Every modern society—every society, I assume—has socially shared commensurating systems that make such judgments possible. The systems enable people to adjudicate the conflicts between and to recognize the limits of different claims across a wide range of fields including knowledge, aesthetics, education, economics, morality, politics, and economics. They tell us which choice to make, how to judge works of art, how to treat people, etc. This has heretofore been a primary way modern societies manage the chaos. There are usually institutions of authority, often hierarchical, that oversee these systems, even as they define the competence and expertise necessary to hold authority.

For example, in the sphere of commodity exchange, the commensurating logics operate through labor and commodities, market exchange and money, as well as the forms of wealth themselves. Oversimplifying the matter, consider the value produced in the physical and emotional labor of domestic life. These values have been commensurated through different systems, including socio-economic logics (in which domestic labor is "exchanged" for security, livelihood, etc.) and religious-cultural logics (in which domestic labor is rewarded through spiritual blessing or familial love). At the contemporary conjuncture, these logics have been called into question by developments including feminism, the condemnation of domestic violence, changes resulting from women entering the workforce, paid domestic labor, immigration, etc.

Starting in the 1950s and 1960s, many of the dominant commensurating logics and institutions have been challenged. Many of the institutions of authority (e.g., education, journalism, politics, science, and the church) have lost their credibility, and their failures have visibly played out in public. Many of the criticisms are well-deserved. These structures of authority were (and continue to be) deeply contaminated, almost intrinsically so, by many forms of power. Refusing serious challenges, they presented themselves as unquestionable. And while some continue to hang on, even to dominate, for the most part, they have left a vacuum in their place, a vacuum that is having serious consequences. We seem to be living in the midst of, or at least facing the threat of, the complete impossibility of commensuration. But there does not seem to be some single crisis at some imagined center which has yet to be located and which is the real cause of all the various crises dispersed across the multiple fields. Facing the inability to make judgments and choices based on some logic apart from the very necessity of making a choice, what is a poor boy or girl to do?

The crises of commensuration have challenged our ability to judge competing claims to knowledge. They have undermined our ability to distinguish between, on the one hand, the contributions of scholars, intellectuals, and experts and, on the other hand, the opinions of pundits and celebrities. The former easily slide into being the latter once they start thinking they can talk about anything under the sun (having read a few books or by relying on their intellectual wit). The rest carve out a small audience composed largely of people who already know of them. Some media outlets have attempted to credentialize their own pundits as "experts." Since their public voices are rarely marked with any acknowledgment of their own value or status, we are left floating in a field of words.

It is not surprising that many people no longer appear to recognize or care about the difference between opinion or belief and knowledge or expertise, between punditry and research, between the reporter (who is supposedly interested in facts) and the intellectual (who interprets them), and between fiction and nonfiction. How do we make the difference matter between, on the one hand, "I heard it from my preferred media sources" or "I have thought about it, even talked to some friends" and, on the other hand, "I have sought out whatever information, explanations, and theories are available, and critically considered what others have said?"

Does the failure of what have been the dominant forms of judgment commensuration mean that there are no other, better possibilities? I doubt that anyone is willing to give up entirely on judgments of comparative worth. There are certainly times when it is important that someone knows what they are doing, that they know something about what they are talking about. In those instances, it is reasonable to demand competence and, in some cases (e.g., a surgeon, a nuclear engineer), to demand even more. How do we go about creating new logics and institutions of commensuration when the current crises have so completely transformed politics? They have dismantled the possibilities of translation, negotiation, and compromise, and are producing new forms of partisanship and extremism. They have changed the calculation of political victory and defeat. The culture wars themselves are largely fought over commensurating logics.

### *Valorizing Experience*

A final account of the sad state of knowledge sees it as the latest expression of some imagined anti-intellectualism inherent in or endemic to the American character. I would rather see it less as anti-intellectualism and more as moments in which experience was opposed to education and expertise. In the present moment, that opposition exists in both the left and the right. At various points across the spectrum, there is a suspicion of reason, elitist intellectual expertise, and the authority of the academy; and there is a valorization of the experience and tacit knowledge of some fraction or configuration of "the people." For some, the people are assumed to be the innocent who have not yet been corrupted by the system, and, therefore, the authority of their experience is determined, paradoxically, by their lack of experience. For some, the people are the outsiders or marginalized whose experience has been constituted by their oppression and suffering, giving them a unique and privileged authority. Sometimes, these two visions of the people may coincide.

This perspective was neatly captured in a conversation I had with a conservative neighbor in rural North Carolina. Knowing his grandson would soon be graduating high school, I asked about his college plans. My neighbor responded, rather caustically, that his family did not see any reason for him to go to college (although, in North Carolina, it would have been affordable). Why, he shot back at me, would I assume that he should go to college? Putting aside my own criticisms of and doubts about the higher education system in the U.S., I responded, rather naively, that people often saw college as an opportunity for young people to expand their horizons, to open their minds and their lives to other possibilities and other futures. For many people, a college education embodied the hope that their children would be able to live better lives than their parents. His angry response was, "Why do I want him to be better than me, to have a different life than I do? What's wrong with me and my life?" I was taken aback and silenced. He saw education as a personal insult. More publicly, recent political rhetoric has rejected as elitism and snobbery the very idea that kids should get a good education for the sake of being educated.

## Media Anti-Intellectualism

It is obvious that the media—the legacy and mainstream media as well as contemporary social media—have played a major role in all of the stories I have just told. But there are stories about the media that are themselves part of the explanation of the current state of knowledge. There are two places the media supposedly present knowledge: The news and their coverage of scientific discoveries.

The story of the transformation of "the news" is a familiar one: As it has moved closer to entertainment, it has become decidedly less informative. Instead of helping people find a way out of the swamp, it is helping create the swamp. They often refuse—in a blatant act of cowardice—to pronounce judgments on competing claims, or even to suggest that such judgments are both possible and necessary.

But there has been less discussion of the ways the media educate—or, more accurately, do not educate—their readers about the processes of knowledge production. The media love the sciences, or anything that they can claim is a science, because it so easily fits into their normal storylines.

They consistently misrepresent the sciences as a series of the latest discoveries or breakthroughs, as if the mere fact of its publication—even the mere fact that someone noticed its publication or wrote a press release—means it is newsworthy and presumably true. But science involves arduous processes (including replication) and contentious arguments through which every finding is judged and its importance understood. The latest paper on any topic, whatever the discipline, is not in and of itself truth.

Anything that can be forced into this mold is science. The life sciences rarely live up to the model of the physical sciences, although the media act as if they do. The social sciences almost never do; but the media legitimate their impressive magic trick of using experimental methods and statistical analyses to achieve practical (e.g., policy) effects to mimic the auratic status of science. The media often even take it one step further when they present social scientists—from economists to psychologists—as if they can directly and objectively predict human behavior. They cannot, beyond the trivial.

Research and scholarship that cannot be represented as scientific, as a series of discoveries, is simply ignored, unless they can frame something as a human interest story (e.g., archeological, anthropological, or historical findings, or literary historical discoveries) or a fashionable event to be ridiculed (e.g., the latest meeting of the Modern Language Association). These forms of knowledge production generally include the humanities and the more qualitative and interpretive social sciences. They used to be called the human sciences, when science meant an organized body of knowledge. They appear messier because they do not, cannot, hide the conversations and disagreements.

The media, and, hence, most people, assume that the human sciences don't advance. They do, but not in the same ways as the sciences. They move forward more slowly, hesitatingly, and modestly, and largely through productive arguments. The media often mock such work as if it simply reproduced the enjoyment of its intellectuals (wallowing?) in a space of constant and never-resolvable arguments. But if you look carefully, the arguments do change, although, sometimes, older arguments return in a new light. Like any science, they advance but not on a single front; they advance in some places and not others, and they advance in different ways and directions. The production of knowledge in any field is an ongoing conversation, advancing and retreating, but always crawling toward better truths and better understandings, rarely arriving at a final shared conclusion.

The media never consider whether the study of human social existence might require tools other than experiments and measurements. After all, it is trying to understand what may be the most complicated phenomenon we know of. Has our understanding grown? Yes. Has our ability to translate it into more popular languages or concrete policy proposals improved? To be honest, not so much. The media constantly lambast the human sciences for their incomprehensible vocabularies. They don't mention that almost every form of scholarship, including the sciences, have their own technical languages. In fact, any expert (including doctors, auto mechanics, plumbers, chefs, and gardeners) have vocabularies that seem obscure to outsiders.

These technical languages serve a number of vital purposes. They function as a communicative shorthand among those working on shared questions or problems. Whether one is a mechanic, a gardener, or a philosopher, it would be much less efficient to operate without them. They also function to allow some people to distance themselves from people's ordinary languages, which encode and reproduce many taken-for-granted assumptions about the world and specific elements within it (from nature to buildings to concepts). For scholars, both mathematical and conceptual vocabularies enable them to put aside the commonsense, if only temporarily. Almost no one rejects the hard sciences because they cannot understand them. The media often employ journalists trained as translators for just this purpose. But people (and the media) seem to assume that because a scholar studies human realities, something with which everyone has some familiarity, they are not allowed to challenge the authority of common sense or to speak in specialized vocabularies. And there is no need for translators. Yet relatively few people blame Shakespeare or Proust because their writing is difficult, and you have to work to understand their words.

I have already suggested that the crises of knowledge are, in important ways, a question of time and the forms of temporality in which people work. I believe that one of the commandments of knowledge production is that it takes work, and work takes time. The media never bothers to ask about how the contingencies of funding and the inequal distribution of teaching loads affect the distribution of time in the academy. The media refuse to accept that they operate in a different temporality than scholarship (and, I might add, than public policy, politics, and commerce). They try very hard to impose their time on the academy, with devastating consequences.

Occasionally, I would get a call from a media outlet asking me for a comment on some event that is happening now. It is bad enough that what they want is not a serious analysis but a sound bite, but they want it <u>now</u>. My usual response is that if they want a comment from me as a scholar, they have to give me time to research the question. I don't assume that I always and already understand everything, just because I have researched some (even similar) things in the past. If they want a comment from me as just another person, without using my status as a marker of expertise, I am happy to give it to them. They never do. Might I say something interesting, even useful, on the spot, as an expert—I would hope so, but that doesn't mean I should offer every thought as a claim to truth. In general, knowledge does not lend itself to immediacy and sound bites.

As academics continue to succumb to the growing pressure to speak too quickly and outside the scope of their knowledge, they undermine the very basis of their own authority. Expertise is always open to being contested, but it nevertheless is based on a claim that you have devoted significant time and energy to studying something, to familiarizing yourself with the various positions, accounts, issues, and arguments surrounding it, and to finding some grounds for choosing to defend some position(s) or answer(s) above others. And that means that you have to allow the possibility of being wrong, without committing suicide. I think of this as the definition of intellectual responsibility. This is the only basis for claiming that our judgments and interpretations are any better than those of any other citizen—that we have done the rigorous intellectual-scholarly work.

But perhaps we should not let that be the end of our responsibilities. The fact is that we are talking about things that matter to people. To whatever extent we think that we do know something about human realities, do we not have some responsibility to offer what we know to the larger arena of the struggles to make the future? If the only way we can imagine doing this is by oversimplification, we will have failed; we need to create new common languages and better stories. That will be the hardest challenge yet.

## The Threat of Relativism

There are two overarching threats to the possibility of knowledge: The claim of absolute authority and certainty and the monstrous face of relativism. Relativism can take many forms. For example, cultural relativism claims that truth and value are entirely determined within a particular culture. Therefore, all judgements, even ethical ones, across cultures are impossible. Every culture—sometimes stretched to every group or even individual—has its own truth.

Consequently, any claim to truthfully represent a world outside of the culture-specific language is impossible. Rather than describing a world, language literally creates the world. Ironically, a famous statement of this argument was offered by a senior advisor to G.W. Bush:[2]

> The aide said that guys like me were 'in what we call the reality-based com munity,' which he defined as people who 'believe that solutions emerge from judicious study of discernable reality' ... 'that's not the way the world really works anymore ... We're an empire now, and when we act, we create reality. And while you're studying that reality—judiciously as you will—we'll act again creating other new realities, which you can study too, and that's how things will sort out. We're history's actors ... and you, all of you, will be left to just study what we do.'

This comment acknowledges that not every effort to construct reality succeeds. It raises questions, therefore, about the conditions that make particular constructions effective. Are they internal or external to the particular effort—or both?

Relativism has many sources, but its roots lie in the academy and modern intellectual debates. In this sense, the human sciences have contributed, perhaps unintentionally, to the crises of knowledge. They have helped bring the monster of relativism to life. Understanding it, however, requires putting it back into the debates, and understanding its relation to at least two other claims: Anti-foundationalism and constructionism. All three concepts have their own histories and variations. Anti-foundationalism was marshaled as an argument against the dominance of logical positivism in the 1960s and 1970s, which had purported to justify science as the only legitimate form of knowledge. Anti-foundationalism argues that there is no universal, necessary, and sufficient basis for all truth and knowledge. Neither empirical observation nor logic can provide the ultimate legitimation for all knowledge.

Constructionism has a much longer and star-studded history; its roots are generally traced back to the late Enlightenment/early modern philosophy of Immanuel Kant. Kant argued that humans inhabit a constructed reality, and that they are, in some part, responsible for constructing the very reality in which they live. It is not difficult to see the problems this poses, for if the human world is constructed, then could there not be different realities? Could reality not vary in time and space? Could it not change?

I want to elaborate the notion of constructionism a bit further since it will play an important role in my own version of slow thinking. Constructionism starts with the assumption that the world is composed of relations rather than independent things. Nothing exists outside of, free of, relations. Relations precede the terms that exist within the relations, for it is only within a specific relation that anything takes on the meanings, functions, and capacities that we then assume exist outside the relation. The relation defines what the elements within it are, and what they are capable of doing (i.e., what kinds of effects they can have). As the relation changes, so do the elements. And relations are themselves not independent entities but always exist in further relations; relations are organized into larger sets of relations. As such, you can describe social existence as the composing of compositions, the assembling of assemblages, and the constant articulation of relations out of relations. Social existence is all about the relations of relations, always changing and always producing change (or fighting against it).

Everything exists only in and as relations, but that does not mean that everything exists in the same way, that there is a single form of relationality itself. Every composition produces specific kinds of relations, which have different capacities and produce different effects; there is no reason to assume that it will always necessarily produce only the same effects. It is not enough to simply describe or explain something as a relation or to say that it is somehow connected to other things. These are questions. What kind of relation? What kind of connections? How are they constructed?

While it may be true that everything is potentially related to everything else, it is not very helpful, for it only reaffirms the chaos. Every level of reality is organized, relations of relations and so forth, from the quantum universe to the emergence of life and sentience, to the production of individualities and populations defined by particular behavioral codes and capacities, to the human and social forms of intelligence and agency, however unfamiliar such organizations may seem.

Relativism has many roots, but the most commonly cited are Hegel and Nietzsche. It says that all judgments are only determined by and valid within the particular constructed reality. In Nietzschean terms, it says that truth depends upon a perspective that exists prior to or external to the production of a constructed reality. As a result, knowledge is always and already contaminated by some prior interests or values. Competing knowledge claims can be understood and possibly adjudicated only by appealing to the different interests they express, justify, and enact.

In the past decade, as constructionist arguments have become more publicly available (and to some extent, been strategically taken up by elements of the right), they have often been presented (misconstrued) as justification for the refusal of evidence, the deconstruction of any and all truths, and the rejection of any possibility of judging stories to be better or worse in anything but purely pregiven political terms. Such relativisms easily lead into a rather paranoid view of the relation between knowledge and power.[3]

Every version of relativism and constructionism is anti-foundationalist; but not every version of constructionism is relativist, or vice versa. My own position is an anti-relativist constructionism. But if constructionism is not—at least not necessarily—relativist, it is incumbent on us to explain why and how we avoid relativism. If we feel compelled to acknowledge the multiplicity of knowledges, cultures, and even experienced realities, we have to consider the consequences of such arguments in relation to the current context of political struggles. How do we explain why all realities, knowledges, judgments, and stories are not equal? It is important to establish the possibility that some stories are better than others, based on something other than politics or common sense. I will navigate my own way out of this quagmire in the form of slow thinking.

## Notes

1  Agnotology is the study of deliberately created ignorance or doubt.
2  Suskind, 2004.
3  It is commonly associated with a simplistic reading of Marx's theory of ideology, and with a serious misreading of Foucault's theory of knowledge/power.

## Reference

Suskind, Ron. "Faith, Certainty and the Presidency of George W. Bush." *The New York Times Magazine*. October 17, 2004.

# 4
# ON THE WAY TO THINKING

There are many ways of thinking, each of which makes the world intelligible, perceptible, and livable. My favorite example is from an episode of *Star Trek: The Next Generation*. Picard is forced to communicate with an alien who thinks with stories as literal events. Instead of saying, "I love you like Romeo loved Juliet," the alien would say "Romeo and Juliet on the balcony," which would be fine if you knew the story of Romeo and Juliet, but it is highly unlikely that Picard would know the alien's cultural references.

As I have said, I do not think my way of thinking, my particular version of "slow thinking," is anything more than a useful way, perhaps even an important way, to answer certain kinds of questions in certain kinds of contexts. It just so happens that I think that this is one of those contexts and the questions I have been raising are those kinds of questions.

Slow thinking is not a seamless, continuous process. It is made up of seven relatively independent intellectual exercises or thought-practices. Each one is itself a way of thinking involving both conceptual and empirical elements; some can exist independently but most usually operate in specific relations and sequences. They are: Conceptual thinking, critical/theoretical thinking, critique, contextual thinking, conjunctural thinking, problematization or the construction of problem spaces, and conjunctural analysis. I invite you to consider these, recognizing that there are others, if only to see where they might take us.[1] Let me repeat: What follows will be difficult, so fasten your seat belts, batten down the hatches, make yourself comfortable, and let's ride the rapids of slow thinking together.

DOI: 10.4324/9781003662587-5

## Conceptual Thinking

Almost every way of thinking involves concepts (although I am not sure about Picard's alien); concepts are the building blocks of thought. Concepts are abstractions that produce identities out of populations or multiplicities. Lines on an x-ray become sub-atomic particles; particular lines become neutrinos. Looked at another way, concepts establish relations among individual entities (whether individual people or buildings). Concepts define how these individuals might belong together. Every concept is a generalization that imposes some kind of unity on a diverse set, but it need not posit any homogeneity, or a single essential property. Consequently, concepts define the first line of defense against the chaos, the first way we encounter the world as organized, allowing us to identify, differentiate, and aggregate the things that "belong" together, although we may not know the basis of the relations (i.e., we may not immediately recognize the similarities and differences). Concepts need not deny or erase the differences; they are simply pragmatic devices for establishing relations (perhaps akin to sets in mathematical terms).

Consider a concept like "reader," which ignores all the differences among readers to abstract out only the fact of being a reader. It ignores the differences among readers: Different readers read different things, in different ways, and so on. Concepts make the relations that we often take for granted perceivable. The identities or unities they produce don't pre-exist the concepts. Sometimes, a concept may reproduce a familiar identity in a slightly different way. Sometimes, it may call a new identity or unity into existence. But concepts also obscure and even erase other possibilities, defining what can and cannot be seen or said. Hence, every conceptual order is fragile and unstable, confronting us with the need for other, perhaps new, concepts, with the need to go on thinking.

Let me take a more contentious example. I am often confronted with claims that "the left" does not exist or, at least, that it has no identifiable content. Presumably, that means it is not a useful concept. Some people refuse the term or refuse to be named by it. They assume it entails commitments to specific organizations and strategies and ideas and practices—e.g., state politics, mass mobilizations, Marxism, unions, etc. They argue that what used to be a more homogenous left is now too diverse and fragmented to be captured under a single sign. They are no doubt partially right about many of these claims.

The composition of "the left" has varied widely, historically and geographically—in local, national, and regional ways—but this is probably true of any political group identity. Although its origins were arbitrary (derived from a particular distribution of parliamentary seats), it has largely functioned as a site of conceptual struggle. Certainly, today, the distribution of issues and positions is rarely clear, but I doubt that it ever was. Nor does the political field exhibit a simple dichotomy between left and right, but, again, I doubt that it ever did. The world has always been too messy for such easy arrangements. Finding allies in particular struggles has become unpredictable? Not new. Passionate disagreements with allies? Not new. No fixed definitions of the left? Not new. Some older left formations no longer seem particularly useful, oppositional, or even progressive? Not new. Some important issues are not so neatly captured by the right/left distinction? Again, not new.

In some cases, people assume that "the left" is necessarily contaminated by hierarchies of power and suffering, that it homogenizes differences under some defined master sign of identity and propriety. Does this happen? In some cases, in some contexts, yes. But that doesn't mean it is always true, or that it has to be true. Besides, no effort to impose hierarchies and negate differences ever entirely succeeds; it leaves gaps, cracks (that's how the light gets in), and dissidents. Why do people often assume the worst of their allies?

The assumed unity and homogeneity of the left has been the exception rather than the rule and, even then, it has always been something of a failed project. Perhaps there have been times when "the left" seemed to name a stable, well-defined set of organizations and positions, or when it tried (unsuccessfully) to impose absolute, insular unity and conformity. But there have also been times when it embraced its own heterogeneity and instability and attempted to encompass its many differences and disagreements.

Ironically, those who criticize the use of the "left" rarely have the same reservations about using other terms that are at least as problematic—such as the "right," conservatism, capitalism, fascism, or neo-liberalism, or a host of social identifications including Black and people of color. Nor do they have an alternative to describe or construct radically progressive alliances. Despite the protestations, I assume that most people "of the left" have some sense of what this strange creature looks like, and if they had to, they could assemble positions, values, concepts, etc. that inform and enliven various left formations, although it might be difficult to say which are essential.

How then might we think of "the left"? Every concept is, following Stuart Hall, a "unity-in-difference." Not "one" but a one that is fractured, always many. It is always heterogeneous and not homogeneous, a unity that is differentiated and always changing. If all you do is deconstruct every unity, all you will have left is fragments, a plurality without relations.

Every collective is an ongoing and shifting project. The language of "the left" as a political identity is an attempt to call a collective into existence; it invites and invokes. It names the ongoing effort to construct complicated and fragile forms of unity out of the myriad differences and contradictions of visions, commitments, priorities, strategies, and tactics. The relations have to be made and given voice, even as the unity is constantly re-assembled. Such efforts always define a project in the future tense. That is the work of the concept of the left. That is ultimately the work of better stories.

Conceptual thinking raises a problem. Concepts organize particulars. But what is a particular at one moment (an individual or a building) might be a concept at another. Or, what appears as a concept at one moment (a neutrino) may appear as a particular at another. My existence as an individual is both that of a particular entity and that of a conceptual abstraction, when I consider myself the unity of my (biological and social) relations. I am the sum of a population and one part of a population.

Thinking is paradoxical! There is no fixed distinction between the particular and the conceptual, an individual and a collective, facts and stories, and so on. Identifying something as a particular means that you have already conceptualized it. Insofar as you are thinking, and we all think most of the time, there are only abstractions.

But not all abstractions are equal. We can construct levels of abstraction, ranging from the most concrete to the most universal. But levels of abstraction are not objectively discrete, stable, and permanent planes. They are more like the spaces marked by the chalk lines on playing fields or crime scenes, interrupting a continuum. It is easy to assume that the concrete is simply and purely empirical with no conceptual organization, while the universal is merely speculative with no empirical content. Every level has its own empirical content, which presents itself through some (if only implicit) set of concepts. It is easy to assume that the higher levels of abstraction are less complex than the lower ones. Every level has its own forms of complexity. While the United States is more abstract than the local Governor's Club, it is no less empirical or complex.

The contents and complexities at each level define the differences that matter and that can be observed and, possibly, measured. Consequently, different concepts will be more appropriate or useful at certain levels than others, as you try to make the "truths" of that level intelligible. This raises important questions. What is the relation between concepts and levels? How do we identify the most appropriate level for the questions we are asking? How do we identify the most appropriate concepts for the level? How do we move between different levels? Can we understand the richness of people's lives at the levels at which quantum mechanics or cognitive science operate? Such questions take us to the next exercise, where thinking becomes self-reflective and critical.

### Critical/Theoretical Thinking

If thinking is almost always conceptual, critical thinking (for short) is where slow thinking begins to separate itself from belief and common sense. The latter are often devoted primarily to defending, securing, reinforcing, or persuading others to accept what they think they already know. There is nothing wrong with this, unless its certainty refuses all other possible paths to knowledge.

Critical thinking is a controlled skepticism that is willing to question whatever is taken for granted. It does not doubt everything. (Descartes tried and it did not turn out very well.) Critical thinking does not attempt to overthrow every assumption, everything that we might take for granted; it does not dismiss all of the good sense—and there is lots of good sense— already out there. It questions whatever is blocking the path of thinking, whatever might be preventing us from seeing other possibilities, other paths. It merely attempts to go on thinking.

This demands a double consciousness so you can stand back from yourself and the dominant forms of common sense.[2] Critical thinking makes the world strange, defamiliarizing it enough to see what work the familiar concepts and stories are doing. It makes you into a stranger in your own land, in a now strange land; it denaturalizes whatever claims to be obvious, necessary, or natural. It opens you up to being surprised. It is a self-critical willingness to have the limits, weaknesses, and deceptions of your concepts shown for what they are. It asks that you be willing to discover that the world is not what you thought it was and that it is not operating according to your assumptions. Critical thinking creates the capacity to hear what you did not already recognize and to see what has remained invisible.

It is a creative act that synthesizes reason and imagination, going elsewhere in order to return to see the world in a different light. Classical Greek thought had a nice image of this: A representative of one community travels to another to participate in some "foreign" activity; then they return to their community to offer an account. The foreign activity is not passively given or received but is actively investigated for its difference. Thinking referred to ways of seeing as active engagements with an other, which could multiply the possibilities of thinking and living, without abandoning all the norms or truths of your own community.[3]

Not to sound too cynical, but it is becoming harder (perhaps it has been for some time) to find intellectuals and academics willing to question their own assumption, including the questions they pose. Do we even know anymore what it means to question our assumptions? I wonder whether most of us— and, yes, I include myself in that—could actually defend them, whether we are willing to wrestle with the angels and the devils that offer themselves up as alternatives.

## A Brief Detour: Anti-Intellectualism on the Left

I recently had a disheartening encounter. A labor activist-organizer whom I respect was sitting in my living room passionately arguing about politics.

Despite our disagreements, I thought the conversation was both productive and enjoyable until she said that if you cannot explain something to a five-year-old, then you do not understand it and it is not worth anything. Was she suggesting that ideas only matter if they are that simple and easy to digest, which is another way of saying that ideas, thinking, don't matter? It is the classic anti-intellectual argument. I assume she would exempt such things as physics, which means that she was basically claiming that human life is easily understandable. She then put the nail in the coffin by telling me that the academy had nothing to say to activists, nothing to contribute to contemporary political struggles. I was stunned but managed—given my wife's glares—to stay silent. I wanted to remind her of Hannah Arendt's statement that "Under conditions of tyranny, it is far easier to act than to think." She probably would have dismissed it anyway.

Such arguments become clearer if we look within the academy. The renowned French social theorist of science, Bruno Latour, once asked: "Would it not be rather terrible if we were still training young kids—yes, young recruits, young cadets—for wars that are no longer possible, fighting enemies long gone, conquering territories that no longer exist, leaving them ill-equipped in the face of threats we had not anticipated, for which we are so thoroughly unprepared?"[4]

This insightful question might be suggesting that critical thinking has misdiagnosed the current context, that the critical spirit needs reinvigoration and new tools, and that it needs to update its analyses to take account of new configurations of power and resistance. It might be reminding us to question our understandings of what's going on, of the battles that need to be fought, and of the best tools and strategies for such struggles.

Unfortunately, the more common reading seems to be that critical thinking has "run out of steam," which is what the title of the essay suggests, and, thus, it ends up repeating a long tradition of left anti-intellectualism. Critical thinking doesn't matter; only organizing matters, only agitation matters. Any ideas worth considering come out of these activities and the everyday thinking of organic intellectuals; the supposed erudition and expertise of the educated intellectual are bogus. They merely reproduce the relations of power inherent in the very claim to represent—know—the world. The rejection of critical knowledge then becomes in itself an act of political resistance, creating an almost absolute schism between knowledge and politics.

This argument could serve as a possible example of critical thinking, calling certain assumptions into question. What are those assumptions? That things are never what they seem, and the (real) Truth is necessarily concealed below the surface by the dominant structures of power. Ordinary people are incapable of seeing or understanding this Truth. As a result, critical thinking is little more than the paranoid search for certainties already known, negative thinking carried to the nth degree.

I am reminded of a (apocryphal?) story about when the U.S. military tried to understand why the residents of a South Pacific island refused to help them exterminate mosquitoes carrying malaria. Their response: If we had mosquitoes as big as those in the pictures you showed us, we would have helped, but ours are much smaller. Are there critical thinkers who fit the description offered above? Yes, I suppose. Is it the only way to practice critical thinking? Not at all.

Does power hide itself? Sometimes. Are the workings of power always visible to everyone (or anyone) at first glance? Unlikely. It is not that truth is hidden, available only to a select few. Rather, it is there, inscribed on the surfaces, but it has to be made visible by connecting the dots in unexpected ways. It has to be made visible not because it is hidden but because our ordinary ways of seeing, thinking, and speaking are not quite up to the task. Critical thinking offers tools to look at the world differently, to see what is already showing itself.

What does Latour (and his followers) offer in the place of critical thinking? Positive thinking: An ethics of creativity and love, a politics "motivated by life;" the support and celebration of every creative, resistant, and alternative community and organization; the construction of new capacities.[5] However vital the connection between critical thinking and these more ethical concerns and modes of solidarity may be, the political question, at least as I understand it more pragmatically, remains unaddressed: How do we get out of here, and go to someplace better? It takes thought and analysis: Of the balance of forces, of the possibilities and constraints of the terrain, and of the strengths and weaknesses of those standing against you. And it requires a historical appreciation of the victories and defeats that have led you to the present context.

It has become all too easy to abandon critical thinking in the contemporary political and cultural context. You abandon it when you fall back onto your own certainties, as if you already know what we need to know, as if the truth of your claims is somehow guaranteed. You abandon critical thinking

- when you refuse to hear ideas that challenge you
- when you judge before you understand, making yourself into the arbiter of political judgment
- when you assume that the task is simply to find the right theory or concept, as if they will guarantee effective politics
- when you reduce everything to a single, simple explanation
- when you take what you see or hear as truth, as transparently available knowledge
- when you begin already knowing what you will find, leaving no room to be surprised or proven wrong

- when you shy away from the difficulties of thinking complexly about complexity
- when you let political passion rule intellect

## Critique

If critical/theoretical thinking shines a different light on reality, critique continues the task by telling one kind of better story. But let's establish one thing first: Critique does not mean criticizing, opposing, or rejecting; it is not about condemning whatever you do not like. It is not simply calling out forms of oppression, nor declaring your opposition to domination. Nor does it involve finding a deeper "hidden" reality—which is rarely actually hidden because we almost always already know it is there. Such practices may have their place, but they do not begin to capture the difficult task of critique.

Critique is a specific practice of thinking, which raises particular questions. First proposed by Immanuel Kant, critique is one of the intellectual tools that defines modern thought. It is not the only one, nor is it only found there. One of the best examples is Karl Marx's critique of the classical political economists (e.g., Adam Smith). Contrary to what is often said, he did not accuse them of offering a false description of capitalism, one that focused only on surface appearances (market exchange) while hiding the true reality (production). He did not accuse them of being wrong but of misrepresentation, inadequacy, and partiality, of confusing a part for the whole. Classical political economy starts its story with markets but fails to see that the beginning of its story (markets) is the end of another. What is it that gives us markets in the first place? What are the conditions of possibility of markets that are not told in the political economists' story? What is "concealed" is not so much hidden as rendered absent by the account itself. And that is not simply the processes of production but the complexity of the whole process, "the circuit of production," which includes not only exchange (markets) but also production and distribution. Because the classical political economists' story takes the market for granted as given, it assumed that it exists universally in nature, as it were, as the basis of any economy. It "naturalized" the market. And capitalism could appear as the end of the history of economies.

Can you see what this implies? Critique brings constructionism into play in the form of contingency. If critical thinking questions what we think we know, what we are willing to assume, then it follows that those assumptions are contingent rather than necessary. Critique goes beyond critical theoretical thinking by attempting to understand how the world and our accounts of it have been constructed.

If reality, at least insofar as we are capable of experiencing it, is a construction, a configuration of relations, then our present reality is contingent. The present did not have to be the way it is—or, better, the way we take for granted; it could have been otherwise. How did the existing configurations of reality come to be? How is reality itself constructed? How were things made to be the way they are? How were they made to seem ... so real, so obvious, so natural, so unquestionable? How have we come to believe what we believe? How is the obviousness of what we take for granted produced? How do some beliefs come to be "true?"

Critique seeks to understand the conditions of possibility (not the same as studying history) of the particular reality and the truth of its accounts. How did it come to be this way rather than that? Why does this appear here but not there? What has enabled it to exist in the way it does, and what are the consequences? Taken together, critical thinking and critique carefully loosen existing relations, seeing the processes by which some relations were recomposed into a new taken-for-granted organization of relations. They attempt to move beyond what is already see-able, sayable, and know-able. They attempt to make visible what we do not yet know how to see or say or even question.

Again, all versions of constructionism are anti-foundationalist. They deny that there is a moment of certainty, a True reality (e.g., as described by science, whether quantum mechanics, informatics, bio-informatics, etc.), behind the constructions. It opposes appeals to necessity and inevitability (it had to be that way, that's just the way things are). It puts contingency—both chance and unpredictability—back into the world so that nothing is ever guaranteed in advance. But it does not throw us into a random universe in which everything happens by accident. There are processes and agencies of determination that work alongside chance. Some of those agencies involve humanity; some involve the ways we think about and describe the world. But not all. Reality—and even the ways we think about it—is produced in the spaces between chance and necessity, between the discursive and the material, through a creative production of ever-changing relations of relations.

But constructionist theories do not deny the reality of the contingently constructed worlds in which we live, worlds in which everything is contingent, everywhere, all the way down. They simply assert that constructions are real. A building is constructed, yet no one doubts its reality. While any constructed reality or experienced world could have been otherwise, a particular world is real and not some kind of weird illusion precisely because it shapes and affects our lives. It has real material effects.

At various times and places, some of these effects will be valuable and important. Their benefits give them meaning, coherence, and an affective power. The constructions themselves—whether of reality or of thought—are productive for a way of life. And their contingency will disappear into their taken-for-grantedness. Their reality becomes natural or inevitable so that we can live comfortably, and people begin to assume they live in a non-contingent reality. Critique does not attempt to deconstruct every moment when the contingent appears to be real, when the construction becomes naturalized, when people believe they have found some Truth. Critique offers a way of thinking that prevents the fact that they are constructions from paralyzing you.

Critique seeks to enable us to inquire into the possibilities for the future disclosed in the present. The French thinker Michel Foucault extended Kant's understanding of critique, suggesting that critique problematizes the present; it makes the present into a problem for thought.[6] More than simply pointing to the contingency of the present, critique demonstrates that it is only the actuality of the present itself that makes us what we are. But the contingency of the present poses a demand and a task: To take up the possibility "of no longer being, doing, or thinking as we are." This is the "heroic" possibility, in the present, of being otherwise, of creating a different present. Critique, then, is a demand to reflect on the specificity or difference of the present in order to imagine it otherwise and transform it—and ourselves—but not by destroying it. (For Foucault, this is illustrated in the life of the dandy, he who creates himself).

But critical thinking returns to haunt critique. The attempt to remake the present can only be carried out from within the present; you can never entirely escape. After all, you can only see what your concepts let you see—and, therefore, what they shape, produce, and bring into focus. Because contingency is everywhere, my understanding of any construction is always figured in advance by things that came before my questions, by the stories that have made me who I am. Your own relation to a situation has already partly predetermined the stories you might tell about it. Your effort to question specific relations, realities, or knowledges was partly written in advance by the stories that have defined your own investments and entitlements. This is the predicament of the intellectual.

One final point: Neither critical/theoretical thinking nor critique are in and of themselves a politics, nor a politics by other means, nor even necessarily linked to a particular politics. But the exacting work they call for is a condition of possibility of effective political struggle and social change (even if the result is not knowable in advance). Thus, unlike some contemporary notions of the scholar-activist, which tend to place intellectuals at the service of already defined politics, slow thinking struggles to retain some distance from politics.

## Notes

1 I would be remiss not to acknowledge that my version of slow thinking is my reading of Stuart Hall's practice of cultural studies. See Hall, 2017a and 2017b, 2019a.

2   For many of the most profound thinkers, who come from situations of oppression, that choice exists alongside and intertwined with the double consciousness that they are forced to live, from which there is no respite.
3   According to the rhetorical theorist Christian Lundberg (conversation).
4   Latour, 2004.
5   But how do we make judgments about the value of different communities or capacities? Doesn't capitalism also seek the expansion of both?
6   Foucault, 1984.

## References

Foucault, Michel. "What is Enlightenment?". *The Foucault Reader*. New York: Pantheon Books, 1984.

Hall, Stuart. *Cultural Studies (1983)*. Eds. Jennifer Daryl Slack and Lawrence Grossberg. Durham: Duke University Press, 2017a.

Hall, Stuart. *Familiar Stranger*. Ed. Bill Schwarz. Durham: Duke University Press, 2017b.

Hall, Stuart. *Essential Essays, vol 1. Foundations of Cultural Studies*. Ed. David Morley. Durham: Duke University Press, 2019.

Latour, Bruno. "Why Has Critique Run out of Steam?" *Critical Inquiry* 30 (Winter 2004).

# 5

# CONTEXTUAL THINKING

Contextual thinking is a concrete application of constructionism. It identifies and investigates a particular reality or region of that reality and refers to it as a context. It does not think of contexts as isolatable, demarcated locations in time and space, often serving as mere background to some more focused investigation. It embraces the complexity of relations and organizations. It refuses to reduce that complexity, as if it were, somehow, whether in the first or the last instance, in the beginning or at the end, all about one thing, or it is caused by or an expression of one thing. Everything is all about money, or sex, or race, or liberalism. Nor will it be satisfied reducing everything to the working out of a binary opposition between two things, a or b, male or female, black or white. Rather, contextual thinking holds to a more modest logic: Yes, it is about a, and (but) it is also about b, and c, and maybe not d, but clearly e .... Contextual thinking even assumes that the nature of complexity varies—both qualitatively and quantitively—from one context to another.

## Contexts and Compositions

Contextual thinking continues the task of critique by looking at the specific processes of construction or composition at work on constructing the contingent reality of a particular context. A context is an organization of relations and relations of relations, a composition of compositions. Specific relations in a context will be able to do certain things and not others, depending on their location in the context. As that location changes and it enters into new compositions, its capacities and effects will change.

DOI: 10.4324/9781003662587-6

I find it helpful to use metaphors to explain contextual thinking: For example, it is a lot like gardening. There are formal gardens, completely structured, and there are wild gardens, verging on chaos. For my wife, who is an amazing gardener, the best garden is in the middle, skirting around and playing with both possibilities and never seeking a fully stable balance, always finding some order in the ever-threatening chaos, but never letting the order destroy the beauty of chaos. And she constantly reminds me that a gardener is never free to do whatever she wishes because there are conditions that set the limits on what is possible: Soil, rainfall, sun and shade, slope of the terrain, etc. A garden is a story told collectively by the gardener, the plants, and the earth, creating a context.

Following on critique, contextual thinking views particular contexts as sites of contestation at which historical realities, which always leave their traces, are made, unmade, and remade. If critique abandons necessity for contingency, contextual thinking abandons universality and transcendence for specificity.[1] To use one obvious example, capitalism is not and has never been a single or stable thing. Even its birth was the result of the contingent and complicated intersections of numerous processes.

Critique is even suspicious of generalizations across contexts. While it may appear that the same relation(s) exist in different contexts, we have to recognize how the supposedly "same" relation is articulated differently, with different effects. It often refers to such supposed equivalences as "family resemblances" or "the changing same." Hence, there can be no general theory of capitalism, or of race and racism, and so on. For example: That some of my observations about the contemporary U.S. political culture have been rightly said of other times and places does not mean that I am saying the same thing, or that it has the same resonances. The specific ways events or statements take shape and the specific effects they produce are the results of the articulations and re-articulations of contexts.

Consider something as simple as listening to a song or watching a movie. What does it mean? What does it do? What effects does—or might—it have? The answers to such questions are not necessary and guaranteed, waiting to be discovered with the right methods. You cannot find the answer inside the text or by questioning the audience, although both are important. Its effects will be determined by how both are placed into a complicated set of organized relations, a context, which will articulate them in specific ways.

The reality of a particular context is never guaranteed in advance; its relations are never necessary and unavoidable; their effects and expressions never inevitable. There were and are always other possibilities. They are the result of processes and struggles, natural and social, of various forms of agency that forge relations and condition their effects. Human beings are certainly part of this ongoing history, but that does not mean that human beings are always in control.

Contextual thinking has implications for how we think about history, power, and even theory itself. It questions the simple separation of the old and the new, the before and the after. Contexts are never simply straightforward continuations or repetitions of the past, nor are they ever complete and total breaks with the past. But things do change. It is not enough to talk about evolution or development. We need more specificity about the articulations of the old and the new. The old continues to operate, sometimes in the same way, and sometimes in different ways because it is placed into other relations, operating in a different context. Things change because new elements and relations come into existence, either by emergence, or by struggles, or by invention. They change the capacities and effects of elements that have moved into the present, taking only some of their old relations and effects with them. The result is that relations almost always have unexpected and unintended consequences—capitalists dismiss them as side-effects—but they are often more telling than the so-called primary effects. The task is always to understand how a balance of the old and the new is constructed.

Contextual thinking understands power at its most basic as the capacity to make relations. It operates through many processes and agencies, and it takes on many forms. Contextual thinking investigates the many technologies, forces, principles, and organizations of power, and how they contribute to the construction of any specific context. For example, you cannot separate questions of immigration from the nature of both domestic and non-domestic labor markets. If you do not want cheap labor entering the domestic market, you probably have to transform both in significant ways. And the story does not end there. Contextual thinking refuses to assume that there is ever a single mode of power (e.g., distribution of resources and wealth, racial formations) determining the politics of a context. It refuses to assume in advance what the political stakes are in any context, or what the outcome of any struggle will be. Such assumptions too quickly let us off the hook of doing the work. The only assumption it makes is that no structure of power is ever completely successful; there is always a crack in everything.

As for theory, contextual thinking dismisses the search for the ultimately right theory, one that would answer all our questions. Such a theory would define our stories in advance, give us certainty, and close down the need for further conversations or, at least, limit them in all too predictable ways. Such a view of theory also lets us off the hook, telling us in advance what we need to know, or simply repeating what we want to hear, rather than leading us to explore what we do not already know and may not expect. Such a theory becomes a sacred mantra to be worshipped and carried abroad.

Instead, contextual thinking recognizes that concepts and their relations are always expressions of the contexts out of which they arise. These concepts and relations attempt to articulate questions not yet fully formed, and to provide answers using the rich resources of thinking available to them. But they also respond to those questions by seeking to recompose the context, offering a different construction of where we are, which makes visible some things—including possibilities—otherwise not seen. At the same time, contextual thinking knows that concepts and their relations are not entirely bound to their origins; that would contradict the assumption of contingency. It does mean that we have to be cautious and reflective when we attempt to re-articulate them and bend them to new meanings and effects, like transplanting a flower into new soil. Concepts are profane tools that you take up, reshape, or put aside depending on their ability to do useful work in a particular context. Contextual thinking teaches us that thinking never stops. The task is to go on thinking.

## Doing Contextuality

Contextual thinking, unlike the previous practices I have described, poses a serious challenge to the organization of knowledge by disciplines. Disciplines are defined around some conceptual object (the economy, the state, social relations, the psyche, etc.). It needs to be remembered that this structure is a relatively recent invention and imposition, a contingent response to a set of conditions. The object of contextual thinking is a context, an articulated network of relations without a center. You may enter the context in any number of ways, and this may still be determined by the remnants of your disciplinary expertise. I entered it through popular music and political culture but that was never where I was trying to go. My efforts took me far outside my discipline into what the academy inadequately calls interdisciplinarity. And since I never knew where I would find myself next, I was never sure where I had to turn, what I had to read, and how I had to do research. This is more than what passes for contextualization and decentering in the academy; it is a commitment to working with the complexity, however far afield it takes you from your starting point. It means that intellectual work becomes an ongoing experiment in thinking.

There is a certain practicality to this task. Contextual thinking highlights the need to think about the questions you ask: Don't start with questions you cannot answer. Don't ask a question if you are unwilling or unable to do the necessary research. And at all costs, avoid conditional (and counter-factual) questions: What if ...? How many of our contemporary anxieties are the result of such questions? Take up a question that matters, that other people (preferably not academics) want answered. Be careful not to take the question for granted. Instead, consider how the question pre-frames or already constructs the problem it is trying to address. Find better ways of questioning the problem. Now you can begin (if you have not already used up all your time).

How has the problem been made into a problem for society? You will need to disentangle it some, because it came to you already surrounded by relations. You have to work through those relations, examining how it has been composed and looking at how it might be recomposed. Now contextualize its conditions of possibility, including what it itself makes possible in the context. Take a break. Do whatever you do to relax. Admit that you can never complete the task, that you cannot even imagine completing it. Redefine it in more provisional, incomplete, and humble ways so that you are not doomed to failure. And then go out and find all the help you can get.

When I taught a class on rock & roll, I tried to entangle a number of historical lines: The music, of course, but that was rarely at the center of our discussions; other forms of culture that contributed to the notion of youth culture (including popular literature, films, styles of dress, dance, drugs, and spiritualism); the distribution of tastes (measured by sales, etc.), and the forms of fandom. But that merely posed the question: What was the significance of the changes in music culture? And for that, the class spent most of its time reading histories (mostly from the bottom) and social analyses (unfortunately mostly from the top) about the changing material contexts of life, especially of youth, in the United States. I hoped that looking at the articulations would allow the class to begin recomposing the broader context and understand the relations between the music and ongoing struggles of power.

Let me offer another metaphor. Contextual thinking is like doing a jigsaw puzzle but under very peculiar circumstances. You are starting with a box filled with thousands of pieces (many of them simply shades of the same color), from an unknown number of puzzles. The covers are gone so you have no knowledge of the original puzzle-images. The pieces are not readable on their own, and any glimmer of where they might belong is always just out of reach.

You take pieces out of the box, and you have to decide where they belong, what they are part of in the larger puzzle. Sometimes, when you take a piece out of the box, it drags others with it; pieces are stuck together, sometimes loosely and sometimes strongly. Do they belong together or is it just an accident of the box? Even when the pieces come to you already embedded within relations, you may not recognize the combinations, nor understand their implications. You have to decide whether to disconnect them. Each piece you place into the puzzle is likely to change your sense of what is going on and modify the significance of other pieces. And to make matters worse, pieces keep disappearing—often pieces you had assumed were absolutely central—and new and often unexpected pieces keep appearing. So, the puzzle is constantly re-making itself. Perhaps it is not an ordinary puzzle but a (Vulcan?) three-dimensional jigsaw puzzle, or Dejarik (holochess, as played in *Star Wars*), or a self-producing erector set.

With each piece you remove from the box, you ask yourself, is this piece pertinent? Is it going to contribute in some significant way to completing the picture? Or at least to completing a more modest task of assembling a small part of the puzzle—maybe a garden in the upper right, or a car at the center? But you cannot avoid asking yourself, how will I know when I have enough pieces to be confident that I am on the right track? How do you decide whether additional pieces might significantly alter your guess about the puzzle? For example, in my own case, the past decades have produced a plethora of valuable historical investigations of various right- and left-wing movements in the United States. But as informative and fascinating as these "backstories" to the story I am telling are, I am not convinced that they would significantly affect—either as a challenge or as an elaboration—my story. Of course, I could be wrong!

But when do you decide that you have enough pieces laid out to make a guess on the picture you are constructing? That is your real starting point and it tells you where you are heading. It tells you how to respond to future pieces, whether you throw them back or not. Where you start matters, because it will open up some possible relations and not others. From each possible starting point, different relations reach out to others. I spent most of Thanksgiving at a friend's house, talking with their 28-year-old son, a talented musician. I have always been interested in how young people find their music, given the sheer number, the chaos, of available choices. He told a story I have heard before. He looks up a band on YouTube (the reason doesn't matter), and if he likes it, he follows the suggestions of other viewers, not the algorithm. In this way, he builds his own musical universe and, with it, a significant part of who he is. And I thought, if he had started somewhere else, his whole musical universe might be different, and he well might be a different person. It all depends on where and how he begins to break into the chaos.

But your puzzle-making challenge is even more difficult. As you set about your task, you realize you are not alone. There are many voices, an audience, off stage, giving you advice and directions. You are in a game show. And the voices keep changing; sometimes old voices change their minds, and sometimes new voices come out of the woodwork, speaking as if they had some secret knowledge. But you can't be sure if they are trying to help you or even working on the same puzzle as you. The result is that you keep thinking you should start over or just give up.

Actually, the analogy of the puzzle is almost a literal description of my own working practice: First, I collect all sorts of disparate elements, based on a nebulous sense of my project. I am never sure how they fit together or if they even do. I start constantly moving the pieces around, organizing them into groups, which I then try to identify, until I begin to find some order in the chaos, some sense of the arrangements and its effects. When they don't quite work, or something changes, I rearrange the piles until I have found some interesting way of composing the puzzle, something that might tell me something surprising, something interesting, something I had not been able to see before. And I begin to compose a story.

There are many ways of constructing contexts and many kinds of contexts. My own choice—somewhat obviously, I hope—is to assemble stories out of stories, offering what I will call a conjunctural story, all the while recognizing that contextual thinking does not carry with it any necessary politics; at best, it can destabilize any assumption that there is a necessary politics to a particular context.

### Note

1 Perhaps paradoxically, contextuality cannot claim to be universally valuable; it may not always be the best way to think about contexts. I am proposing it as a useful—contextual—response to a contextually specific set of problems, a way of thinking contextually about contexts that seem to demand such thinking.

# 6
# THE DISCIPLINE OF THE CONJUNCTURE

We are not done, although I am sure you wish we were. And I am afraid things will not get any easier. How do you distinguish contexts? How do you find a context suitable for a particular task? There are two ways of answering the question: Levels of abstraction and scale. I have already described the first as stretching from the fully abstract (time zones) to the entirely particular (this person in this house writing this chapter on this computer, listening to this music, etc.).

Scale approaches context in terms of spatial and temporal relations and reach, such as size, distance (most commonly the global, the regional, the national, the state, the regional again, the local), and duration. Often, scale is mistakenly equated with abstraction, as if the global were necessarily more abstract and the local more particular. I am sorry to say that this is wrong (and I cannot say that often enough)! Every scale can be treated both concretely and abstractly. Speaking about the global may pose unique conceptual challenges, but it is not devoid of empirical realities. And speaking about the local may offer up a host of empirical realities, but it is not devoid of conceptual abstractions. Similarly, every level of abstraction will have its own measures of time and space, defined less by distance than by its relation to other levels. And, as I have said, every level of abstraction has its own forms of empirical realities as well as its own forms of abstractions.

We tend to think of both scales and levels of abstraction as ladders, but neither is laid out in a linear hierarchy. Each is more like Escher's paintings, with their mind-boggling geometries, or the moving staircases of Hogwarts Castle in the *Harry Potter* books/movies. I imagine multiple levels in simultaneous, complicated, and sometimes even impossible arrangements. The image of the ladder seems to leave the in-between spaces empty, but the

DOI: 10.4324/9781003662587-7

interesting questions are all about what happens in between, in the relations that are constructed among them.

## Conjunctural Thinking

A conjuncture is most commonly thought of as a particular social context, defined in scalar or spatio-temporal terms, such as the nation-state. It is located somewhere between the immediate event and the long duration of the epoch: An event is a matter of years, maybe a decade at most, usually in a particular place; an epoch lasts for centuries or even millennia, usually over an expansive space. A conjuncture is generally measured in decades, its spatiality somewhere in between. But that will only get us so far.

While I find this useful, a conjuncture must also be understood as a particular level of abstraction. Its salient difference from the event and the epoch concerns the nature of the complexity and the kinds of interventions or determinations, as well as the kinds of stories (understandings), it allows. It might be expressed this way: In the event, the density of the relations is so high as to be almost overwhelming. Consider an event like Trump's electoral victory. Trying to construct a story capturing all the elements, forces, strategies, constituencies, etc. would be (almost?) impossible. An epoch, on the other hand, has a low density. It is no less complicated, but the relations are attenuated and more difficult to locate. Neither allows for the precise mapping of relations at the level of detail necessary for the construction of stories aimed at certain kinds of significant interventions.

A conjuncture is a level of abstraction somewhere between these two. That doesn't mean that conjunctural thinking ignores the levels of the event and the epoch. Each has significant effects in the conjuncture itself: Epochal processes and structures are articulated conjuncturally, and specific events are not only affected by conjunctural processes and structures but can have profound conjunctural effects. For example, Christianity is a powerful epochal force having profound conjunctural effects; and the presidential candidacies of Donald Trump are events that have resonated throughout the conjuncture. In fact, to some extent, conjunctures are constructed as populations move through particular events and the stories that help them navigate their way.

No context is an island; every context is related to other contexts, vertically, horizontally, and transversally. And depending on the nature and strength of the relationships, contexts affect one another in many different ways, across broader geographies and histories. Every context carries with it an exteriority that has effects within its spaces.

But the conjuncture is a construction; it is not there, objectively given, waiting to be taken up and described by some dispassionate, neutral observer. Conjunctural thinking produces the conjuncture in the very act of (re) constructing it, although I do not mean to suggest that the thinker is somehow in control. It is more like carving one complex composition (a conjuncture) out of an already existing, even more complicated, composition.

It is here that slow thinking becomes political. Its questions are political ones: What is the present conjuncture? How is power organized and naturalized? How can we organize political struggle? Conjunctural thinking refuses to assume that the natural state of politics is a war between two cohesive and homogeneous camps, each seeking total victory over the other. It also refuses to assume that the natural state of power is one of complete fragmentation and dispersion. And it refuses stories that simply present history as an endless dialectic of power and resistance. Instead, conjunctural thinking understands the relations of power—at least modern power—to be an ongoing struggle to maintain or transform the existing state of affairs; different power blocs attempt to arrive at or impose a "settlement" that would establish a stable balance in the complex field of forces, however fragile and temporary that balance may end up being.

The choice of conjunctural thinking is exactly that: A choice. It is a wager that this level of abstraction/scale is a useful and effective way to conceive of a context, both intellectually and politically, especially in terms of the relations of governance, institutions, movements, and populations. The conjuncture offers the possibility of stories that are capable of identifying the changing balance between the old and the new, the changing compositions of relations, and the ways those compositions come to serve the forces constantly fighting to win, hold onto, or simply temper the dominant position. And its stories promise, as well, to show how the conjuncture might be recomposed, to open the possibility of beginning to repair the world.

Conjunctural thinking rethinks the concept of crisis, returning in part to the demand for interdisciplinarity in contextual thinking. Most contemporary thinking assumes a society is the sum of a number of distinct domains— the economy, the culture, the state, social relations, etc. Each stands on its own, with a high degree of autonomy. Using critique, we know that these domains have been constructed and their independence naturalized. That is, they have been shorn of lots of the relations that embed them in the totality of the society. They have been disembedded. And yet, they continue to be embedded in society. If you will forgive my semantic playfulness, the nature of their continued embeddedness partly defines the forms and degree of their disembeddedness. For example, the particular way the activities commonly thought of as economic are dispersed in our lives partly defines the way the economy seems to exist as a realm unto itself. Remember: That this autonomy is constructed does not mean it is not real (i.e., it has real effects). The question is, how has this autonomy been produced and naturalized? How have certain activities been produced as self-producing, regulated as self-regulating?

But the construction of autonomous realms is never successful. Modern life and thought are continuously having to confront the fact that, despite their apparent disconnection, each domain is continuously shaped by its relations to the others. When one domain is seen to "interfere" too much with another, it may become a public issue. Often, these uncontrollable articulations will upset the straight lines that claim to neatly transect social reality: The economy over here, social differences over there. They will create crises. And those crises will not stay still in one place. They will travel, meander as it were, in nonlinear distributions, all over the conjuncture. If you were to map a crisis, it would look like a spiderweb. At points of maximum density, people will say: Here is a crisis. But the crisis is everywhere, and it is moving. (I have already elaborated one such crisis, a crisis of commensuration.) These webs of distributed crises trouble the ways life is lived conjuncturally.[1]

Such ways of life are themselves constructed. Previous thinkers have described these compositions, for example, as life-worlds and ways of being in the world. Insofar as they are conjuncturally specific, I will refer to them as "habitable landscapes." There may be more than one landscape available in a conjuncture. They may overlap or compete. They may be made available only to certain populations, or they may be lived differently by different populations.

A habitable landscape is a messy and (you guessed it) complex terrain. Despite the often seamless way in which it is lived and traversed, a landscape is both fractured and organized; its unity is the effect of particular kinds of compositions, with specific effects. These compositions—I will refer to them as regimes or formations—are constantly producing the habitable landscape through forms of what we causally think of as culture.

On any particular landscape, some experiences, behaviors, actions, and even feelings are possible. Others seem inevitable and obvious, and still others seem impossible or unimaginable. They are held together by the positions people occupy. Philosophers refer to these as subject-positions or subjectivities. They are the places of self-consciousness. They are the centers of the circle that defines our perceptual and experiential universe. They are the points from which we speak ("I") so that our speech becomes an expression of our intentions and thoughts. They are the points at which we are addressed by different stories. We like to assume that they all come together at one location, defining our true self, but that seems less and less likely these days.

When the seamlessness of a habitable landscape is interrupted by the articulation of numerous distributed crises and that articulation begins to take on a density of its own, whether intentionally or not, the entire conjuncture can become a unique problem space. The existing stories cease to work and new stories have to be found. This is an organic crisis.

### Constructing Problem Spaces (Problematization)

A conjuncture puts forth its own questions and demands. It may even seem to constitute itself by the problems it poses. To fail to listen to these questions, although there is often more than one way they can be heard, is to fail to grasp the conjuncture while you are constructing it. Sometimes, one or more particular problems emerge and gain a certain weight that inflects the entire conjuncture. Or rather, they define the story you feel called upon to tell: The story of a problem space.[2] That is to say, something is being made into a problem before your very eyes. The question is, how is it being problematized?

The conjuncture of postwar America can be understood as the intersection of two problem spaces. The first involves changes in the very nature of the habitable landscape itself, although it is more easily thought of as the changing place of culture in the political struggles of the postwar conjuncture. Of course, culture—matters of discourse and expression—is important in most societies in numerous ways, especially in modern societies (where the use of state violence was supposedly constrained). But in the current conjuncture, the struggles over and around culture have become unavoidable; they have become constitutive of what appears to be a new, or at least historically specific, form of social crisis and political struggle. Consider this statement from C. Bradley Thompson, a respected conservative intellectual:[3]

> If you think the political system is corrupt, what you're really saying is the American people are corrupt. And if you're saying the American people are corrupt, then what you have to do of course is change American culture. And the way you change culture is through ideas.... If we're giving tens if not hundreds of millions of dollars to political campaigns and we're giving one-tenth of one per cent to trying to change the intellectual culture of this nation, you are by definition going to lose.

It is captured even more succinctly in Breitbart's (the right-wing news service) motto: Politics is downstream from culture.

But I want to suggest that as early as the 1950s, a particular problem space was taking shape around an increasing separation between two dimensions of culture: Affect and meaning. The result was that affect itself, which had largely existed relatively unnoticed, well-integrated into culture and everyday life, was increasingly becoming a problem, at first implicitly but fully visible by the late 1970s. The conjuncture was reshaping itself or, rather, it was possible to re-story it as a problem space of affect. (See the next chapter.)

The second problematic involves organic crises, which are not unique to this conjuncture. In different conjunctures, they take shape in response to specific articulations of the multiple webs of crises that spread across the entire space of society. An organic crisis arises when an entire social formation becomes uniquely and extremely unstable as a result of not a single crisis, but an accumulation and condensation of multiple, expanding, and deepening crises and struggles. The crises intersect and strengthen each other. The result is that no existing settlement is able to establish itself and stabilize the social field.

Such an "organic crisis" can endure for decades. (Others have referred to it as a mega-crisis or a meta-crisis.) An organic crisis disrupts and unsettles the most taken-for-granted terms of social reality, especially of political possibility. It calls into question a society's understanding and imagination of itself and its sense of identity and purpose. It problematizes the forms of belonging by which "the people" are constructed and the defining values of the society. It challenges the common logics by which people understand and value their relation to and place in the world.

The organic crisis itself becomes the ground on which politics has to be fought. A significant dimension of the specificity of postwar American political culture has been shaped by the fact that it has given rise to two organic crises, to a doubled problem space constructed around the question of modernity. Or, to put it differently, what it means to be modern has been problematized in at least two distinct but overlapping ways.

Whether considering the growing separation of meaning and affect within culture or the appearance of politics as an organic crisis, the construction of the conjuncture as a problem space involves competing attempts to articulate the structural and experiential crises into new stories. We have to understand these stories, where they come from, how they connect to older stories, and how they work or fail to work, if we are to move forward.

### Conjunctural Analysis

Understanding (and perhaps transforming) a conjuncture through its stories is not as straightforward as my presentation might suggest. Unfortunately, it is never that neat; the stories insist on mixing it up, merging together, interfering with each other, even rewriting each other. The world is messy, and it is impossible and even undesirable to try to keep the messiness out of our thinking.

Like critical thinking, conjunctural analysis requires us to look at the world differently. It is a bit like considering the Nazca lines or ancient geoglyphs, without the capacity to stand above the conjuncture; you are stuck on the ground, in the conjuncture, like everyone else, but you have the tools of slow thinking at your command. Conjunctural analysis is an orchestration in which all the exercises are made to resonate and harmonize together. This conjuncture-specific composition aims to let you see things happening across the surface of the conjuncture—in the existing configurations of the conjuncture, in the dominant stories, in the struggles over the balance in the field of forces, and across the relations of the problem spaces. Together, they make telling other stories possible. Others will have to judge whether they are better stories.

Conjunctural analysis—slow thinking—is committed to the rigor of intellectual work. It does not abandon "objectivity" just because it is an unreachable goal. We can continue to reach for better truths, not because we have put our interests and passions aside, but precisely because we have interests and passions, because we want to repair the world. We need the best stories (built on the best thinking we are capable of) to make sense of where we are and come up with the possible strategies that might move society somewhere else. To accomplish this, we have to use the best resources available, even if that sometimes involves using the master's tools, because you don't get to pull alternative tools out of thin air; but that does not mean we cannot criticize and critique them, re-configure them, and put them to new uses.

Conjunctural analysis refuses to allow political desire to undercut intellectual rigor. It refuses to bend intellectual labor to the demands of politics, to allow politics to define the trajectory of thinking. It demands that there be some autonomy of intellectual work, some gap between the intellectual and the political. Politics pulls analyses in directions it has determined, creating a neurotic sense of inadequacy in which we assume that if we could just be political enough, in just the right way, we could guarantee the truth and efficacy of our analysis. Our intellectual work would become inherently political, and our politics would become necessarily true. But that would mean conjunctural analysis has a guaranteed political content or agenda, beyond the demand of the freedom to follow thinking wherever it leads.

But conjunctural thinking is political. Its politics resides in the first and the last instances. In the first instance, it is in the questions we ask. While conjunctures may pose their own questions, what we hear is partly determined by our political positions. In the last instance, conjunctural analysis seeks to open new possibilities, to fabricate the context anew, to repair the world. But like everything else, it cannot guarantee where its analysis will end up, or how its stories will be taken up. All it can do is to go on thinking and keep the conversation going. Between the first and last instances, in the analytic work of constructing better stories, truth is constructed and increasingly lost and responsibility is taken and increasingly abandoned. Politics may inform the heart of conjunctural analysis, but its soul lies in its faith in better thinking and better stories.

## Notes

1  They are often, but not always, grounded in contradictions in the material infrastructures of the social organization, but they are more than structural weaknesses.

2   Scott, 2004.
3   Reported in Purdy, 2015.

## References

Purdy, Jedediah. 2015. "Ayn Rand Comes to U.N.C." *The New Yorker* (March 19, 2015).    www.newyorker.com/news/news-desk/new-politics-at-the-university-of-north-carolina
Scott, David. *Conscripts of Modernity*. Durham: Duke University Press, 2004.

# PART II
# You Want It Darker

# 7

# THE PROBLEM SPACE OF AFFECT

There are specific forms of compositions that transform a material landscape into a habitable landscape, that make a reality livable for humans. We generally think of them as cultural and equate them with languages and other organized systems of signs. We assume that their primary effects involve the production of cognitive or semantic meanings, which enable people to communicate, represent an outside reality, or express an individual's intentions. What distinguishes human life from other forms of existence is that humans live in a meaningful world.

I want to open up the field of culture beyond what we normally think of as linguistic or semiotic behavior to a broader and more diverse range of compositions; hence, I will describe them as discursive or expressive formations or regimes. And I want to expand their effects beyond the production of meaning. Instead, their unique capacity is to produce relations—effects—at a distance. In other relations, effects are generally produced by one body (loosely understood) acting on another; it's not the sun that warms your skin, it's the electromagnetic waves. But, you object, it's not the music that produces an effect, it's the sound waves. And yes, the sound waves produce an effect on your body. But that is only a part of how music works; music produces so much more. (I will return to this in a moment.)

Cultural regimes can produce different kinds of relations and effects. But exactly what kind of effects a particular cultural regime has will be determined—you guessed it—contextually. It is affected by other cultural regimes as well as many other compositions, forces, struggles, etc. All these relations together organize and alter the habitable landscape, defining our realities and our ways of living in the world.

DOI: 10.4324/9781003662587-9

## Affect and Discourse

And this brings me back to my earlier assertion that some cultural regimes operate primarily affectively. To that end, I return to music. There is a reason music often serves as the example par excellence of an affective formation. Every piece of music is an orchestration of sound, articulating mind and body, self and other, including the world, in profoundly ineffable ways. It can rush over us like waves, sometimes soft and calming and sometimes overwhelming and dangerous. Or it can hit us like particles of energy—abrupt and singular, each note, line, or voice individuated in its unique vibrations. Yet whether like waves or particles, music forms a fragile space that engulfs us and haunts us; a space in which, if only for a few moments, we can surrender our existence to its rhythms and textures. Music creates a momentary possibility of living. Music binds and bounds us, while holding back the chaos; it places us somewhere between pure harmony and total cacophony.

Always a unity-in-difference, an orchestration brings together different sounds, including lyrics, to compose or articulate what we loosely call feelings. Different instruments carry with them different capacities of sound; they are the voices that make up the musical assemblage. Particular musical styles, and even particular works, have their own harmonics, keys, scales, frequencies, rhythms, textures, and resonances. There is no pre-defined balance among the voices; that is worked out in any of its possible performances, or, I might say, contextually and, sometimes, even conjuncturally. For example, think about the changing resonances of popular music styles over time. Who would have thought that the music of my youth could become the background for commercials?

Music articulates relations. The first point of connection is the ear, but it is not the ear that hears music. The ear is always entangled up with the rest of the body. And the body is tangled up in all the relations that define where we are located on a habitable landscape, that define who we are at various sites on a habitable landscape. It is a character or position in one or more of the stories you live in that hears music. Sometimes the character will hear but refuse to listen. Imagine a string quartet with a saxophone, or folk rock with a jackhammer, or opera with bongos. There are no guarantees whether a particular orchestration will create a habitable soundscape, or, if it does, for whom. There is no guarantee whether anyone can "feel" it. Remember "Da Doo Ron Ron?" Maybe some people could not feel it, but maybe they could feel other rock music. Maybe they could not feel rock but they could feel other music (e.g., jazz—which would make the difference between rock and jazz very important to them). I have to admit that I could never feel opera. I had to learn to feel heavy metal, and I am still working on country. You dance to the symphony of sounds and feelings that you are caught by, that transform you—and when it works, it can offer a new experience of living, transmuting time and space themselves.[1] Yes, maybe that only happens at the best moments, but anyone who loves music has known the experience of moving to a different beat, of experiencing a different landscape.

As I said earlier, I had initially thought of affect, following the early Freud, as a matter of the quantitative intensity of an investment or relation to something.[2] I realized that this easily led to a rigid dualism between meaning and affect, between reason and everything else (feeling, imagination, superstition, etc., as if these were themselves equivalent). I did not think they could be so easily separated. They appeared to be more intimately connected, inseparable if not indistinguishable, within a culture and, hence, within a habitable landscape, for most of modern history. Affect is a constitutive dimension of our lived reality; without it, we would not feel alive in any context, in any world.

I had to rethink affect beyond its natural or biological reality, without denying that this is obviously necessary. But it did not guarantee or even explain the full richness, the deep effects, of affect. Affect is neither spontaneous nor disorganized, despite being often represented as an irrational eruption through and disruption of the organized spaces of meaning, reason, and power. Affect does not exist outside of discourse, and it is not some ineffable, magical excess that escapes understanding. The sense organs undoubtedly have limits on what they are capable of perceiving, and the brain has limits on how much information it can process. But what they perceive and how information is processed are not innate. It is the result of habits of the eye and the ear … and the mind. And those habits can be changed. Affective realities are made and made into habits.

But it is easy to understand why people fall into such traps. Over centuries, we have lived in a tradition that valued meaning and rationality and assigned affect to the less than fully human (e.g., women, children) and, ultimately, the infra- or non-human. It developed sophisticated and elaborate vocabularies for the former, and only vague and truncated vocabularies for the latter. We have extraordinary nomenclatures for logical forms and errors, for scientific arguments, for rhetorical figures, for geometric shapes, etc. But we can't distinguish between the anxiety I feel waiting to hear if this book will be published, if my medical exam will be okay, if my son is well, if my retirement is safe, if my son has a future, or if the world is safe. How do you describe the difference between feeling that you have no control over your life and feeling that everything is a threat? We call them both anxiety, but they are likely to feel very different. In fact, while I can imagine explaining what reason is (a system of rules that lead you predictably from one set of statements to another?), I can't begin to imagine explaining what feelings are.

Consider something as simple as consent. It establishes an affective relation, independent of whatever it is you are consenting to. Consent does not necessarily entail agreement with any actual content. Do we understand what people are doing when they consent? What is the opposite of consent? Is it refusing to consent or something more active? Actually, consent can be passive or active, dispassionate or passionate, or anything in between. And there are many modes of consent: Enthusiastic, limited, grudging, hopeful, hopeless, disaffected, negotiated, ironic, recalcitrant, (self-)righteous, desperate, forced, cynical, and desperate; but also willful neglect, passionate indifference, active avoidance, escape, etc. Without knowing how someone is consenting—the specificity of the affective relation—it will be difficult to locate its likely effects.

While affect (as relations and effects) is a part of every cultural formation, what particular place it has, what particular role it plays, and how large or determining that role is will vary and change. There will be discursive regimes that seriously attempt to eliminate all affective effects (!) and claim to have done so successfully. Most scientists and mathematicians come to mind. On the other hand, we think of affect's primary home in the arts—visual images, musical bars, behavioral snapshots, literary figures, synesthetic experiences, etc. The arts foreground affect, increasing its presence and importance and multiplying its resonances. In between science and art stands everyday life, a habitable landscape constituted by both meaning and affect (and more).

Affect is historically constructed and, as a result, how it is constructed can always be contested. It is differentiated (e.g., anger vs rage, emotions vs moods). And it is structured (e.g., emotions might be arranged into joy, sadness, fear, and anger). It is constructed partly by every cultural regime and, more powerfully, by specific, powerfully affective, discursive formations; it is taught implicitly in everyday habits.[3] You have to learn how and when to be happy, to feel pleasure, to be angry or outraged, to be bored or apathetic, etc. Discursive regimes define the possible and necessary organizations of our affective lives, both personal and shared, within a particular conjuncture. And hence, it makes sense that you might have to learn to hear—to "feel"— heavy metal or country or opera. It means, on the one hand, being able to open up to the resonances of a particular regime (from some position). And, on the other hand, that regime has to be able to insert itself in hearable ways at that position on the habitable landscape. For a long time, the stories I lived in just didn't let me hear (feel) country. But country also hadn't found ways, at the time, of making itself hearable to me, to a certain kind of subject-character. Things change. Learning to feel the music means being able to hear the harmonies negotiating with the cacophonies, and taking up a position on the particular landscape it constructs. You may not succeed: You may not hear it, you may not feel it, you may not be able to live it.

Affective relations and organizations are crucial to any habitable landscape. They constitute the ways we are attuned by and to the world. Affective relations make a material landscape habitable by making it into more than the sum of the relations and formations that compose it. They function as the glue that both holds them together and stitches the various populations they produce (e.g., individuals and groups) into the landscape.[4] Affect provides the stickiness that binds relations into larger and larger compositions tied to particular spaces, each with its own sense of coalescence, coherence, or consistency. Affect is the elusive—but neither invisible nor always disappearing—condition of the possibility of relationality itself. Affective articulations are what hold the lived world together by constituting a sense of unity (and hence of sanity) or, at least, by holding back—even taming—the chaos always lurking on its borders. It is crucial to the unity of a habitable landscape because it binds together the totality of the habitable landscape. And in doing so, it is what defines the vitality, the animus, the energy of the lived. Affect constructs the livedness of the lived, but it can do so in many ways, according to its different possible articulations.

## Problematizing Affect

Occasionally, affect has become visible in its own right. The use of "affect" in politics is hardly new. Greek rhetoricians called it pathos (and, to some extent, ethos). Affect has been crucial in so-called democratic politics through appeals to emotions, charisma, and patriotism, or through tactics of fear, demonization, and populism, or in what John Maynard Keynes called "the animal spirits." The successes of the various conservative alliances of the past 50 years owe much to what they learned about affective politics from the popular left of the 1960s.

Affect has also always played a major role in commerce. The roots of its current forms lie in the early-20th century rise of consumer capitalism and the birth of an increasingly self-conscious system of advertising, marketing, and public relations. It was no doubt carried forward by the rapid development of a consumer-oriented, technologically based media environment, culminating, at the moment, in digital and social media.

I want to return to the idea that a conjuncture can come to be, can be made to be, a problem space in which a particular relation is problematized. Such a problem space began to emerge around affect in the 1950s but gathered strength in the 1960s Movement's reimagination of the relation of culture and politics.[5] By the 1980s, it had become palpable, even unavoidable, and it has continued to gain strength ever since.[6]

Specifically, what was problematized was the growing power of affect in the habitable landscape. This was the result of the disarticulation of affect from other forms of cultural relations and effects. It identified an ongoing process whereby affect was disarticulated and delinked, especially from matters of meaning. To offer one example: As I am editing this, a number of journalists are writing about the relation between the traditionally accepted measures of economic well-being and people's feelings (measured in public opinion surveys) about their economic well-being. They claim that the usually predictable correlation between these has disappeared over the past decades.

It is not that this disarticulation is complete, that affect has become autonomous. Affect has not freed itself from all relations to other discursive effects. Things are never that simple. A better description would be that those relations have been loosened or weakened, making affective relations more powerful and even more frequently dominant. The result has been a reconfiguration of the ways in which many discursive formations operate and relate to one another, enabling them to take on different shapes and capacities. I do not know if there is an end-point when affect will finally achieve complete autonomy. I will leave that to those who enjoy speculating about the future.

I am trying to describe an ever-increasing separation of how you feel from the object of the feeling, of what matters from its actual value, and of an investment from its meaning. I will refer to this as the quasi-autonomy of affect, which has progressed far enough that it has transformed the habitable landscape. Given my description of the role of affective relations in the landscape, it threatens to undermine the very possibility of a habitable landscape. Instead, it has fractured the landscape. We increasingly find ourselves living much of our lives on a quasi-autonomous affective landscape. This might help explain some of the feelings of the strangeness, and so on, of the contemporary world.

This quasi-autonomy is both historically constructed and real. It has not just happened accidentally, although I do not know whether there were any strategies or conspiracies involved. I do not know why it happened. I can hypothesize that it may be partly a result of the endless proliferation of everything—from knowledge to morality to cultural tastes—combined with the loss of every standard by which choice can be justified (i.e., the crisis of commensuration) and the threat of relativism.

In the ensuing chaos, everything becomes equal, equally worthy of one's attention, concern, or investment. Equivalence reigns, and significant difference fades into the background. References to tyranny and democracy, violence and charity, can be interspersed with advertisements for luxury goods. Claims that "American independence begins with ..." can be followed with whatever corporate product is being sold today. Talk shows can have the president followed by pet-trainers.

Like the habitable landscape, there may be multiple affective landscapes in any conjuncture, and any affective landscape may be lived differently. Every affective landscape is organized, but each is constantly being reorganized by both internal and external relations and, sometimes, struggles. Neither the affective landscape nor its elements are intrinsically political; they have to be made political. Nor do they have a particular politics; that, too, has to be articulated. Yet, the very existence of the affective landscape as a unique conjunctural event has come to play a crucial role in contemporary political culture, and there continue to be struggles over the politics of its component relations.

## Living in an Affective Landscape

There are many possible responses to finding yourself in an affective landscape, from living as if without will, to living as if willing were all that mattered. There are various forms of apathy: Passive apathy accepts the democracy of everything and decides that nothing matters, that no investments are possible in a flat world. Exhausted apathy (or desperate boredom) is too tired to care about anything. Cynical apathy marks differences and invests in some things but is suspicious of everything. Desperate apathy knows that there are too many problems, and that everything you do to solve one problem just creates or adds to other problems, so why bother (friend?). Conjunctural apathy only cares about the immediately local and the abstract future, but nothing in between. Passionate apathy loudly proclaims (to no one but yourself?) that the only thing that matters is maintaining your apathy.

Ironic cynicism allows commitments but takes everything with a grain of salt; every claim to truth or value is put in quotation marks, inflected with a question mark. It is hesitant but not paralytic. There is also a more playful but disempowering cynicism, a happy acceptance of the inevitable. If you are sailing on the Titanic, go first class. The glass is half full, but it is full of urine.

Redemptive nihilism suggests that the only hope, the only possibility of salvation, lies in the very choice to act, regardless of what the choice is. Perhaps this is the context of the darkness (doomscrolling, horror) of so much of contemporary youth culture, partly as a response to the increasing banality of violence, stupidity, hypocrisy, evil, mediocrity, and arrogance. They see cause for pessimism everywhere (and no doubt feel it) but do not make it into a problem or treat it in purely negative terms. Instead, it becomes the world they have to live in and work with—possibilities of change and mobility.

In caring resignation, people still care about the declining state of things but have given up on and exited from both the established systems of governance and their own power to enact change. The world tends to collapse into an increasingly personal space and time, and the future recedes into the present. Perhaps it is a re-articulation of the 1960s "be here now."

And finally, the most frightening (and common?) accommodation is a fundamentalism, in which all that matters is that you make a choice and how strongly you make it. Whether and how something matters, demands our attention, or earns our faith cannot be justified by anything but your commitment. What choice you make is unimportant. That way, you will never be let down. It is the right choice because you have made it. Your commitment is the only thing that can define truth and righteousness (and, ultimately, all that can guarantee success). Something is right because of how passionately you are committed to it. The advertising slogan "Where there's a will, there's an A" captures this perfectly. It does not matter if you have fulfilled the assignment or if what you have produced is crap. Everyone can succeed if they try hard enough and, if they do not succeed, it's because they did not commit with enough energy and passion. Competence and merit are irrelevant.

### Revisiting Structures of Feeling

I want to consider how the four structures I previously described have been developed as they have been displaced onto an affective landscape. **Hyper-inflation** on the affective landscape transforms fundamentalism's sense of absolute certainty into a **fanaticism.**[7] In fundamentalism, failure belongs to the chooser; their investment was insufficient. But now, the equation is reversed: Failure is assigned to those who oppose you, the enemy. If your absolute commitment is not enough to achieve full (hyper-inflated) victory, then you are being prevented from winning. "The world we live in equally distributes talent but not opportunity." The enemy must be denying you the opportunity. (Unfortunately, talent is not equally distributed, although it does require opportunities if it is to be realized.) Failure means that you are a victim of external forces that oppose your righteous and well-deserved goals, like the government, or liberals, or those "minorities" calling for "social justice." Or capitalists, racists, or well-meaning liberals. Failure is always someone else's fault, like the teacher's, who doesn't recognize the strength of your effort and commitment. If others seem to win the rewards that you deserve, then it must be that they are being helped by your enemies.

Fanaticism sees itself as a victim under constant attack. It offers a paranoid economy of superiority and inferiority, of good and evil, of the deserving and the undeserving. The result is an absolute, hyper-inflated sense of partisanship that saturates every aspect of life. Your choice is the only possible choice; any other choice is by definition abhorrent. Those forces that oppose you, as well as those groups that claim what you have rightly earned, are evil; they cannot be allowed to continue to thwart your efforts. They must be negated and, sometimes, too often, this can justify their extermination, because their evil cannot be dismissed as mundane and ordinary; it must be absolutely negative. Obamacare is not just a mistake—it is the new slavery or Nazism. And Trump is the nightmare that cannot be allowed.

Feeling victimized increasingly ends up in expressions of hatred, resentment, and rage, enacted with varying degrees of brutality and cruelty. It can lead to actions ranging from psychological acts of bullying, contempt, meanness, and intimidation (e.g., trolling) to the physical infliction of suffering, including neglect, impoverishment, incarceration, and murder. Most recently, it has appeared in practices of shaming and humiliation, without seeking to elicit the guilt that might accompany self-criticism. Anything you need to do to win—including following the devil—is righteous because you know, with absolute certainty, that your cause is righteous.

The roots of this culture of cruelty may lie in the terror of public exposure and the self-hatred that might come from having to put yourself in the position of victim in order to legitimate your truth. You offer your own suffering to justify the suffering of others and even your own efforts to inflict such suffering. Your suffering is the privilege that gives you the right to make others suffer. You defer the humiliation of loss and victimage by humiliating others, by diminishing their status and capacities, destroying their sense of pride, and reducing them to a lower state of being. By mortifying another— and taking pleasure in it—you assert that you are not a loser or, better, that you appear to be a loser only because the other side, the devil, cheats. Get thee behind me Satan!

It has been drummed into our heads that we live in an age of **anxiety** (and it is obviously so much worse than before; so says hyper-inflation).[8] It affects so many individuals, who are caught tightly in its grip. Anxiety disorders are among the most common form of invisible disabilities in the U.S. It can take many forms, from the uncontrollable repetition of unwanted thoughts (OCD) to the automatic leap to the worst-case scenario (awfulizing) to the obsessive demand for order. For many, the only thing preventing them from being overwhelmed by anxiety (or from giving into the depressive reality that nothing matters) is the constant sense of busy-ness, as they drown in the time soak of the endless tasks, inconveniences, distractions, and annoyances, and, sometimes, little pleasures, of modern life.

But anxiety has declared itself to be a social and public problem, a constitutive element of a shared affective landscape. It is everywhere. Anxiety—as a hyper-intensity—often goes hand in hand with depression—as a hypo-intensity—since both make you feel unable to escape from or gain control over whatever is happening, and something is always happening, if not right here, then just over there. Anxiety locates you within a landscape of dread, of often-shapeless and invisible threats just waiting for you. It saturates everything and renders you powerless. It easily slides into paranoia (but a little paranoia is probably useful).

Anxiety is a state of being, making a landscape (unin-)habitable. It has no particular time or place, and no object. The source of anxiety today is life itself. Anxiety—rampant, universal, and banal—incorporates everything. (If it becomes focused, it easily spirals into fear and panic.) Rather than creating singular moments that explode through and thus remove themselves from some sense of a supposedly normal life, anxiety makes everything into an emergency waiting to jump out and take over your very being. Always experienced in the present, anxiety operates in a future perfect tense. It creates the state of emergency as the new normal, in which every crisis is banal and extraordinary. The fact that anything might suddenly become a crisis already makes it so. The thought that something could be a threat in the future makes it a present threat. Anxiety is reflexive: Anxious about being anxious, knowing there is no place to hide. It is living in a perpetual state of disquiet about life, living in a constant state of exhaustion.

Contemporary **narcissism** similarly saturates the entire affective landscape. What might have been a contradiction in previous moments, between individuals being held responsible and being entitled, has been reconciled in a hyper-inflated sense of individualism. Narcissism haunts both the body and the mind. You are responsible for your health and happiness. And you are entitled to whatever it takes to deliver on the promises. The body is a fragile thing and must be protected; it must be allowed to protect itself. Everything becomes a potential symptom, threatening you with all sorts of illnesses, many of which you have not heard of. (Deep down, you know that they only exist because some company has found a cure.) Everything in your house might be a threat, but you can take responsibility by buying the right product. Things you never associated with health can now be treated with health products. You have to become a health puritan. And you are empowered to become your own health professional who can make demands of your doctors and bring your own lists of diseases, tests, and drugs. Or you can skip the doctor and go online, not only for drugs, but for the medical and psychological treatment you want.

Do you worry that you don't look young enough or that you do not have the "right" look? Beauty aids and cosmetic surgery and the never-ending parade of diets and exercise regimens, plus all the forms of body-art, are supposed to give you the ability to shape (sculpt) and decorate your body and control your appearance. Even young people have to work to have young bodies. It is not enough to look young, you have to feel young, and that means having the energy and, to some extent, the body (skin condition, teeth, muscles, flexibility, etc.) that goes with it. That means giving up many of the pleasures that you may think make life worth living or, at least, enjoyable. Supposedly, you will rediscover (or maintain) the pleasures of things you could do when you were young. But why do I need to be able to do the things I could do earlier in my life? I used to love to dance. Now my body tells me that it is probably not a good idea. Maybe I could dance again, but I doubt I would find anything like the pleasure I once had. Pleasures change with age and context. There are other things that give me pleasure now, and they do not demand the pain of re-working my body. Besides, the exercise and health regimens required seem designed to change the chemical state of your body and are more likely to produce other forms of enjoyment. And those forms have one goal: A healthier life is a longer life. But no one ever tells you why you want to live longer. And society does not afford the opportunities that would make such a long life extraordinary. Why do we have to improve the state of our body for a future that may not come?

I do not mean to sound too cynical, or to deny that such efforts may be worthwhile. They seem reasonable and natural; they feel right. They do seem to define the reality of a healthy body and a vital and well-lived life. But it is worth reminding ourselves that those feelings and truths, that reality, are relatively recent constructions within the affective landscape.

The new narcissism has also changed our relations to our mind and spirit. Consider a controversial example: "Mindfulness," or some combinations of meditation and yoga, is a key part of the self-care industry, and one example of the omnipresence of "therapy speak." Before mindfulness, there was centering, and, more recently, there is resilience and self-empowerment. They suggest that the solution to your personal problems, often the result of your relations to the world, comes from you. Live in the present moment (an old hippie misappropriation of an even older Buddhist idea); free your mind and your body. Let the pressures of the world (the past and the future, the real struggles that do and should demand our attention) dissolve. The answer to life's anxieties, complications, and problems is in your head and body. And they are in your control. Don't change the world, change yourself. And if and when you fail—because you will—the world and the problems it poses are not going away—then you are still the problem. This is the paradox of self-care in the present conjuncture: Accept who you are, accept that we are all damaged, and embrace your dysfunction (since it makes you who you are); and yet, you must constantly overcome yourself! Is this another in a long line of anxiety-producing demands for self-improvement? More thinking might be useful.

Like all forms of narcissism, contemporary narcissism involves personalization, although carried to an unimagined extreme. "The personal is political" is transformed into "the political is personal," giving rise to a new individuated micro-politics. The result is the sacralization of personal experience and feeling, which trumps knowledge and expertise, leaving the definitions of offense, victimage, and even violence entirely in the hands of the supposedly offended party. It has enabled all sorts of problematic claims, such as "I have no evidence but I in my heart I know ...." Recent attacks on affirmative action provide a clear example: Those who were not accepted or hired feel that they are—individually and specifically—being punished. They know that if only the minority candidate (as if they had a specific individual in mind) had not been chosen, they—specifically—would have been. As fallacious as this may be, it makes sense if affirmative action is really all about you and only you.

Similarly public social spaces have been personalized (rather than having disappeared). Every time you think you have something uniquely public, all you find is the personal. The personal overwhelms and colonizes everything. The world revolves (at least it should) around me because it really is all about me. The public has not disappeared; what used to be thought of as the public has become a resource to be filled by the personal.

A problem arises when you try to understand the personal. Perhaps the more salient question is, who is the self in an age when people no longer believe in authenticity? Or has narcissism altered the sense of authenticity? Perhaps people today live in a state of inauthentic authenticity, pretending to be authentic, but knowing full well that it is only a mask, a brand that they take on for their own reasons. Or perhaps they live in a state of authentic inauthenticity, in which they believe that their authenticity lies in their power to create themselves. After all, they are constantly told that they can be anything they want to be, that there are no limits to their possibilities. This is hyper-inflation of the self as both empty and infinite. The self is an emptiness that can only reach beyond itself. Authenticity only exists in the absence of limits, easily displaced into a sense of personal omnipotence.

Authenticity gives individuals the right to see themselves reflected in the world, by becoming the very images they see reflected back at them. Their authenticity gives them the right to whatever is promised in those images. So what if all they want to be are the manipulated players in a virtual media reality, a privileged mirror image of the media world? They have a right to the white teeth of Hollywood movies; and to pets who will be their children. Disappointing, but could it be authentic?

But there is another, seemingly contradictory, side to contemporary narcissism. It points back to older forms of authenticity in which an individual is defined by their own truth, which has yet to be discovered. People are cajoled to be the best they can be. (Recent ads have proposed this should be true of your pets as well.) This suggests that you have intrinsic promises to keep. A recent series of ads asserted that I had to become "who I really needed to be in life." At the moment, the most popular way to discover that seems to be through some retrievable genetic ancestry. Even our pets answer to the call of the wild. We get our love of flowers from a distant ancestor and our stubbornness from yet another. Apparently, affective narcissism has no need to reconcile this contradiction, and people live not with it, so much as between the two forms.

Finally, the affective landscape is characterized by a profound **time warp** or **temporal alienation**. We feel lost in time, not quite sure when we are. The very structures that have organized time (past, present, and future) seem out of joint and the present feels out of place, out of time. Time itself is becoming strange, and we are estranged from it.

Temporal alienation has broken every possible meaningful relation of the present to the past, and the reliability of the past as a source of wisdom. We are overwhelmed by pasts that never existed, haunted by pasts that could never have happened. It is not so much a general amnesia of the past but an active forgetfulness and a recuperation of an entirely malleable past. The spectacularization of the trivial, the ordinary, and the lie, the many images of apocalypse, each with its own temporality (e.g., in Christian, leftist, and environmentalist forms), representations of the past as a perpetual repetition or mimesis of the present or as the anxiety of unknowability—all of these separate us from a comprehensible past.

For example, what does it mean to be held responsible for doing acceptable things in the past that are now unacceptable? It is a basic principle of modernity that laws cannot be retroactive. But apparently, that has changed. Yes, in retrospect, you can see the horrible error in your ways, but … imagine the apology: I apologize for not having had the foresight to know that what was then acceptable and normal would become totally inappropriate decades or even centuries later. What does that do to the temporality of responsibility?

And this holds equally true of the future. The future has been rendered irrelevant and even unreal, and with it, the very possibilities of human agency. It is as if we can act now only to prevent what we already know is going to happen. Or we act after the fact, when it is already too late. It is as if it is always too soon or too late. There is never a right time to act. The very idea that the present has some responsibility to the future gives way to the radical uncertainty of unintended consequences. The understanding of debt as a claim on the future fails to see its contemporary financial logics; it is not even that the future collapses into the present but that debt itself is a process of endless—atemporal—circulation. The very premise of time itself seems naive or impossible. In the face of the very impossibility or at least emptiness of a future, we live it as melancholia in the future perfect (progressive) tense. The future has always been uncertain and unpredictable, but what happens when that uncertainty seems predictably certain? What happens when the future itself disappears beyond every possible horizon?

Ultimately, temporal alienation negates the very existence of the present. It is as if time itself were stuck. It is not that both the past and the future no longer exist in the present; it is not that they exist only in the present. We are, as it were, stuck in the present, stuck in time, all dressed up with no when to go. It is as if time itself has stopped, leaving us with the haunting absence of a present. Arrested development?

Yet people often complain that time has speeded up (but only for some people, in some circumstances, and sometimes). In the 1970s, people talked about how important decisions were being controlled by "the news cycle" and, as its speed was increased by technology, it became increasingly harder to formulate or respond to stories. Today, technology has given us instantaneous processing and communication, shrinking the time for any human response, shrinking the space of the present beyond human perception. And yet, just as often, time has slowed down or, at least, seems to be constantly repeating itself, giving rise to the eerie experience of always having been here (now) before, a constant life of déjà vu.

Perhaps the present does not feel present because we have lost any sense of agency, any sense of our ability to act to bring about change. We feel "stuck." We cannot locate ourselves in the processes of change, and we can no longer grasp their temporalities. The very nature of change itself is changing. It is not surprising that people feel—in all possible senses—out of time, living the "forever now" as a kind of melancholic echo.

## Conclusion

It is not surprising, given this affective landscape, that people feel affectively exhausted, suffering from a fatigue that encompasses every aspect of their lives. It easily gives rise to a life of languishment, of holding in a place constituted by some minimal definition, or even the absence, of well-being. Jimmy Carter described it as a national malaise. And the easiest response appears to be the celebration of the very fact of survival, endurance, resilience, the capacity to wait it out. This is a commitment to the inevitability of staying the same, of staying in the same place. Or, in a wonderfully paradoxical response, we can live out the contradiction wherein the world will keep getting worse (no matter what we do) and yet we remain committed to doing the right thing— acting in environmentally and politically progressive ways, although we are already defeated.

The affective landscape plays a crucial role in contemporary political culture. It is central to the visible successes of the right, the more limited successes of the left, and the fragility of the center. It poses numerous traps and hazards, but also new political and cultural possibilities.

In the story I want to tell, the right seems to understand the importance of culture and, whether explicitly or implicitly, the significance of the quasi-autonomous affective landscape. Many of its practices can be understood to operate on the affective landscape, taking up and re-articulating the structures of feeling I have identified here (as well as others).

The left ... not so much. It has a long history of distancing itself from matters of culture and affect. It needs to think about how its own positions, strategies, and tactics are shaped by and reshape the affective landscape. It needs to consider when and where it may be reproducing particular structures of feeling or ignoring the right's manipulations of them. It is not a matter of blame or complicity or even of strategy, but of the possibilities of articulating hope out of an increasingly forlorn affective landscape.

## Notes

1   In fact, a great deal of contemporary entertainment—exemplified by gaming and video performance—seems to be trying to make the visual function more like music. Or consider the apparently necessary presence of multiple television screens—often with different programs, often without sound—in bars and restaurants. It reminds me of the commonly noticed overwhelming sensorial landscape of many Asian cities.

2   For the academic reader: I was unsatisfied with the attempts to synthesize Gramsci and Lacan. I wanted to return to the underdeveloped, founding works of Raymond Williams and Richard Hoggart, but I needed new theoretical and analytic tools. See Grossberg, 2010.

   At the time I began writing about affect, there were not many other scholars engaging with the concept in the cultural and political context. The most significant was the queer psychoanalytic theorist Eve Kosofsky Sedgwick. Later, I became increasingly wary of psychoanalysis's underlying universalizing impulses and its reduction of the social to the psychological.

   I was drawn to the work of Gilles Deleuze, especially his interest in Nietzsche and Spinoza—the Jewish Spinoza was one of my own intellectual heroes. I was wary of the ontological and speculative impulses, even though it produced some important and interesting work, especially in feminist, black, and decolonial studies. Instead, I turned to the more historical ontologies of Heidegger, Deleuze and Guattari, and Foucault. I aligned myself with scholars attempting to integrate affect into a cultural studies tradition.

   In recent decades, affect has come to define its own interdiscipline and, all too often, become something of a magical term, providing the key to ... well, just about everything. There is also a lot of work that largely depends upon a commonsensical approach to emotions, etc., and a (liberal) social psychology, in which affects are individualized and under-theorized. The result has, unfortunately, too often been a continuation of the banal argument between humanism and anti-humanism.

3   There may be exceptions, e.g., biologically determined or socially necessary affects. There are interesting debates around this topic.

4   Affect then is the second glue, alongside stories, that stitch relations.

5   The music has often been said to define a generation, mainly by the media, but I think it is still accurate. There was something about the music of the 1960s that spoke to kids, something that made it matter in new ways, both quantitively and qualitatively.

6   There probably have been other instances when affect became a problem, disconnected from meaning. Certainly, 18th-century Enlightenment efforts to separate thinking or meaning from affect was one among many discourses that impacted the relation, although it was by no means completely successful, especially in the realms of ordinary people's everyday lives. Affect was more rigorously problematized in the late 19th and early 20th centuries by various

figures in the arts, although it often remained marginal in philosophy, and I am uncertain about its relation to everyday life.

7   I wish I could, to some extent, bracket many of the immediate negative connotations of this term. I use it to describe a particular affective structure or orientation.

8   This discussion draws on Preston Adcock's dissertation research, *High Anxiety* (Chapel Hill: University of North Carolina, 2025).

## Reference

Grossberg, Lawrence. *Cultural Studies in the Future Tense*. Durham: Duke University Press, 2010.

# 8
# THE PROBLEM SPACE OF THE MODERN

Before I can begin my story, I have to lay the groundwork of a second problem space. It involves a unique doubling of organic crises around modernity, or the question of being modern.

To repeat myself a bit, an organic crisis signals that the driving questions of a society have been transformed as a result of not a singular and sudden historical rupture but the many changes and struggles that have altered the ways people understand their lives and the challenges they face. It expresses a shared sense that society has failed in some major ways, and thus expresses a vitally felt need for radical social and political change. It demands a new vision, a new set of values and relations, and perhaps even a new reality or habitable landscape. This is a moment in which, to use Gramsci's often quoted description, "the old is dying and the new cannot be born; in this interregnum a great variety of morbid symptoms appear."[1] Organic crises are highly transformational moments, when people no longer feel comfortable in or confident about how they have been thinking and living, but they also cannot give up the old ways, at least in part because they cannot see an alternative. What had been a knowable and livable reality, a taken-for-granted habitable landscape, has been shaken to its core by the flood of chaos and contradictions that have seeped through its boundaries.[2]

Not surprisingly, people's responses are often confused and contradictory. They commonly feel frustrated, dislocated, angry, insecure, insignificant, and helpless. They grasp at outlets for relief and release, whether psychologically or socially, whether thoughtful or desperate. They seek answers—whether old or new, whether generous or violent and vitriolic, whether forms of commonality or hatred—that will help them navigate their shared discomforts and discontents.

DOI: 10.4324/9781003662587-10

An organic crisis does not simply arise by itself, nor is it objectively given. It has to be actively produced or resisted through political struggle. There is no guarantee that such an organic crisis can or will be constructed, how it will be constructed, or whether it will succeed in reconstructing people's understanding of the conjuncture and their ability to navigate it. Different political projects offer their own diagnoses and stories of the crisis (or they may fight against its construction). Each offers its own vision of how to reconstitute a sense of societal unity and re-establish a sense of equilibrium, identity, and direction. Each proposes to settle the chaos by offering a new balance in the field of forces.

The two conjunctural organic crises and the struggles that surround them are significantly different—and that difference may be terrifying to some. They often contradict each other. Yet they are also closely related and there are significant continuities between them. And despite the fact that the second was aimed as much against the forces organized around the first, the first continued to exert itself alongside the second.

Both crises arise out of challenges to, and against the perceived failures of, America's presumed status as the exemplary modern society, with all the governmental, social, and normative structures necessary to sustain it. The first organic crisis emerges primarily as an attack on postwar American liberalism and the liberal state. It is framed around two questions: What does it mean to be modern? What is the best way to be modern? The second organic crisis confronts the failure of all attempts to construct a modern society and state (including the proposed settlements to the first crisis). It too begins by asking what it means to be modern, but then poses a more radical set of questions: Why should we want to be modern? Is there an alternative to being modern? How do we escape modernity?

By describing the contemporary conjuncture as a problem space of the modern, I am not suggesting that the modern has not always been a space of contestation and struggle. I simply want to focus on the particular ways in which these struggles have defined the contemporary political culture. If I am going to introduce stories that problematize America's modernity, it makes sense to take a detour into the daunting task of talking about the modern. This is a subject that has launched thousands of essays and books, and hundreds of intellectual careers. I am going to be brief and gloss over the nuances of the many debates over the modern.

There are numerous ways the modern has been understood: As a process (modernization), as an emerging cultural practice and norm (modernism), and as a state of affairs or way of living (modernity). The modern or modernity—I will use them interchangeably—almost always marks itself as different from some other group or period—from Antiquity, the Middle Ages, the primitive, etc. Whatever the difference is, it is usually assumed to be visible in many if not all of the elements comprising a modern society or habitable landscape, so we talk about modern design, modern warfare, all modcons, etc.

The question is, what is that difference? Often, one change is taken to be essential and causally responsible for everything else. Modernization and development theories put all the weight on economic growth and technological advancement. Theories of governance focus on the transformation of the state from absolute sovereignty to democracy. This enabled the emergence of civil society, with new kinds of individuals and subjects, and the replacement of violent coercion with the creation of ideological consensus. And this in turn called forth new forms of power and control, such as surveillance and population management. Cultural theories identify some underlying concept or logic that permeates all social life. The Enlightenment posited that it involved epistemological concepts, such as reason, autonomy, individualism, science, etc. Others argue for more historical principles, such as literacy, cosmopolitanism, or difference.

Phenomenological theories emphasize changes in the basic structures of human experience—time and space. They might focus, for example, on the fact of rapid and expansive change—"all that is solid melts into air"—and an attitude to such change. To be modern is to make oneself at home in the maelstrom, to embrace and even desire change. Some have concluded that modernity invented history as the time of change, understood in largely linear (and often teleological) terms.

But traditional societies also change and often seek change, while, on the other side, modern societies always embody and embrace traditions. Moreover, change is never completely harmonious. It never exists without resistance. More concretely, the modern is the product of over four centuries of negotiation, struggle, and war, established through a series (both synchronic and diachronic) of compromises, forged on top of the resistance and the blood, sweat, and lives of those who opposed it in the name of tradition, daily life, freedom, or alternative visions of society and futurity. History is always a matter of encounters between the old and the new, the familiar and the strange, and in the case of European modernity, that must include its global colonizing efforts—both its victories and its failures.

Stories that identify the modern with a single difference or essence raise important questions. Is everything in a modern society itself modern, i.e., does it express the essential difference? Does the aura of being modern pass onto non-modern things in a modern society? If supposedly non-modern societies assimilate modern elements, does that make them modern? Were they already modern but simply did not know it? Or conversely, if something (capitalism, democracy) is modern, does every instance of modernity have to exhibit it? Do non-modern societies, such as Antiquity, have their own unique differences and are they also expressed in their various elements?

We might do better with one of the more complicated stories of modernity that recognizes a necessary plurality of changes, features, and conditions. They see it as a complex reality or habitable landscape, a composition of variable and somewhat contingent relations operating at different speeds and scales. Like any landscape, it is an organization of intelligibility, feelings, power, and value. But what makes it modern is precisely that it is more: It is an organization and promise of possibilities. In that sense, the modern is always an aspiration. That perhaps explains why so many people have desired to be modern and have imagined what it would mean, given their present situation. In such stories, there is no universal modernity. There is no one way to be modern. Modern societies can and do look very different. Every iteration of the modern is a hybrid, comprised of variations on a set of themes.

Such stories often produce their complexity by capturing as many of the themes from the kind of simple stories I have described. Nothing wrong with that, but it raises a question about what modernity refers to in the two organic crises. For the most part, the modern has European (western) origins. Those societies that have been called, and may have called themselves, modern are both constructions and real. But in using the concept of modernity to name certain societies and not others, are we claiming that only those societies that have some roots in or some connection to European modernity can be modern? Does that become the essential defining (albeit circular) feature of the modern? You can only imagine other ways of being modern within the terms of already existing forms. Rather than actually problematizing the modern, such accounts take it for granted.

What would it mean to problematize the modern? What is at work in the conjunctural crises? How might slow thinking help us? The common picture of European modernity is real, and its power is just as real. But it is a construct that has to be—and, in the organic crises of the conjuncture, has been—questioned. We cannot simply accept its universalizing and normalizing claims. European modernity is more amorphous than is commonly assumed. It has been taken up and inflected in many ways (e.g., bourgeois, romantic, and revolutionary moderns), but it has also been inseparable from any number of counter-, alternative, and anti-modernities within the west. It has been adopted and appropriated, in specific territories, by other struggles, resulting in even more competing visions and realities of the modern. European modernity has always been contradictory, more fractured, than it claims. It is characterized by progress and catastrophe, order and chaos, civilization and barbarism, emancipation and control. It has always been changing, always on its way, always resisted, always becoming something other as it comes to rest in and reorganize a variety of contexts.

But if there is already so much complexity and contingency in the concept and the stories, is it possible to say where the boundary between the modern and the non-modern is located? Or do we admit that it is simply arbitrary, or a simple matter of power? Or might we think about it as that which is being contested in the organic crises? What if we thought of modern societies as having family resemblances that warrant them being described as modern? There does not have to be any essential features, a necessary origin, something that transcends each and every instance of a modern reality. There is only a changing same. There could be other points of origins and other paths into significantly other forms of modernity. Some might have taken hold for a while (Al-Andalus) only to eventually be defeated by external forces. Others have been interrupted and redirected by their encounter with the Euro-modern forces (e.g., Japan and China). And still others may have themselves provided the fertile ground for the emergence of European modernities. Even American history, despite its obvious European roots, might fruitfully be seen as an encounter among competing modernities, not all of them of European origin. Perhaps that would give us insight into the contemporary problem space of modernity, especially as it has been articulated on the affective landscape.

## Notes

1 Gramsci, 1971, 276.
2 Since writing this, I have begun thinking that the transitional moment maybe giving way to more concrete visions of an alternative future. The struggles defining the possibility of a new settlement have become ominously clear.

## Reference

Gramsci, Antonio. *Selections from the Prison Notebooks*. New York: International Publishers, 1971.

# PART III

# In the Dreams That We Dream, We Ask What Have We Done?

# 9

# WE'RE ON A MARATHON (PRELUDE)

Almost everything is in place to begin the story I want to tell. It will not explain the present moment, but it may help account for how we got here. It is a backstory of the conjuncture that stretches from the 1950s to the present in the U.S. My starting point is somewhat arbitrary; there are earlier conjunctures intimately connected with the one I am describing, stretching back at least into the late 19th and early 20th centuries. For example, in the first third of the 20th century (largely due to the First World War and the Great Depression), many people lost faith in the institutions of governance and authority and in the possibilities of democracy. Some even turned to political models of dictatorship, etc. as the only viable solution.

My backstory addresses only the political culture, partly because I think it has been often ignored. There are other backstories that would only enhance and enrich mine. Returning to my metaphor of the puzzle, I want to describe my story as part of a conversation of conjunctural stories, hopefully working together. I am doing what I can to assemble the puzzle, working on particular—what I might call—roaming transversals. Puzzles are not so neatly organized that they can be divided into rows and columns. As others' work is added to mine, or to other roaming transversals, the resonances move through and recompose every piece in the puzzle. Changing metaphors in mid-stream, the transversals are like ingredients in a recipe. They give new flavors and textures to other ingredients even as they themselves take on new flavors and textures. The final result is greater than the sum of its parts. My aim is to make the conjuncture more visible in a way that may be useful and that may help others continue the composition. My hope is that you will see this as not simply my opinion, nor as a conclusion I had reached before the

DOI: 10.4324/9781003662587-12

demanding efforts of research, analysis, and thought, but also accept that it is incomplete and no doubt wrong in some places. I like to call it experimental objectivism.

My story has three scenes or conjunctural moments that blend unevenly into one another, although I will pay most attention to the last two. I will offer, at best, summaries of the more extensive analyses I have presented in previous works. I have chosen to think of them as moments of a single conjuncture rather than as separable conjunctures. This will allow me to weave my story through the two problem spaces on which I have elaborated. It is a story of how the affective landscape has been and is being mobilized and deployed around the emergent organic crises of modernity.

Let me introduce you, briefly, to the three moments. The first, from the 1950s to the mid-1970s, was dominated by a particular version of the liberal state and the so-called liberal consensus. This consensus was built on the country's economic and technological successes (however unequally distributed) and a sense of cultural pluralism. It assumed that American liberalism was the best possible set of compromises to realize the promises of modernity. It was, however, fraught with ideological and political contradictions. And it was confronted by a plethora of resistances and oppositions from both ends of the political spectrum. The attacks, however, were unable to construct an organic crisis. But the emergence of the 1960s movements and the counterculture of the left, as well as of a new conservatism, set the stage for the second moment and the coming organic crises. Additionally, this first moment also saw the first signs of a quasi-autonomous affective landscape, marked by numerous contradictory affects, including complacency, optimism, boredom, terror, paranoia, spiritualism, etc.

The second moment, from the mid-1970s to the end of the century, began with the collapse of the liberal consensus under the weight of the many attacks and its own failures, and the ensuing struggles to bring down the liberal state. The political culture seemed to call forth an organic crisis and a struggle for a new settlement. This was the moment of the new right, and of neo-liberalism, globalization, and identity politics. But in a broader sense, it was defined in large measure by a struggle over how to be modern. It was a modern struggle over the meaning of modernity, a "best practices" of modernity, if you will.

The third conjunctural moment, beginning somewhere in the late 20th century and the beginning of the new millennium, gathered together a wide range of already existing forces and cultural regimes to problematize modernity itself. It made the very existence of the modern itself into the problem. Hence, the solution demanded more than its mere reconfiguration. It demanded an escape from, and alternative to, modernity. The parable of the burning house returns in full force. This time around, the moral of the story is that the house of modernity is already on fire. It has only itself to blame. The best choice is to leave the failure that is modernity behind. But since the house is beyond repair and the fire might spread, the first thing to do is tear it down.

I need one more piece for my puzzle, one ring to rule them all, to weave the story of the three moments together. Remember that the aim of conjunctural analysis is not to discover the evil that you already knew was there, nor to discover some hidden conspiracy of power that others can never see. It is to make visible the relations that we are not yet attuned to, relations for which we need to think otherwise.

I do not want to tell another story in which the conjunctural political culture becomes the scene of a polarized battle between parties, movements, ideologies, or policies. In a sense, that is where any story has to start. It might begin with actually existing, taken-for-granted groups—for example, the reactionary right and the so-called woke left—but that almost inevitably ends in stories of blame and complicity. It might start with the clash of ideologies (e.g., liberal, conservative, totalitarian/authoritarian, populist/identitarian, socialist/communist, anarchist/syndicalist), but it is unclear how far that story can take us. It might start with substantive policy debates (e.g., the role of bureaucracy and the "deep state," economic regulation, social justice), but such stories are likely to collapse the distance between movement and state politics. Or it might start by presupposing some imaginary battlelines separating the left (including progressives and even more centrist Democrats at some moments) from the right. As I said, these are reasonable places for any conjunctural story to begin, and mine begins with the kind of polarized struggles presupposed by all these stories. But it refuses to end there.

But the point of conjunctural analysis and the effort to tell a better story is not simply to end where you began. It is to find a different configuration of the conjuncture that lets you see something you might not have expected. My research leads me down a different path to a different conclusion, however temporary and partial. My story draws attention to some surprising formal parallels between supposedly opposing forces and positions. My story constructs the political culture as a struggle among competing affective tendencies or logics. These describe affectively formal operations, with no necessary content.

These tendencies articulate a relation between the affective landscape (or particular structures of feeling) and the organic crises. They set out the possibilities and limits of political action and struggle; they dictate the norms of political behavior. They define the nature of an acceptable balance in the field of political culture, and therefore, set up the end-game, defining any achievable balance that might be sought in the larger field of forces.

My analyses identified four affective tendencies, each with its own history. Each is manifested or expressed in many ways in various political groups and practices. They often work in hybrid ways, appropriating elements from one another as necessary for specific circumstances. A liberal tendency offers a logic of pluralism, tolerance, and compromise. It is what remains after the ideals of consensus-building or of a representative democracy collapse. The more American liberalism seemed to fail, the more liberalism became an empty—affective—logic to be either attacked or nostalgically defended.

To understand the hegemonic tendency, we might begin by thinking of a multi-party parliamentary system in which power has to be constructed through temporary alliances and, sometimes, tactical compromises. An affective hegemonic tendency reimagines the balance in the field of forces according to a distributive logic of concentricity. Society is re-organized and power re-distributed along concentric circles, moving out from a center of power toward an ever-receding periphery. The distribution is accomplished through processes of negotiation (but need not require compromise). The farther issues or groups are from the center, the less power they have and the less likely they are to be able to influence the center or to demand the right to negotiate for their own advantage.

Once again, as various attempts at this affective hegemonic settlement failed, the organic crisis remained. And two other simpler affective tendencies emerged as dominant. Both have long and active histories. Both took center stage largely by invoking the second organic crisis. Both were quickly connected to older stories of polarization and identity that had been operating, with varying success, since the beginning of the conjuncture. Both operate with a strong binary logic, as what Gramsci called a war of maneuver. It describes a battle between two cohesive and homogeneous camps, arrayed against each other across a single frontier. The difference between the speculative and the pseudo-revolutionary tendencies is whether the frontier is temporal or immediate.

The speculative tendency is the empty logic of utopianism. (I suppose it could also be dystopian but I find it hard to imagine politically. Perhaps that is generational?) The attraction of utopian politics is in the picture it paints of another habitable landscape, whether located in the past or the future. It is its ability to excite our imagination, to tell a story into which we can enter and imagine a life, that makes it so powerful. I don't know if we have lost our faith in utopias, but we have lost our faith in the concrete possibility of any particular utopia. The result is an affective logic built on the negation of the present as an abstraction and the affirmation of the alternative as abstract possibility. The alternative is presented without any details other than that it is not the present. Concrete analysis gives way to formal speculation. A formal frontier separates the present from another—unspecifiable—time. It is an empty—affective—logic of negation and escape.

The pseudo-revolutionary tendency has its roots in what may be the oldest conception of politics: A war between them and us, between friend and enemy. We know who we are; we know who they are; we know what the differences are. (And we must forget about the internal differences.) We (think we) know why we are fighting, so let the battle begin, whether it's countries or classes or races or .... The only thing it establishes with certainty is that the frontier exists. The result is an affective logic that expresses itself as what I have called fanaticism. The enemy is real because the frontier is real. For example, white people are the enemy because racism is real. Those with privilege are the enemy because we are oppressed.

Chapters 10-13 present a somewhat discontinuous history of America's political culture over the past 75 years, framed by the two problem spaces. They are organized by the domination of particular affective tendencies during specific moments. They are also often angry, judgmental, and pessimistic. My sense is that the band is playing on while the ship is sinking, and we don't seem to be able to talk about it. We don't even seem to be able to hear each other, to say nothing of listening (and I suppose that those who disagree would say the same thing to me).

I know there are a myriad of intellectual and activist experiments that have been going on and continue to go on. I know that people find ways to express their outrage and to protest whatever injustices they see in the world. I know there are movements, groups, media outlets, etc. that serve the wide variety of positions and politics. I have met many people who are asking lots of questions, doing a lot of reading, and seeking more effective and appropriate forms of theoretical, diagnostic, and political practice. I know that in 2025, there is a movement of outrage, anger, and hope that is being compared to that in the 1960s. I am not yet convinced. And the country continues to go to hell in a handbasket.

I know there are many people—on both the right and the left—who feel dissatisfied, even alienated, by the dominant tendencies shaping our political culture; they seek another way to be political, another politics. In the final part of the book, I introduce a fifth—popular—tendency. It operates with a logic of articulation or composition. It embraces uncertainty: The future is never guaranteed! It starts by understanding where people are and what they feel rather than telling them what they should feel. It listens to the stories they live in, and how those stories construct a habitable landscape for them, before it tries to change the stories. It recognizes that people are complicated and have complicated places in many stories. It understands that they can be moved into other stories and political positions, but not if we begin by condemning them. The popular tendency recognizes that we might have to change if we are asking people to change themselves. But in this conjunctural moment, the point is not to champion this tendency against all the others. That would merely create another frontier. Rather, its stories have to engage with and re-articulate other tendencies. A popular tendency will not seek total victory but modestly accept the possibility of a re-imagined balance in the field of forces. And the point of my story, in the end, is not simply to tell a better story but to make "hope practical, rather than despair convincing."[1] Call it a hopeful cynicism.

## Note

1 Williams, 1989, 240.

## Reference

Williams, Raymond. *Resources of Hope: Culture, Democracy, Socialism.* London: Verso Books, 1989.

# 10

# WE STUMBLE AND FALL

The Liberal and Hegemonic Tendencies

## The First Moment

The first conjunctural moment, the moment of "American liberalism," was built on the industrialization of the early 20th century and the New Deal. It was key to the United States cementing its leadership of the western world and becoming the self-proclaimed model of a free, prosperous, and democratic society. This particular—liberal—version of a modern society believed itself to have accomplished a stable (managed) consensus around the so-called corporatist compromise between capital and labor (in which labor was rewarded as profits increased). It enabled the normalization of a limited welfare state and the public provision of a narrow range of services. There was a celebrated sense of economic prosperity and the promise of political freedom. It is often thought of as a golden moment of both rapid growth and an unusually equitable (for capitalism) redistribution of wealth. It created the largest and wealthiest middle class ever and a high degree of economic and geographic mobility for many working and lower middle class families. There was a sense of accomplishment, relief, and superiority following the wars and a desire for comfort and convenience; yet, it was in many ways contradicted by a generalized political paranoia, only partly the result of the Cold War, and the experiences of conformism and boredom. Still, while the "American dream" had changed, it still shone, somewhat dimmer, as a beacon on the hill.

However, liberal modernity was simultaneously riven by the contradiction between its own assumed accomplishments and the real limits of its claim to shared prosperity, freedom, and justice. There was a deep sense of frustration and anger among at least two heterogeneous populations: First, those who

DOI: 10.4324/9781003662587-13

were excluded from having the promises fulfilled; and second, those who, for any number of reasons, simply rejected the vision of modernity embodied in liberalism. Consequently, liberal modernity was attacked as soon as it settled in. There were struggles against capitalism, labor struggles, civil rights, anti-racist, and black power struggles, anti-colonial and anti-imperialist struggles, and anti-nuclear weapons and anti-war protests, as well as feminist, environmental, countercultural, and bohemian movements. For many of these, their energy and unity were partly drawn from popular culture, and their visibility often depended on the growing power of media cultures.

For some who resisted, liberal modernity was a failed accomplishment. They demanded that the liberal state do more to live up to its ethical principles and political ideals. For others, liberal modernity was inescapably compromised. They identified its contradictions (from both inside and outside the dominant class fractions) and challenged some of its fundamental structures of power and ideologies, some of the defining features of its claim to modernity. And for others still, liberal modernity was an undesirable project. They sought to escape its power or to create safe harbors in the midst of devastation. And despite the commonly told stories, the opposition to liberal modernity was not limited to the left. Different right-wing—conservative and reactionary—positions, some with long histories, were (re-)emerging and organizing against liberalism.

The "golden age of liberalism" was short-lived; liberal modernity never became the stable and popular social arrangement it imagined itself to be. But its resonances have continued to play a powerful role in political culture. Liberalism continued to be a battleground for decades. And some might say that it continues to be so.

To understand this, we need to recognize that this first moment was shaped by the first expressions of a quasi-autonomous affective landscape. Liberalism as an ideology was slowly being replaced by an affective tendency offering a balance in the field of forces around a logic of pluralism and its corollaries of tolerance and compromise. It told stories of the world in terms of strict oppositions but assumed that reconciliation was always possible. The threat of war would be managed by détente; bureaucracy and expertise would serve common well-being; the law would meet the demands for change. Its fantasy was to enable "to each his (or her) own." It imagined "a thousand points of light," an image used by both Arthur C. Clarke and William S. Burroughs long before Bush's PR team made it into a campaign slogan in 1988. It assumed that an almost natural harmony of feeling could be achieved.

Given that this was only the beginning of the emergence of an affective landscape, the liberal affective tendency was not yet strong enough to manage the field of political investments. American liberalism was unable to reconcile the contradictions between its ideological politics and an emerging affective politics. Many of the attacks on liberalism voiced an underlying but still poorly articulated set of affective demands. But what was rapidly becoming an ideological nostalgia made it difficult for some political groups to abandon their faith in politics as a matter of substance, ideas, and policies. Consequently, American liberalism could not untangle the emerging affective contradictions, which might have allowed it to confront the material limits and inequalities of postwar America. It could not rescue the already failed project of liberal modernity. And yet it did not disappear. While it proved incapable of sustaining either the right or the left, it has continued to play an important role for a large part of the population of the country for decades, pulling in toward a center, until that center collapsed under pressure from other tendencies.

## The Second Moment and the New Right

By the mid-1970s and early 1980s, one of the dominant stories that emerged out of the battles over liberalism was that liberalism had lost. Liberal modernity had collapsed under the weight of its own failures. To a large extent, it became obvious to many people. America was in an unsettled moment, living in the ruins of liberalism. Many thought, at the time, that this second moment was or, at least, began as the worst of times: The time of Carter's national malaise, the oil crisis, hostages in the Middle East, stagflation, the Contras, crack cocaine, the apparent re-legitimation and overt resurgence of public expressions of racisms (e.g., the 1991 beating of Rodney King and the OJ Simpson trials) and the re-animation of anti-racist protests and even violence, etc. Yet it was also, in some respects, apparently the best of times, marked most clearly by the collapse of the Soviet Union in 1991 and the end of the Cold War.

A new battle emerged: A struggle to construct and respond to an organic crisis, the reverberations of which continue into the present. Various groups offered competing visions not of a different society but of better (non-liberal) forms of modern governance, better ways of being modern in, outside of, and beyond the liberal consensus. There was nothing apocalyptic or catastrophic inherent in the stories that were told or the settlements that were offered. For the most part, the struggles over this organic crisis did not really threaten to overturn peoples' sense of normalcy.

This is perhaps understandable if we recognize that liberalism subsumes a number of practices and formations. It referred, first, to a laissez faire political economy in which markets were allowed to regulate themselves. Second, it referred to a set of Enlightenment values, especially forms of individualism, rationalism, progress, etc. Third, it identified a move from a system of governance that attempted to control people's behavior with physical force to one that increasingly used the social power of norms and normalization. And finally, especially since the 1950s, it heralded a form of governance that attempted to control people's conduct through forms of expertise, policy, and the law. In the struggles around liberalism in postwar America, the second—a system of values—remained largely taken for granted, although particular values were challenged, redefined, or reprioritized. It was, however, the last— a system of regulation through law—that came under direct challenge from the right (and some elements of the left).

The leading force in these struggles, largely through political culture, was a new conservatism that had emerged in the 1960s. This "new right" fought to undermine liberalism using two transformative insights: First, political change demanded a strategic, step-by-step program, to minimize the power of the state. This would require it to re-imagine and reconstruct the assumptions and institutions of American society and culture. Second, culture had become the key battleground of contemporary politics. But it also understood, whether consciously or not, that culture was becoming increasingly affective. Operating on the quasi-autonomous affective landscape, the new right operated with (articulated) a different affective tendency, re-imagining the possibilities of political balance in terms of hegemony rather than pluralism.

Conservatism has a long history in the U.S.; it has taken many forms and identified many enemies. It has often deviated from other national versions in significant ways: It has often held libertarian and even anti-democratic suspicions of the state. It has often existed adjacent to evangelical and fundamentalist Protestant denominations with a history of "awakenings," as well as virulent strains of anti-Catholicism and anti-Semitism. It has frequently embraced (or timidly negotiated with) overtly racist and white supremacist groups. And it has often presented itself in paranoid stories of a nation under attack, imagining both internal and external threats to America's very existence. Recurring bouts of xenophobia and anti-immigration politics have gone hand in hand with over-the-top expressions of patriotism and isolationist ethno-nationalisms. That paranoia has often extended to the corrupting, anti-American forces of modernization, concretized in the growing power of cities, which have corrupted the moral values and virtues of the true American citizens, usually located in small towns and rural communities. The Cold War enabled the new right to identify the "obvious" presence of communist sympathizers in the various left movements of the 1960s with anti-American sentiments. It was even able to eventually transform important liberal icons into "neocons," who wanted to use U.S. military power to change the international face of the world by engaging in "nation-building."

Ironically, Richard Nixon's defeat of Hubert Humphrey in 1968, partly the result of the left Movement refusing to support Humphrey because of his position on the Vietnam war, helped empower the new right, despite the fact that Nixon was never thought to be a true conservative. His political position was at best ambiguous. He broke the postwar Bretton Woods agreement (partly to fund the war in Vietnam) while welcoming global capitalism. He placed anti-communism at the center of American patriotism and explicitly used (dog-whistle) racism to bring Southern white voters to the Republican Party (his "Southern strategy"). He began the war on drugs, ensuring that many young black men would be ineligible to vote and condemning many black families to further impoverishment. And he tried to reconstruct the political field as a populist conflict between a silent majority (the good, honest, ordinary, hard-working folk of the country, who trusted their own faith and experience) and the urban-cosmopolitan, liberal, educated, and secular elites, including the media. Hia Vice President Spiro Agnew famously described the latter as the "nattering nabobs of negativism." They arrogantly thought that their education, their knowledge (including their faith in science), and their expertise not only guaranteed that they held the truth, but also gave them the right to define what other people should do and how they should live, embodied in their defense of big government. Sound familiar?

While the presidential candidacy of Barry Goldwater in 1964 had made the strength of a resurgent American conservatism visible, the extremism of his views, the ruthlessness of his campaign tactics, and, ultimately, his decisive defeat convinced young conservative intellectuals (e.g., William Buckley Jr., Russell Kirk) that the right had to do more work to prepare the ground and educate the American people. At the same time, the Goldwater-Johnson election marked the beginning of a crisis for moderate Republicans, who saw themselves being increasingly marginalized within their own party. Already, there were signs that the middle was collapsing under the stress of what each side saw as a polarization of extremes.

The new right not only took up many of the left's criticisms of liberalism, it also studied, appropriated, co-opted, and clawed back many of its tactics and rhetorics in service of its own strategies. For example, the left's "do your own thing" had come from and was taken back into a more conservative libertarian notion of liberty as non-interference. At the same time, using their knowledge of and connections to the media, the new right was able to influence how the left movements were represented both in the short term (especially addressing older generations, the working classes, and rural populations) and in the long term.

The more urban, university-centered, largely bicoastal baby boomers were, unfortunately, quite parochial, often assuming that they were the entirety or, at least, the rightful representative of their generation, if not the country. The patriotic right was able to tell its own stories of Vietnam and the 1960s left, portraying the protests as the work of anti-American communists, black troublemakers, and privileged, unclean, perverted—possibly homosexual—cowards. They were not fully successful, but what success they did have was not limited to rural and small-town communities. While not everyone living in less dense areas went to the right, many were open to the possibilities. And not everyone living in dense urban areas (nor every person of color) went to the left. This was perhaps the beginning of the culture wars.

Conservative intellectuals like Buckley and Kirk argued that the right had to gain a better understanding of the state of the nation and its culture, including the thinking that animated both the mainstream center and the various lefts. This meant investing in the work of scholars and intellectuals. But the right also had to reconfigure the forces of conservatism, assembling a new and potentially more fluid coalition for the conjunctural moment. They began reconfiguring conservative ideas and practices, with the explicit aim of establishing a new "ruling bloc," an alliance of anti-liberal and anti-leftist interests, that could lead the country in a new direction. This ruling bloc was to be flexible; its membership would change as conditions warranted. It brought together, for example, new conservative intellectuals, capitalists, evangelical Christians, neo-classical economists, etc. It was held together as much by affective allegiances as by ideological enemies. (i.e., liberalism and the left). The initial success of this effort came in the form of the presidency of Ronald Reagan, although there was a lot more work to be done.

This new right was constructed by the interactions among a number of distinct commitments. It reached out for support (especially funding) from and created alliances with other groups, which they included in their stories as being under attack. Hence, it could convince them to contribute to its strategic plan. Many of these (e.g., religious movements) were predictable. Others were less so. For example, conservatives had traditionally rejected capitalism as the destroyer of values. Instead, the new right embraced it (as the counterpoint to communism), especially its free market and anti-regulation advocates. In 1971, the Powell Memorandum ("Attack on the American Free Enterprise System")[1] warned capitalist CEOs that their interests were under attack. They needed to increase their political influence through donations, lobbying, the media, and the establishment of think tanks.

The new right presented itself as an umbrella organization, a changing coalition of conservative factions, with a relatively open and inclusive formation, internally both disparate and organized. This was later embodied in Ronald Reagan's 11th commandment: Thou shalt not speak ill of any fellow Republican. Despite continual internal fractures and fights, the new right constantly forged new relations among and between movements, institutions, and parties, continuously configuring new unities-in-difference. At the same time, it held the more extremist, reactionary, and violent groups of the right on the margins—but rarely explicitly renounced them.

The new right set about the task of constructing an organic crisis and proposing its settlement with a well-thought out strategic plan. It left open to debate questions about immediate tactics and questions about how far to go and how quickly. It understood that politics demanded patience. It saw itself fighting a long war to win back the country. For example, after Roe v. Wade, Buckley often reminded his audiences that it might take 50 years to outlaw abortions, and that it would entail very difficult and painful struggles. But he assured them that it would be done because it mattered so much. (He was essentially correct.)

Strategizing assumes that achieving any goal might well require using different tactics at different times or sites, moving step by step and stopping at way stations on the route. It also means planning for contingencies (including unpredicted actions by the opposition) that might require new tactics, for which you are always well-prepared. You aren't surprised; you are ready to pounce on any mistake or opportunity, or anything your opponent does that you can weaponize against them. And this will sometimes mean working with people you don't agree with or even like. The new right took the time, often using partial failures and incomplete struggles, to strengthen itself. Rather than move to another struggle, it could see the tactical value of occasionally retreating from the playing field, only to return to the same fight but with different tactics and appeals. No doubt, such resoluteness was enabled by copious amounts of money and deeply (affectively) committed supporters.

None of this suggests some secret plot or conspiracy, a cabal delivering orders from the shadows (although I am sure smaller conspiracies did exist). For the most part, the strategizing was there for all to see. I recently saw that some progressive journalist had discovered emails and other documents planning the attack on diversity at particular universities (including my own). This was—he screamed—a conspiracy. No, this is politics, strategic politics. Panic has become the hyper-inflated default response to good—however despicable you might think the content—strategic politics.

Strategy depends on the long road through institutions. The new right operated largely through dispersed organizations and movements. Each was understood pragmatically, as goal-oriented rather than as just an agent of agitation or resistance. The new right's shifting roster of organizations combined grassroots activism, policy development and advocacy, and electoral campaigning. Sometimes, these organizations were called upon to multitask, providing intellectual cover, tactical descriptions of concrete goals, and planning for various contingencies (e.g., the chaos of the 2000 Florida election). They were also carefully managed so as not to create too much duplication or conflict.

These institutions were tasked to formulate not only alternative (non-liberal) policies and solutions but also tactics that could be used to define and win battles. Some were also meant to find ways to manage the relations between state and movement politics. And others had to hold the more extremist right-wing groups—reactionary, traditionalist, white supremacist, and neo-fascist—in the margins, even as they appropriated and re-articulated some of their commitments, giving them a "friendly" face.

The individuals and groups who participated in these institutions and campaigns talked to one another; they read many of the same things and argued about them. They assembled something like playbooks. They identified possible crises and issues, and how the latter could be used to create the former. They provided compelling facts, examples, and rhetorical strategies and potential policies and legal precedents that could be used when the circumstances demanded.

Saving the best for last, the new right embraced the primacy of culture; it was committed to radically changing the culture of politics and the politics of culture. Part of this entailed a commitment to gaining a better understanding of what was going on. And that meant investing in serious, rigorous scholarship and intellectual investigation. Remember the last item in Powell's list. Capitalist donors funded think tanks, many of which have endured and continue to produce and publish important research, proposals, and policies. Conservatives created magazines, some of which were intellectually exciting and often encouraged disagreement and debate more than anything on the left did. When conservative intellectuals published works, the conservative media took them up, promoted them, and did everything they could to make them visible to the mainstream, to make them popular.

But the new right was also apparently willing to accept that politics was going to be fought out on the emerging affective landscape. It weaponized—and monetized—cultural issues (previously called social issues) such as school prayer, pornography, homosexuality, education, diversity, and, most intensely, abortion. And then it affectively hyper-inflated images and slogans, articulating them in and through various structures of feeling. Rather than winning ideological consensus (except in the vaguest terms), it sought to win people over by telling stories that could pull them into particular sites on a recomposed affective landscape. It understood that the power of culture was in the stories that were told and in their ability to speak to people, to invite them into their spaces, and to reconstruct an affective landscape in which people could find livable places for themselves. It understood that public discourse and media are wonderfully pliable tools for the dissemination of stories, that stories operate contextually, and that they can be bent to different purposes. It understood that people hear and understand particular statements and stories only in the context of the stories which they already inhabit.

The new right adopted many of the practices of consumer capitalism and the media, as well as of the 1960s countercultures' re-appropriation of them. And if they were, at the time, largely cut out of the spaces of mainstream popular culture, they found other ways to enter and speak affectively. This became the premise of Rush Limbaugh's radio talk show when it went on the air in 1988, and of Fox News when it premiered in 1996. Campaigns were increasingly driven by cognitively meaningless but affectively powerful images like "morning in America" and "a thousand points of light." Both could serve to intensify particulate pieces of the affective landscape and reconstruct the maps of what mattered to people.

Using the simplest of ideological markers (e.g., liberty, family values, free markets), it affectively linked and even equated issues. It pulled people from one position into a broader set of commitments, creating new and powerful mattering maps. Any single issue could be offered as a metonym for some sense of unity and totality. And with the same tactics, the new right largely controlled the image of the left as well, which spent more energy on internecine and sectarian arguments than on forging an alternative sense of its own unity-in-difference.

The new right learned how easy it was to control the public conversation by appropriating pieces of (the other side's) stories and recontextualizing them in its own stories. The result was the production of very different affective resonances. Then it could link them to already-felt fears and doubts (which it had constructed) and to values meant to assuage any feelings of guilt people felt (e.g., local control, parental choice, family values). Once begun, it doesn't matter if people know what you are doing, or even if you confess to it. You can admit to the big lie, as long as the story is affectively powerful enough. You can claim the moral high ground even as you face constant moral scandals. (Reagan was, after all, the Teflon president.)

The new right sought to exacerbate people's affective frustration with institutions and policies. The new right did not spend much energy policing voter registration rolls; instead, it waged an affective war against voting itself. It tried to convince people that their vote didn't matter, to the point where they would not vote. Whether because the future is unpredictable, ruled by unintended consequences and chance, or because the system is rigged and corrupt, or because one vote can't make a difference, the conclusion was clear. There is no possible reason to vote.

If you want to dismantle a public institution, first appeal to the desire for lower taxes (presented as an immediate increase in income). Less government income means fewer services, which means greater deficiencies and more frustration. This will make further cuts in taxes and/or privatization seem reasonable, forcing people to take up the burdens of the inadequate services, making them more likely to abandon the institutions themselves. (And for heaven's sake, don't remind them of how much they already rely on government social services, or how much the state requires them to do things that are beneficial!) It's a brilliant strategy: Because institutions are not working to our satisfaction, ensure that they cannot work by undermining the extent to which they do work.

The new right had only to put the finishing touches on the attacks on liberalism from the first conjunctural moment in order to construct an organic crisis; that came about largely through economic (stagflation) and cultural (moral) panics that cemented the feeling that the country was in crisis. Liberalism as the dominant American way of being modern had failed. What previous criticisms had ignored—had, in fact, exacerbated—was that liberalism attempted to govern by regulating people's behavior through the law. What was needed was, first, to minimize the role of the state in all aspects of life (i.e., deregulation) and, then, to reimagine every sector of modern life that had been corrupted by liberalism, including politics, the economy, culture, education, the arts, social relations, international and military relations, etc. While many critics of the new right argued that it hypocritically attempted to control people's moral life, they failed to see that this was done as a matter of political culture rather than regulation and law. They imagined themselves to be offering not merely a vision but a blueprint (however many disagreements there were) of a different way of being modern. And while some looked back in history for sustenance, many were attempting to respond to the very organic crisis they were attempting to construct against liberal modernity.

The new right's proposed settlement was an expression of a hegemonic affective tendency, which reorganizes society on principles of distribution. Hegemonic politics are commonly assumed to work through ideological consensus-building; those seeking power have to convince people to agree with their world-view. But hegemony is better understood as an ongoing struggle to win people's consent—consent to allow a particular ruling bloc to lead the society out of an organic crisis. People do not have to agree with its ideology or with any specific policies.

Hegemonic struggles for consent are waged by telling stories that speak to people, stories in which they can recognize themselves, stories in which they can find a place to live. But those stories still have substance and content. They define the organic crisis by identifying specific causes in, for example, the liberal state, and offer often nostalgic images of their proposed settlements (e.g., Reagan's morning in America). And they incorporate and belittle other stories as simply more of the same.

But the more affect saturated the political culture in the second moment, the less substance mattered in the stories. The crisis became increasingly abstract and its settlement more ambiguous. And more consent, already an affective relation, was given to stories aimed at bringing people into an affective landscape that was being actively reconstructed by those very stories. The stories constructed a different way of organizing the now affective political culture (and with it, a different way of living in it). They expressed an affective hegemonic tendency, which makes hegemony into a formal—distributive—logic. It distributes issues, struggles, and crises, as well as the populations that are gathered around them, in what can roughly be described as concentric circles. These differ in how close or far away they are to or from whatever is attempting to become the new center of power.

That distance presumably correlates with a distribution of power and status. The center may negotiate with some groups on some issues, depending on how near they are, and offer them some of what they seek, even if they are not among the center's priorities. (It sharply distinguishes negotiation as a strategy from compromise as a tactic.) But there are always some groups with whom it will not negotiate, whom it will not even recognize as belonging to the nation, whom it will try to keep off the field of forces. And there will always be some issues and crises that it refuses to acknowledge or even erase.

As the new millennium approached, the nation was exhausted. The stories it told of the previous decades described it as tumultuous, deeply troubling, and often problematic (with lots of pleasurable distractions). As Fukuyama (1992, 48) put it, "We arrive ... exhausted, as it were, from the pursuit of alternatives we felt had to be better than liberal democracy." The new right seemed to have lost much of its energy, and its victories were dwindling. Or perhaps it had won its next victory. It seemed to have taken control of, if not become, the Republican Party. And because it had, it came under attack, not from the left or center but from the right itself. New generations of conservatives, often with close ties to the reactionary groups which the new right had suppressed, accused it of making too many compromises and becoming itself too compromised. The fact that it may have been part of a strategic plan did not matter.

This new right expressed different, more fundamentalist, affective tendencies. It opened itself to the more radical and intense stories of polarization that were increasingly flooding the nation. It refused any logic that allowed the possibility of compromise. And it argued that the continuing deterioration of the nation evidenced that the organic crisis, as it had been framed in both the first and second moments, was unable to carry the burden of what was happening. The nation faced a new organic crisis. A new organic crisis had to be constructed. It would locate the crisis in modernity itself and propose to reject the very project of modernity. Here, the crisis is even more abstract and the settlement is defined, most frequently, almost entirely in negative terms (i.e., not modern). Enter a new politics of "us and them," embodied in the speculative and pseudo-revolutionary tendencies, articulated through ever stronger attacks on modernity and attempts to undercut its very ability to govern affectively and effectively.

## The Second Moment and an Uncertain Left

During this second moment, the left was significantly less visible. And it was (not so neatly) divided between those who thought the fundamental crisis of American society and politics revolved around capitalism and those who thought it revolved around questions of culture, identity, and oppression.

I will postpone my discussion of "identity politics" to the following chapter and consider only the economic left here.

The visibility of an economic left, focused on national and even global economic concerns, grew rapidly, beginning in the late 1970s. The country faced a series of economic shocks, culminating in "stagflation" (inflation + stagnant growth), coupled with various foreign policy challenges. The responses were largely dictated by a rejection of Keynesian liberalism in favor of a revitalization of (neo-)classical liberalism or, as it came to be called, neo-liberalism and its soulmate, globalization.[2]

While the economic left regularly protested against neoliberal claims and policies in the United States, it was also committed to a worldwide effort to disrupt the normal transnational operations of institutions such as the WTO, the IMF, the World Bank, etc. Many of the left's most visible successes were the result of well-planned, large-scale demonstrations, which also served as spectacles that could be seen around the world.

It is difficult to describe the economic left's efforts to construct an organic crisis without simultaneously pointing out why they were unlikely to take hold. This doesn't deny the important political work it did; and it potentially holds important lessons for the third moment as we face a global (environmental) crisis from within a still-national conjuncture. Whatever its successes or failures, the left of this second moment is a vital part of the backstory I am trying to tell.

The economic left attempted to construct its organic crisis in purely economic terms. (It was not until the third moment that identity politics was able to mount something like an organic crisis.) There were always serious ambiguities in the economic left's efforts. What is the relation between neoliberalism and globalization? Is the crisis national or global? Can an organic crisis be global? Do we have the necessary analytic and political tools? More to my point, what role do neoliberalism and globalization play in the story? Are they the cause of a crisis waiting to be constructed? Are they already in a crisis not yet visible? In either case, what kind of story might call people into the crisis and a particular settlement, and how can it be constructed?

If the economic left was going to build an organic crisis around, for example, neoliberalism, a constant reference point, it would need some sense of what it refers to: If it is a description of purely economic relations, is it: A new form of capital accumulation, a return to primitive accumulation, the marketization and monetization of previously protected regions of social life, deregulation and free markets, a fiscal policy such as monetarism, stock valuation measured solely by profits, all of these, some specified number of these? Maybe it's about governance: The expansion of corporate power, the regulation of labor markets, economic citizenship, global imperialism? Or is it more of a social thing: Placing risk on individuals, reducing individuals to monetized flows, reducing all value to market value?

There are still more questions. Is it an actual set of policies and are they mere proposals or are they already in place? Or is it simply an ideological fantasy or a long-term project? Would it be important to know the effects of introducing specific economic changes and policies to already existing economies? Would existing social, cultural, or political relations matter? Would neoliberal changes make everything they touch neoliberal? How would anyone know if and when neoliberalism failed?

If the organic crises were a crisis of neoliberalism, then its near spectacular failure in 2007 (admittedly in the third moment) should have done more to disrupt the balance in the field of forces. In 2007 (and visibly lasting through 2009), as a result of deregulation and speculation, a large part of the financial sector fell into crisis, resulting in a major recession, vividly demonstrating the precarity of both the national and the global capitalist systems. When the U.S. government (as well as its western allies) responded, predictably, with measures to support failing banks and corporate capitalism, the anger was palpable as ordinary people suffered while bankers and the wealthy seemed to come off unscathed.

Many on the economic left thought that the financial crisis would be the straw that broke the camel's back; that this was the beginning of the end of neoliberalism (if not capitalism as we knew it). The whole edifice was about to collapse. It did not! The left acted as if the dominoes would fall and re-arrange themselves all on their own. They did not. But this was not some inevitable conclusion or simply the result of capitalism's resilience (although I am sure that played a role). Rather, the left was unable or unwilling to take up the task; it had no strategy in place by which to articulate a real economic crisis into an organic crisis; maybe all it could do was occupy spaces or escape into green entrepreneurialism.

It had little understanding of an organic crisis. This economic crisis could have been articulated to any number of other social crises as well as to the affective landscape in different ways. The moment presented an opportunity (even a demand) to challenge not only the forms of economic dominance but also the broader set of political and cultural forces. It was a moment when the various crises and struggles spread out across the terrain of life in the U.S. might have been brought together and fused into an organic crisis and a different way out of (liberal) modernity. But it was not the left that led the way.

Before leaving the second conjunctural moment, I want to point to another division within the left, which prefigured the affective tendencies of the third moment. It was expressed in the difference between a horizontal politics (an expression of the speculative affective tendency), generally associated with the economic left of the moment, and a more antagonistic binary politics (an expression of the pseudo-revolutionary tendency), generally associated with the identity politics of the moment. Again, I will only talk about one—a horizontal logic of organization. It remains a logic of distribution but refuses the concentricity of a hegemonic logic. It offers a logic of fragmentation, a social or communitarian dispersed politics of anarchy.[3] It rejected structure, formal organization, and the power of hierarchies. On the one hand, it offered a politics of the local (understood in largely spatial terms), especially participatory, democratic decision-making. On the other hand, it recognized the need for local movements to come together, not as an articulated unity but as a pragmatic show of force. Any attempt at a unitary articulation is an assertion of power. Power had to be understood and responded to as always dispersed and local. It treated all struggles as existing on a common— horizontal—plane. And it often won important local battles and impacted local communities. It drew communities into new stories and new political positions, and even into new political possibilities.

## Conclusion

As the country entered the 1990s, both the right and the left had failed to successfully compose the organic crisis, to establish a new settlement or balance in the field of forces, or to offer a compelling reimagination of the modern. No story was able to achieve anything close to a stable and sustainable position. The organic crisis never quite came together; it remained always only partially visible, largely ill-formed, and poorly expressed. What were offered as major changes turned out to be little more than small alterations. Neither the left nor the right could escape the constrained space of possibilities that was the inheritance of liberal modernity.

These failures pushed the crisis of modernity even further and opened a third conjunctural moment, with its own dispersed crises added to the mix. It now seemed that the organic crisis had changed. The first organic crisis is no longer up to the task. It can no longer capture the depth and breadth of the horrors of the present. We can no longer find a settlement by simply searching for better ways of being modern.

A second organic crisis was taking shape. Exactly what shape it would take, and what settlements would be possible, was the new battleground of political culture. But this organic crisis was different from your typical organic crisis (if there is such a thing). It has all the makings of an epochal crisis. It challenges structures and commitments that, in one form or another, have been in place for centuries. It poses a politics of "the long durée." It defines any possible settlement as an attack on modernity itself, in all its possibilities, whatever its essence. And yet, the organic crisis is lived in the conjuncture. The stories that construct it will have to reconcile this paradox. They will have to find new logics and new affective tendencies.

## Notes

1 Lewis F. Powell Jr. was appointed to the Supreme Court by Richard Nixon in 1971.
2 Globalization has existed at different times, in many different forms. In each form, globalization is a hybrid of old and new and local and foreign processes and structures. In each form, globalization has produced a myriad of effects benefiting (and damaging) various constituencies, although it is always the capitalists (and the powerful) who gain the most.
3 At the transnational level, it often presented itself as a movement of movements, which had also been used as a self-description of the 1960s movement. In the 1980s, this seemed to mean simply a gathering of various regional and national protest movements.

## Reference

Fukuyama, Frances. *The End of History and the Last Man.* New York: Free Press, 1992.

# 11

# WE FIND WE'RE ALONE

## Stories of Polarization

Nations are rarely homogeneous; they are probably always internally differentiated. And there are probably stories that represent—construct—those differences. Stories may make them trivial or foundational, humorous or tragic, justified or prophetic. They may tell of their harmonious co-existence, or of their bitter confrontations. Such stories of differences are a necessary part of making sense of the world. But there are many kinds of stories of differences, and they operate in many different ways. There are no guarantees that particular differences will offer useful ways of organizing the social field. And there are no guarantees as to which stories will actually take hold, or in which stories people will find places to inhabit, or how they might enter into a story.

There are even many kinds of stories that tell of a nation divided. Sometimes, such stories reach back to precedents: To times when we assume similar stories were told—the Civil War, the Gilded Age, the 1960s. Perhaps, we find comfort in thinking that we are retelling the same old stories. But they are never exactly the same old stories. There is always something different each time these stories are told and their "truth" is constructed.

The most powerful and damning stories of division are stories of polarization, which render the nation as absolutely divided between "us and them." In these stories, the many differences amongst social groups and possible constituencies are distributed and condensed into two starkly drawn homogeneous camps. No differences matter except the single difference between the two camps. Each side knows its cause is right and even necessary. This binary difference is imposed on what might otherwise be seen as a highly diversified population. Each camp has its own essential and necessary identity

DOI: 10.4324/9781003662587-14

and political position. Each has some content. And the frontier is so clearly marked and so powerful that nothing can cross its boundary.

Stories of polarization (and their offspring, populist stories) have played an important role in the political culture of the current conjuncture, even if the term itself was not used. They were there in the 1950s and 1960s, often as expressions of vitriolic forms of social paranoia and hatred. Nixon's attempt to popularize a populist story set the stage for them to come into their own in the second conjunctural moment I have just described. They were bolstered by an increasingly capitalized media and increasingly statistically defined social sciences. The latter claimed to provide an authoritative, institutionalized way of representing the nation back to itself, through systems of statistical polls and surveys. But until the third conjunctural moment, polarization stories still existed in tension with other stories. They were not yet the unquestioned foundational stories of politics that they were to become—completely affective and omnipresent.

## The Third Conjunctural Moment

The third conjunctural moment arrived around the new millennium, marked by forces that re-articulated the affective landscape. A new technological revolution affecting people's everyday lives reshaped the possibilities of communication: The world wide web became the primary platform for information, social media became the new community, and first cell phones and then smart phones changed interpersonal relations. But technology also threatened disaster: Many people panicked that Y2K would bring about the end of the world as we knew it.

But the political culture and the field of political struggles were also reconfigured by a number of events, especially when taken together. In 2000, George W. Bush defeated Al Gore to become 43rd president of the United States. The election was all but decided in Florida (in the "hanging chad fiasco") or, more accurately, by the Supreme Court. There were arguments about whether the Supreme Court had violated the Constitution, which leaves elections in the hands of the states. But something much more consequential had occurred. Perhaps people didn't realize it at the time, but this was a shot fired across the bow, announcing the beginning of naked hostilities. The rules of engagement were changing, and the Republicans were prepared for any contingencies that might upset their game plan. Wait—they had a game plan? In retrospect, that seems obvious. Was this a conspiracy? No, but it should have alerted Democrats (who seemed more invested in saving the system itself) about the changing struggles over political culture.

The terrorist acts of 9/11(2001) announced the arrival of the new millennium with a bang (no pun intended). This introduced or, rather, re-articulated a structure of a feeling of fear and insecurity and made questions of security and surveillance not only national priorities but everyday realities. They also gave the right what it had been lacking for some time: A Satanic enemy opposed to everything America stood for and which, like communism, was not tied to a single nation-state. It was an enemy threatening from all sides, including from within, creating new kinds of paranoia, hatred, and demonization. It was also easily attached to the figure of the immigrant, despite the fact that those entering at the southern border were rarely those being represented as terrorists. It also gave the left a new figure that could be generalized into more encompassing images of oppression and American guilt.

Less commented upon was the growing and constant barrage of reports of violence across the country: In schools, in restaurants, on the streets, government standoffs with various extremist cults and domestic terrorists, and, almost as common but less commented on, police violence against blacks and other minorities. The right somehow wove these dispersed acts into stories that defended, in affectively absolute terms, the 2nd amendment.

The new millennium saw the beginning of the war on terror, aimed against the so-called Axis of Evil. In 2003, Bush ordered U.S. armed forces (with a few, mostly unhappy, allies) to invade Iraq, under the pretense that it was amassing weapons of mass destruction. The war lasted until 2011, destabilizing the entire region, even though it was established early on that there were no WMDs. Once again, one of the most important lessons went unheeded. The threat of war elicited some of the largest protests ever seen, both in America and around the world, and they continued long after the war began. Bush took no notice of them. He was not swayed by them, and he did not respond to them. He stood by his certainties (even when proven wrong) and his moral absolutes. The people had spoken, at least enough of them that it was reasonable to expect their government to take some account of them. It did not, and they became irrelevant to political decision-making. The stories declared that this was done in the cause of morality. Bush was more concerned with the possibilities of civilizational wars and the Axis of Evil. This was the first death knell of representative democracy.

In 2009, Barack Obama became the first black president (and perhaps the first intelligent and articulate president in a while). This was historically momentous, if only for its symbolic power. The response to Obama was profound. On the one hand, he elicited a powerful affective investment from the left (despite his centrist, neoliberal policies) and was treated by many as a prophetic—almost messianic—figure of liberal possibilities. On the other hand, the right, which often ignored his policies (except for those they could label as socialist), often used the figure of a black urban president to mobilize deeply racist and anti-cosmopolitan sentiments.

Almost simultaneously, and not entirely coincidentally, the Tea Parties appeared; the media quickly brought them into the political and electoral mainstream. The Tea Parties comprised a de-centered, national movement of autonomous local groups. They had no formal national leadership or organization, although there were several organizations that claimed to represent various coalitions. And national leaders qua spokespersons quickly appeared to answer the media's calls. The Tea Parties saw themselves as an insurgency, as renegades who challenged the state and the "normal" practice of politics from both outside and inside the Republican Party. They accused the Republicans and the new right of continuing the normal (i.e., liberal) practice of governance and of compromising the principles of a truly conservative agenda. The Tea Parties did not appear to want to take over the Republican Party so much as hold it to the fire. Obama and the Islamic fundamentalist/terrorist became the symbolic figures through which the frustrations of the right were expressed, and eventually re-articulated, ironically, away from conservatism into another politics, commonly referred to as reactionary.

The Tea Parties were not, however, the embryo from which that new politics sprang forth. They were more like the door through which movements that had been largely marginalized and even silenced by the new right could enter onto the stage of mainstream political culture and find an affective coherence. They embraced the Tea Parties' rejection of the "RINOs" ("Republican in name only") who had abandoned their principles out of fear, cowardice, and corruption. They looked back to appropriate the paleo-conservative's emotionally charged, anti-elitist, and anti-establishment appeal to a rigid moral nationalism. And they drew heavily, even more than the new right, on the symbolic and performative tactics of the 1960s left movement.

It was also during these years that a re-invigorated and reconfigured identity politics (increasingly an expression of the pseudo-revolutionary tendency) began to shake up the left; sometimes referred to as woke, a term with a long history, going back at least to the blues singer Huddie Ledbetter and the black intellectual and activist Marcus Garvey. It was taken up by the Beats and made popular again through the success of Erykah Badu's 2008 hit, "Master Teacher." It was around before Black Lives Matter made it a cornerstone of their politics in 2013, and the right immediately turned it into a term of derision.

Finally, albeit later, the Covid-19 pandemic (2019) and the subsequent lockdowns and protests presented a unique historical and existential challenge unlike anything people in the U.S. had experienced before. It demanded that people re-arrange their lives—their work, family, and play. It changed the ways people experienced public spaces and, for that matter, private lives. It demonstrated the government's complete inability to respond in anything even approaching adequate ways. It was, for many, the nail in the coffin of both liberal governance and its existing opposition. Yet neither the left nor the right had found the stories that would mobilize a new politics. Neither was able to draw people into their stories of an organic crisis with enough passion. Neither was able to win people over with their stories of a possible settlement.

## Affective Polarization[1]

These events, as well as others both earlier and later, reshaped the affective landscape of the third moment. They have foregrounded polarization stories. They have made them into affective stories of absolute certainty and absolute difference. The difference is no longer defined by some essential feature or content, but by the frontier itself. Each side exists and functions as a collapsed symbol of the polarization story itself. The identity of each camp is only defined by the existence of the frontier.

The news is everywhere, beating us over the head, and it keeps gaining strength: The United States is radically polarized. Stories of polarization tell us, over and over, that the nation is radically divided. They have permeated every aspect of life (or so it seems), driving the nation, if not families, apart. These stories, when they are not simply based in assumed identities, offer statistical averages, mostly measured by elections or opinion polls on particular issues that are mistakenly generalized. Almost everything that happens in this moment is captured by stories of polarization.

I am not saying that polarization stories are not true or that polarization is not real. It is constructed and it is real, because it has real effects. It does feel like the nation is so sharply polarized that it is beyond repair, and that the line separating the two camps is almost always predictable and impenetrable. And it feels like this rigid boundary through the heart of the nation is becoming ever more powerful as it spreads across our lives. Yes, we are polarized. We can see it, we experience it, we feel it. Perhaps its most frightening effect is that we are increasingly defined by our political identity, which seems to trump all other ways of defining who we are. But it is not the only way of understanding what's happening, and who we are, and it did not have to become the dominant, commonsensical story. It is the story we keep repeating to ourselves, the story that we keep hearing from the media, politicos, and friends. It is the story that most of us have come to inhabit.

But the story's apparently accurate representation of our world is the result of its own agency: It constructs the world in its own image. It is the story interpreting the data, making sense of our experiences for us, and organizing the field of political culture by reorganizing the affective landscape. It is an endless loop of "confirmation bias." The story does most of the heavy lifting, positioning people on the affective landscape so that they see the world through its lens. Unfortunately, it is very difficult to escape the stories of polarization. But it is not, in the first instance, a matter of escape or even of truth. There are questions about how it has been made to seem true, natural, and even apolitical to anyone who looks. There are questions about how it works and what it does. There are questions about how it is heard, taken up, lived, and used.

Polarization stories make it impossible to understand the other camp. They render the space of the center, the messy space in-between, unhabitable, a no-person's land where you can only feel detached from the vital struggles of our age. The middle-ground—I do not mean compromise—of complication and disagreement disappears. It is the ground that the great scifi author Robert Heinlein once described thus: "I never learned anything from a man who agreed with me." It is a space of flexibility and limits. I will reach out this far but no further, but I will reach out, beyond my own comfort zone. It is where complications and contradictions flourish and proliferate, and where new relations, new configurations, and new possibilities emerge.

Stories of polarization permit each side to blame the other for everything under the sun. The right blames all the crises facing the nation on the intentional, indoctrinating efforts of cosmopolitan and multi-cultural elites. These elites, and those supposedly oppressed minorities they support, have assumed the power to create an interventionist state in the past century by fostering both relativism and a conspiracy of ideologies posing as Truth. The left blames the right (often alongside capitalists) for being fear-mongering liars spreading misinformation and conspiracies, which succeed only because of the gullibility and stupidity (sometimes measured in terms of education) of its supporters. For either side, the other camp opposes the founding values of the country and represents absolute evil, that is, they are locatable on the contemporary affective landscape of fanaticism. Each camp presumes that only its feelings matter, which further legitimates their transformation of opinion into the certainties of moral judgment. Polarization has become not only a description but an explanation and a self-fulfilling prophesy, a conspiracy theory in its own right.

Each camp usually accuses the other side of conspiracies. Stories that portray the other side as being lost in conspiracies are perhaps the simplest way to dismiss it. Both sides have their own conspiracy theories. The right believes in stolen elections and liberal child-sex networks. The left is constantly talking about cabals, capitalists, white supremacists, and The System. Admittedly, some of the right's conspiracies (pedophilia in fast food restaurants) seem weird and obviously fabricated, especially in their details. But those on the left have become increasingly intense, especially in their abstractness: It's all in the necessary conspiratorial evil attributable to anyone who would oppose obviously beneficent values—social justice, democracy, equality, etc. versus racism, sexism, homophobia, etc. The stories on either side are built upon an impossible conjoining of a vision of reality as constructed (which necessarily ends in relativism) and an absolute assertion of truth, resulting in what I would call an affective authoritarianism.

What makes a story a conspiracy? What makes some stories acceptable and others dismissible as conspiracies? Why do people take them up, and what does it mean to live inside one (or more)? Do those who believe in a conspiracy story think it is crazy or paranoid? Conspiracies are real, and there might be some truth in the paranoia of conspiracy theories, but a conspiracy rarely gains total victory because there are so many—often competing—conspiracies. A conspiracy theory has all the answers in advance, assuming they are always obvious (and they are to anyone living in the story). A conspiracy story is the ultimate form of paranoia. It is infinitely expandable, potentially taking over every aspect of people's lives (and, hence, often linked to "cults"). It is, consequently, the perfect genre for stories of polarization!

What sort of work do such affective polarization stories accomplish in the third conjunctural moment? How do they work? There are at least two key effects that are important to understand. The first is surprisingly simple and visible for all to see if you can step outside the stories for a minute. Polarization stories link things to create a sense of affective unity within a camp. While many different issues, values, enemies, and struggles may be entangled at some level, they are not necessarily related. There is no guarantee that a person who holds a position on issue A will hold some supposedly corresponding position on issue B; that correspondence has to be made. For example, there is no reason why people who oppose abortion will necessarily oppose gun control. Yet there does seem to be some truth to it, and that truth has to be made. That is the first job of polarization stories.

Their second job usually requires the media. As I have said, the terms "left" and "right" can easily become too vague, broad, dispersed, and varied to be of much use. Yet stories of polarization demand that a clear binary opposition is constructed. In any political struggle, there are always people and groups who seem more committed and active, affectively invested in the struggle, more than most participants. They are usually strongly anti-establishment and often represent themselves as revolutionary (without necessarily implying violence). They occupy what statisticians refer to as the long tail of the curve of political positions. They are almost always marginalized, ignored, trivialized, denigrated, or excoriated by the mainstream media, dismissed as too extreme, too dangerous, too irrelevant, too self-indulgent, or, sometimes, too much fun (to be taken seriously).

The increasing power of polarization stories has made the long tails into the darlings of the media. They become the new metonyms of the left and right. The stories of polarization work by identifying such opposing groups and making them into the images or symbols of the polarized space of politics. As a result, they dominate the public, popular sense of the political and cultural battleground.[2]

Today, the media generally refers to these, for example, as the reactionary or MAGA right and the woke or social justice left. For this metonymizing to work, two things have to happen: First, the long tails have to be privileged in the media, so that they come to define not only the leading edges or vanguards, but the most visible and vocal representatives of their camps; and second, their tactics and rhetorics have to be presented in ways that emphasize their extremism, even to the point of exaggeration and parody. This enables the media to present their extremism as irrational but understandable or justified but misguided. And it allows the media to condemn them outright when it has to.

The media (as well as political campaigns) often use a specific synecdochic practice in which a particular example—usually of hypocrisy, failure, lying, or corruption—stands in for a much larger class of related but less obvious instances. An example is taken out of its context or separated from other examples that might muddy the story. And then it is exaggerated, (hyper-) inflated, as if nothing else exists or has existed except this one single act. That one act now defines the other entirety of the other side as liars or incompetent. It can be extended: Take the most extreme version of a position (and whatever tactics accompany it) and let it stand for everyone who might agree with some version of the position. Such thinking is, it should be obvious, like free candy to the media. Cost-free, it sells. It is pure clickbait.

The right's stories suggest that the "woke" left has captured the entire left, not only the progressive left but the liberals and the Democratic Party as well. A few true cases (e.g., of "call-out" and "cancel" cultures) justify the claim that they all use such tactics of fear and intimidation, indoctrination, and authoritarianism. The left's stories similarly take the most extreme cases—e.g., of violent racism, electoral cheating, or corruption—to describe the entirety of the right. The more the long tail becomes the face of their respective sides, the more their affective articulations and tactics bleed into and saturate the larger struggles that they are positioned to both lead and represent.

Now there are only two sides—left and right, defined only by the affective frontier dividing them, battling it out for the heart and soul of America. The newfound obviousness and affective absoluteness of polarization stories have made them a powerful force in political culture. Many people who do not necessarily support such "fundamentalisms" nevertheless find themselves caught up in the stories of polarization, mesmerized and, yes, perhaps intimidated or even somewhat paralyzed by their public power.

Polarization stories have transformed the political culture. They have pulled people into their efforts to reconstruct the affective landscape and, at the same time, opened up the possibilities for affective stories about the second organic crisis of modernity.

### Polarization and Identity Stories

Most societies, and perhaps even smaller social groups within them, have (or strive for) a sense of unity or belonging together, which can be self-consciously named. For example, some tribal societies simply referred to themselves as the people, or even the human being. Some identified with a place (the Israelites) or an ancestry (the children of Abraham) or a special relation to the sacred ("the chosen people"). Such names refer to the communities with which people identify. They identify with other people because they tell the same stories, regularly engage in similar behaviors ("rituals") and habits, and share common experiences. Sometimes, belonging involves shared forms of suffering. In some cases, that suffering remains within the collective, an occasion for ritual commiseration and charity; for example, Jews have long suffered from anti-Semitism, but they did not politicize it until after the Holocaust. After the holocaust, being a Jew becomes an identity. In other cases, under specific conditions, that suffering becomes the condition of possibility for a political struggle, and the community name may become, or be made into, an identity. Belonging is made to matter in a different way. Such communities construct their own lineages and traditions, their own styles and values, and their own stories and languages. Their commonality is entirely cultural. And I would argue that it is not a matter of identity. Although, under certain circumstances, it may become, or be made into, an identity.

It is easy to look at such communities of belonging and assume that they are identities, as if the category of identity has always existed and always in the same way. Its reality is obvious in the very fact of naming. But when we talk about identity politics, is that all identity is? Moreover, once you assume identity is real, it is easy to assume that particular identities (e.g., gender and race) are real and have always existed in the same way. Whatever variations may appear don't matter very much.

I have already suggested that identity, and its categories, are constructed. Different stories produce different realities and experiences of identity itself, as well as of different identities. Identity in some form has likely appeared in many societies at various times. There may be family resemblances among different configurations and articulations of identity and identities. That doesn't mean it was the same thing, or that it functioned in the same ways.

Identity plays a crucial role in the contemporary conjuncture, across all three moments. They are central to the ways people understand themselves and others. They impact almost every aspect of how people live their lives. But we cannot take the conjunctural reality of identity for granted. Its specificity has had unique and powerful effects, defining the key question of contemporary modernity: Who am I?[3] Without understanding this, we are likely to fail to grasp the possibilities and limits of struggle and change. And failing to acknowledge them can easily result in dead-ends.

The conjunctural construction of identity exists at the tense intersection of two stories. Any identity formation, any conjunctural construction of identity and identities, will define how identity exists and functions and what identities can be seen, can matter, and can be legitimately recognized. It brings the two stories together, giving each its own affective importance and operational logic.

First, identity might be something people possess, whether they know it or not, whether individually or collectively. It is constituted by some property that is the necessary and sufficient—i.e., essential—definition of who I am. That property might be determined by genetics, ancestry, appearance, or, most recently, experience. Hence, my identity is fixed, once and for all time; it cannot be denied or taken from me. It is unproblematic. Yet assumptions about the nature of essential identities have varied widely, often becoming a seriously contentious issue.

Second, identity might be defined relationally, usually described as a system of differences. Certain differences and not others are made to matter for a variety of reasons. Who I am is defined by my place in a network of relations with others. This is true, but generally uninteresting for our purposes at the level of the family but also at the level of social relations, where people are distributed into categories that can only be understood in the contexts of their relations with, their differences from, the others. Here, identity and identities are more likely to become a problem. For example, we might think of LGBTQIA+ as an attempt to change the field of differences and expand the network of social relations. There is a long history of contexts in which communities have been reconstructed as identities within relations of negative differences.

Neither of these stories is, by itself, entirely unique to the current conjuncture. But the current conjuncture changed the nature of the field of difference. It makes all relations into particular and simple binary differences: X/Y. Compare contemporary differences (e.g., black/white, Jew/Christian, immigrant/American, even civilizational wars) that contrast two parts, as it were. And it defines those relations in the negative. We are not them; they are not us. (I am not suggesting that there were not earlier instances of such configurations.) Contrast that, for example, with anti-Semitism as a case of everyone (all sorts of differences that don't matter) against the Jews. It is less a binary division than a synecdochic one: The whole against the part. I think perhaps AIDS was used to construct gay populations in a similar way. Hence, it is not surprising that metaphors of diseases are commonly used.

But that is insufficient. Identity in the current conjuncture is also constructed by collapsing the two stories, equating identity as possession and as difference. The essential property is located within binary relations of negation. The answer to the question, who am I, is answered with a contradiction: I am who I am because I possess something that makes me who I am and, yet, I am who I am because I am not the other.

The result is that the very notions of belonging and identification, of difference and identity, have become contested. Their meaning and reference, their relations, and their political valences have been destabilized and re-asserted in various ways. Their realities seem to dissolve into one another. How is the affectivity of belonging articulated to the constitution of identities? Do identities exist outside stories, whether determined by, for example, genetics, or ancestry (apparently, you can now have ancestry and genetic tests for your pet—as one ad put it, you can "finally know who [your] dog is, enabling her to be the best dog she can be"), or appearance? Do identities pre-exist differences? Does an identity belong to the individual as a pre-determined, guaranteed characteristic, something the individual possesses? (In that case, class was not an identity since it was not a feature or quality of an individual, at least not until quite recently.) But since the individual has many features that, taken together, make up who or what they are, which are necessary and sufficient for—i.e., essential to—the definition of identity? Or does identity involve a feature essential to the group rather than the individual, perhaps bound up with its collective subordination and suffering and expressed in a naturalized culture, or an inescapable past? But would this mean that identity cannot exist outside of difference? Isn't identity always more complicated than a system of binary differences would suggest?

There is still more to the conjunctural story of identity, perhaps the most important part. Many societies have used identities and differences as markers of fundamental inequalities and used them as mechanisms and justification for the unequal distribution of power and resources. They have often led to irrational forms of hatred, hostility, violence, war, and even genocide. At the very least, they produce particular identities and differences as a matter of power and politics, and a site of struggle in political culture.

The United States has a long, uninterrupted history of constructing differences in ways that enable a wide variety of forms of hatred and oppression. We can take as an example racism, since no system of differences articulated to power has been more visible than those organized around race (and its slippery relations to ethnicity, which has often been subsumed into race) and racisms—from segregation and ghetto-ization to lynching and extermination. The forms and practices of differentiation and othering change over time and space and, at any moment, they will be organized and distributed in particular ways. We might say that both racism and anti-racism are constitutive of U.S. history.

In the U.S., at different times, race has been and continues to be defined in biological, epidermal, ethnic, and cultural terms; moreover, U.S. racism has never been limited to "black" populations, but has been extended to other groups; at different times, different populations, usually first encountered as immigrants—(with the exception of Indigenous peoples and the descendants of African slaves) including Jewish, Irish, Southern and Eastern European, Asian, African, and various white and brown people from Latin America, the Caribbean, the Middle East, and South Asia—have been represented as black, and have been on the receiving end of racism. Unfortunately, the hatred of these groups rarely disappears completely; sometimes it is submerged, only to reappear when circumstances allow (e.g., the current revival of anti-Semitism). In other words, there are many forms and practices of racism, resulting in many constructions of race.

Part of the uniqueness of the current conjuncture is the undeniable centrality of the politics of identity. And its importance has only grown as it has moved through the three moments, arriving as perhaps the central and defining struggle of American politics (alongside but included within the struggles against MAGA and the oligarchs in 2025). At various conjunctural moments, identities and the politics surrounding them have taken on specific shapes, powers, and functions. The first conjunctural moment, emblematized in the civil rights movement and liberal feminism, offered a pluralist politics of tolerance and compromise.

In the second moment, the politics of identity was a matter of distribution. Various identity groups had to fight for the right to be included among the oppressed: Feminists against the claims of the working class; black feminists against the claims of white women; homosexuals against, well, pretty much everyone, etc. As it became less of a fight and more of a voluntary embrace, identity politics expanded to encompass gender and sexuality, mental and physical disability, race and ethnicity, and nationality, and the list keeps growing. Each specific identity category can proliferate, for example, LGBTQIA+ (lesbian, gay, bisexual, transgender, queer (or questioning), intersex, asexual, and others, including pansexual and Two-Spirit). The plus leaves the identity open, a safety value for later adjustments. Obviously, such a proliferation is in many ways a good thing. Yet the result is that there is always some group that may be missing—and the arguments by absence ("You didn't talk about …"), never a good thing, never end. What about kids? My research documented a change in America from a country that overvalued its kids (in the 1950s and 1960s) to one that seriously mistreated them, often viewing them as dangerous criminals, incompetent or incomplete humans, and even threats to national security, by the 1990s. These days, some people seem to think that animals are an oppressed group, sometimes implicitly suggesting that we should treat our pets better than we do our children. (Or have I just done what I have just accused the media of doing, offering a metonym?)

What has happened to identity politics in the third moment of the conjuncture? It has been almost completely captured by stories of polarization. Stories of identity and polarization call up and call upon one another, reinforcing and multiplying their affective strengths. Polarization can be subsumed under the category of identity, and identity can be expanded to fill the spaces of polarization. Identity stories have returned, in rather surprising ways, to the simplest binary logic of negation (while trying to hold onto the additive series of recognized identities). All sense of complexity and nuance disappears from both sides. All binary differences are collapsed into a single opposition between the oppressor and the oppressed, the powerful and the powerless, the privileged and the suffering.

Identity is no longer defined by the possession of some shared, essential property, but by one's place in and experience of larger historical forces that possess the individual and locate him or her as part of a group: Most commonly, the experience of being oppressed as a result of, for example, coloniality, racial capitalism, etc. This now constitutes the ground on which politics becomes the cornerstone of identity even as identity becomes the ground on which political virtue is established. Privilege is directly correlated with power; either you have it or you do not. Oppression is equated with subordination, suffering, and the complete lack of privilege. And the difference is absolutized. In the end, there can be only two, created by assuming a natural distribution between the privileged (e.g., white) and the oppressed (e.g., people of color).[4]

But there are serious dangers here. Consider the ways terms like "white," "privilege," and "people of color" are used in these stories. Which identities are included as people of color? Is every ethnicity, race, or sexuality eligible? Why latino/as (often white) but not Jews (Semites, the oldest and longest oppression)? Who gets to decide? What role does a history of oppression play? Who judges what is oppression? Can some group be both oppressor and oppressed? Does such a concept of identity assume that all suffering is equivalent? How do you measure or commensurate the suffering or the privilege attached to different identities? Who suffers more and whose suffering is more immediate? Which is worse: Enslavement, genocide, or a million small cuts? And finally, this conjunctural articulation of identity and polarization cannot prevent its own logic from being reversed: Each side feels that it is the oppressed (maybe there is yet another oppressed sitting in the corporate HQ). The oppressor becomes the oppressed. A war carried out in the name of freedom or liberty, individualism or democracy, American greatness or justice, and equality easily slides into a war for revenge that simply reverses positions of power. It seems that many people want to story these virtues without actually practicing them. Cynically, I think the right is continuing to play out its strategic plan; the left, not so much. Can rights be claimed by any group that claims an identity? Do they have to be recognized and/or granted by every other group? Are they natural or legal? Are they the prize to be won in victorious struggle or electoral victory? It will take courage to find our way out of these stories and ways of constructing the reality of identity and identities.

## Conclusion

The unique presence and power of polarization stories in the third conjunctural moment arise partly out of the failure to establish and resolve the first organic crisis of modernity. While that crisis—the need to find better ways of being modern—continues, a new organic crisis began to take shape, calling for an end to modernity, whether through negating and overturning it, or escaping it. This second crisis challenges the modern itself; it questions the desire and need to be modern. It seeks something that is not modern. It seeks logics and ways of thinking other than those that have defined the many faces of modernity.

It is an organic crisis that imagines itself to be a shift in what I might figuratively call the tectonic plates of a longer epoch that can only be measured with the conjunctural tools available to us. It is a crisis that makes it feel like the terms of political power and struggle, affective sociality and hope, and epistemic consensus and dissensus are changing. It also feels like the field of political possibilities and imagination has both expanded and contracted in frightening ways. This second crisis seeks to overturn the old order—and all its ways of doing things, its values, principles, and logics, just as modernity overthrew the Ancién Regime. Its actions may appear incomprehensible or dangerous (and they may well be) when judged from the still remaining remnants of the modern order, but they claim to exist in their own reality. Some modern principles will be thrown out (e.g., democracy and equality, forgiveness and measured response), while others are so radically turned on their heads that they seem ludicrous (e.g., competence or freedom).

As I have said, the struggles over this second organic crisis have given rise to and been shaped by two affective tendencies, each with its own history. These tendencies, while not having captured everything and everyone in the political field, have become increasingly dominant. And for the moment, they appear unstoppable. They are reshaping the affective landscape and the possibilities of a new balance in the field of forces. And they exist seamlessly alongside stories of polarization.

Both tendencies embrace the quasi-autonomy of the affective landscape as the ground of political culture. They seem intent on pushing it even further. They attach themselves to and rework specific structures of feeling, both qualitatively and quantitively. They seek to redraw the landscape as well as the ways people navigate it. And, I must say, they have political struggle on a road to nowhere, feeling that there is no way out and no creative middle left to occupy. Living inside either tendency often means having to constantly and immediately make your commitment and loyalty visible and hearable. People can viscerally feel the pressure to publicly perform their claim to be included in a political identity.

I ask you to recall that these tendencies carry only a formal politics. Although they can be linked to particular groups and movements—and I will certainly do so at times—I am not interested in the groups themselves (which are often full of contradictions) but in the tendencies expressed in their practices and discourses.

The speculative tendency (ST) escapes the modern by negating or rejecting what it assumes to be its essential element. Having escaped the modern, it seeks only the formal possibility of alternatives to modernity, the possibility of radically other habitable landscapes or lived realities. Its affect is affirmative. It constructs an absolute, moralizing frontier between the modern and the non-modern. It is often highly abstract and largely creative. It tends to be intellectual and, unfortunately, often, academic. (Forgive me if I start drifting in that direction.)

I have already referred to the pseudo-revolutionary tendency, several times. (Again, I hope you will have forgiven me.) I do not intend PRT as an insult (although I understand its connotations). But can you, in fact, think of a revolution (especially within modern times) that has worked; that has not had to go through hellish violence and, even then, did not still end up far from the imagined revolutionary vision (even if it sometimes ends somewhere better than where it began)? No? Abbie Hoffman once wrote a book called *Revolution for the hell of it*. What he did not realize is that revolution is often the hell of it. Why do we have to constantly reimagine repeating the same problematic cycle over and over? Why do we like the idea of revolution so much, but not enough to actually subject it to critique and criticism?

The PRT constructs a totalizing, moralizing war against everything modern. Refusing compromise, it embraces the Black Panthers' slogan: If you are not part of the solution (as it defines it), you are part of the problem. It rarely promulgates a positive program for what the future would look like. It does not offer much sense of how we get from here to there, or even where there is. Its affect is largely negative. The PRT is almost entirely defined by its antagonism to modernity, which becomes the home of infidels and the antichrist. It has to be destroyed.

I know that my description of the PRT will land me in trouble with the left (but they will gladly accept it as a description of the right). I will be accused of offering caricatures, or at least of doing what I accuse the media of doing in stories of polarization: Letting the long tail of the curve serve as the metonym for a larger movement. To whatever extent I have done that, I apologize. This is certainly not my intention; rather, I am trying to build my story by researching the stories we have been telling ourselves in the political culture. And I think I have good evidence that the PRT plays a major role in the third conjunctural moment. People will claim that its power has diminished in the face of Trump's scorched earth politics. There is some truth in that, but I continue to see the effects of the PRT in the stories shaping the political culture.

Let me emphasize that I do not equate the content of these tendencies as they are being enacted by the right and the left in this third conjunctural moment. They could not be more different. But in the story I am telling, I am interested only in formal affective parallels that may result from different political positions operating as expressions of the same tendency. It is only one way of describing—one part of a richer story of—what's going on, of making visible the conditions that both enable and constrain the possibilities of a viable, alternative conjunctural politics.

## Notes

1   This discussion draws on Nicholas Gerstner's dissertation, "Divided We Stand? Stories of Polarization." Chapel Hill, 2025.  Gerstner identifies four logics of polarization: direction (the North Star); bending (light); continuum  of intensity (polling); and opposition.
2   There may be some extreme groups that violate whatever limits the media has set on itself and that it hesitates to cover for various reasons, for example, violent militia of the right.
3   My friend, the Australian intellectual Meaghan Morris, once told me that identity is America's most successful export.
4   There is a reflexivity of privilege: The privilege you take in calling out privilege can prefigure how you see the conjuncture.

# 12

## WE BEG WARMTH FROM THE SUN

The Speculative Tendency

The speculative tendency (ST) plays a crucial role in the third conjunctural moment, although it is less visible than the increasingly dominant pseudo-revolutionary tendency (PRT). It starts with an absolute and generalized condemnation of modernity; even more, it may even express a determination to overthrow it. And out of the ashes of modernity, it configures the outlines of a possible future. In other words, the ST is the affective re-articulation of utopian thinking in the face of the second organic crisis of modernity. Utopian thought generally describes its utopia in concrete terms. But its relation to the present, i.e., the nature of the change that leads to utopia, is abstract and speculative, simply attributed to either a great expanse of space/time or a catastrophic event.

The ST renders both relations abstract. Both the utopia's relation to the present and the utopia itself are defined in abstract or highly general terms. The ST negates a specific abstract idea or logic essential to the modern. The utopia is then defined by its radical difference. It remains largely abstract and conceptual, although the right's expressions of ST are generally more detailed. ST seeks its utopia as the non-(a-, pre-, post-)modern. A future only becomes possible when the present and its history have been negated and erased (or somehow overcome and transcended). What is left is the possibility of a world that is anything but a modern world.

The ST emerged in a slightly different form in the first conjunctural moment, in the various spiritualisms, nativisms, communalisms, and non-western religions that were part of the 1960s Movement. What was unique, at least at that moment, was the performative nature of these commitments; that is, they were lived and made publicly visible in practices, rituals, appearances, and lifestyles. The ST receded from public view in the second moment, but

DOI: 10.4324/9781003662587-15

continued to flourish in, for example, the back to nature movement, the "social and consciousness movement," intentional communities, and more institutionalized forms of meditation. The ST also played an important role in some environmental movements.

The ST is generally thought to lean toward the left, although many operating under its influence find such political identifications too doctrinaire. Actually, it can be and has been inflected to a variety of political positions. In fact, how its politics are shaped is a matter of some urgency. For example, movements in popular culture have evinced a growing nostalgia for simpler, more pastoral, less mechanized, communal ways of living, which has been taken up by right-wing stories that celebrate rural life against the urban and cosmopolitan life. While numerous left stories during the second moment seemed to be trying to capture such a longing, such articulations seem to have been displaced in the third moment.

I will identify three forms of the ST in the third conjunctural moment; there are certainly more (and they are not so easily separable). They all have a home in the academy, but they have all resonated with some political movements. They all start by identifying the essence or foundational moment of modernity, which, when negated, will be the crack that brings modernity down. The first two understand the modern as a philosophical project defined by the European Enlightenment. Each sets out to tear it down, brick by brick. The third understands the modern as a political project, these days, most commonly, coloniality. The project has contaminated the entirety of western modernity and has to be overthrown or somehow undone.

## The Enlightenment versus the Pluriverse

Thinkers have been challenging European Enlightenment thought since, well, the Enlightenment. But the Enlightenment was no less complicated than the modern. Like the modern, there were actually many enlightenments, each a composition, a unity-in-difference. "The Enlightenment" was a construction, an abstraction from a more fluid, contradictory, and heterogeneous set of enlightenments. Each instance was shaped by its own geographies, cultures, and social conditions; each responded to the changes it confronted with whatever intellectual resources it could muster. To make matters Worse, the concept of the Enlightenment assumed that many distinct and sometimes contingent challenges (e.g., reason, humanism, subjectivity, individualism, agency) were equivalent or, at least, stitched together into a seamless, harmonious whole.

The first expression of the ST challenges the Enlightenment's monological view of the world: There is only one reality, one truth. Everything else is hallucination and superstition. ST asserts that other worlds are possible, even that they may already exist.[1] For a while, it found a home in the

World Social Forum. Let me repeat a story told to me by the anthropologist Mario Blaser: A whale swims into an inlet around which an indigenous tribe has made its home for centuries. The tribe is being slowly decimated by encroaching development. They know the whale is the tribe's founder returning to lead their fight to survive. They will perish without the founder's strength. Greenpeace comes to rescue the whale. They know it will die if it is not returned to its pod. Being the inheritors of the Enlightenment, it's easy to dismiss the tribe's claim as mere faith. But what if it's not? What if Greenpeace's supposed knowledge is? Which side are you on? Do other worlds exist? Might they be outside the physical laws of modern worlds? Are there worlds inhabited by other forms of animate beings, even ones in which inanimate beings are sentient? Even worlds in which inanimate beings communicate with the people inhabiting their world?

The notion that "other worlds are possible," commonly described as "the pluriverse," has a powerful affective appeal. It is more than the appeal of utopias. It speaks directly out of our sense of the crisis of modernity. But just because it tries to speak to the heart of the contemporary crisis, it raises important questions about the stories we might tell in our efforts to repair the world. Let's assume the pluriverse is not just a metaphysical (ontological) prayer but a claim about the possibilities of other habitable landscapes. Is it anything more than the dictum that we should not continue doing what we have been doing for centuries? The most common response is to live in harmony with the universe. Do we know what that means? Where do we look for an answer? And just to play the devil's advocate, why are we supposed to live in harmony with the universe? Perhaps we are the agents of entropy, bringing chaos and disharmony into an ordered universe. Perhaps we are the agents of order, bringing structure into a chaotic universe. Or maybe, like the Jedi, humanity is meant to bring balance into the universe. Does anyone know?

Does every possible world have a right to exist? Certainly, there are some we should not tolerate. We end up back in liberalism: Tolerate every reality unless it threatens others or denies others the right to exist. Tolerate tolerance and don't tolerate intolerance. Or perhaps, tolerate every reality that lives in harmony; but isn't that a new kind of moral puritanism, just one that we find acceptable? Is there only one way to live in harmony?

Finally, there is something paradoxical about the pluriverse (if not the ST itself). How do we set about changing worlds, or our way of being in the world? What is humanity's role in making? discovering? uncovering? opening? another world? After all, we got ourselves into this mess, in part by thinking that we are the masters of the universe; that we make reality. If we assume that we are responsible for escaping modernity and finding other worlds, aren't we still imagining ourselves to be in control? So we haven't really escaped the Enlightenment because we still have to grab the reins of change—again. This is a very modern dilemma indeed.

The pluriverse makes a surprising formal appearance in a particularly resonant re-articulation of a reactionary theory known as "traditionalism." It is most visible in the work of the influential contemporary Russian political philosopher Aleksandr Dugin, a Heidegger scholar and advisor to Putin.[2] Traditionalism generally attacks democracy and liberalism (hence it is often described as illiberalism). It advocates for autocratic and authoritarian, if not totalitarian, governance. Dugin links it to a radically re-conceived sense of nationalism. He offers a "fourth political theory" against the continuing influence of western Enlightenment. Since the end of the Second World War, the world has been organized around a specific figure (*nomos*) or law, namely, a three-world model (capitalist democratic, communist, and non-aligned or developing).

Dugin argues that their differences have been understood within the terms of the Enlightenment itself. But this way of organizing the differences is no longer useful and has, in fact, collapsed. He condemns the remnants of the declining western control. Its Enlightenment/liberal values have become nothing but nihilism, hypocrisy (because its so-called democracy is actually the rule of minorities), and the ultimate form of "titanism," which he defines as "the revolt of the earth against heaven." Finally, putting the nail in the coffin, the west does not understand the essence of difference. It assumes the terms are comparable and, hence, it can understand them as negating each other. It assumes the terms exist in the same reality, refusing to acknowledge the possibility of true otherness. The other is not the same but different. It is different because it is other.

He calls for a new multipolar nomos—akin to a pluriverse and opposed to western notions of universalism, akin to the earlier rejection of monologism. This new nomos involves at least three empires, each defining its own reality, its own values, and its own systems of truth and power. None can be judged according to the logics and principles of the others. Not coincidentally, one emergent empire will be a neo-Eurasian religious nationalism with Russia at its center.[3]

## The Enlightenment versus Ontology

A second, anti-Enlightenment version of ST locates the essence of the Enlightenment in the assumption that human thought is incapable of grasping the truth of reality or existence.[4] The clearest expression of this version of ST is the highly academic and difficult "new ontology" of the French thinkers Gilles Deleuze and Félix Guattari.[5] Deleuze himself offers a highly speculative set of universal claims about the essential truth of the universe. Bear with me, please. Reality is not a collection of fixed, isolated objects, but dynamic processes of change that involve the making and remaking of relations. So far, his theory is just another version of constructionism. These processes are not so much processes as events or "becomings." They are defined only by their energies or intensities. They are pure potential, capacities to produce particular relations and effects. If we think in terms of bodies, a body is only what a body can do. That is, the truth of a body is nothing but its capacities to affect and be affected. Consequently, everything that exists, exists in the same way: As potentiality or capacity. Reality is only the multiplicity of such events. But unlike other constructionisms, you cannot distinguish among events or relations, or between causality and agency.

There are a number of ways this ontology has been articulated to the realm of power. The first largely abandons the task of diagnosing the present in its conjunctural specificity. All power is the imposition of structure on the infinity of becomings as potentiality. Hence, power is always the negation of reality itself. Modern power privileges some hierarchically or centrally located figure of authority as the locus of power against the dispersed power of the multiple. Any organization of reality and life is the enemy of the vitality of the universe and, hence, of life. Modern power is evil in and of itself. Power as structure itself has to be continuously negated, disallowed, and "deterritorialized." Even those structures that reside within us—the fascist within ourselves—must be destroyed. If all structure is fascist, then the only acceptable form of political opposition will be processual, fragmented, horizontal, and radically democratic (in which everything is equal). This ends up as an extreme anti-politics.

Even as a recomposed utopianism, what would it mean to imagine a social existence in which there is no organization, no structure, and, in fact, no power? Would such a world be anything other than chaos, madness, and death? Would many people choose to die for fluidity or multiplicity, although many have been killed for enacting them?

A second, slightly less absolute ontological politics harkens back to Max Weber's description of modernity as the disenchantment of the world. It suggests that there is a politics embedded in the very poetics of re-enchanting the world. There is a politics in returning our sense of uncertainty—and magic, if you will, or whatever it is that makes the world "shimmer" in ways we cannot explain. The sense of fluidity and multiplicity is not meant to define a specific conjunctural politics, but to shift our perceptions of the world, to open us to the potentialities that surround us, to motivate us to re-imagine our places in the world, and to change, however slowly, our way of being in the world.

Finally, some intellectuals and activists have attempted to connect the ontological and the conjunctural as related levels of abstraction. Ontological concepts are put in the service of conjunctural analysis. In the collaborative work of Deleuze and Guattari, for example, they use ontological concepts (and invent others) not so much to diagnose the conjuncture, but to tell a story about how the conjuncture was produced out of the universe of potentialities. And the story ends up offering a better understanding of the conjuncture than where it started. How did this particular form or particular institution of power come to be real, and how was it made (without crediting or blaming only humans)? It is, in a sense, the question of critique recomposed.

The space between the highly abstract level of speculative ontology and the less abstract level of the conjuncture is precisely the space that the ST leaves empty. It takes a lot of work to move through that space and to construct the necessary conceptual relations. Ontological concepts by themselves cannot describe conjunctural specificities, nor can they be morphed into political practices with intrinsic political value. Unfortunately, lazy thinkers let ontological concepts magically leap across the distances between levels, pretending that ontology can explain everyday realities.

The anti-politics of this new ontology is mirrored by an anti-Enlightenment theory on the right, sometimes called "the Dark Enlightenment" or Neoreactionism (NRx). Often presented in an ironic and intentionally confrontational style, it was initially proposed by the postmodern theorist Nick Land and the software engineer Curtis Yavin, under the pseudonym Mencius Moldbug.[6] It describes itself as neither left nor right, because neither is able or willing to fully renounce and escape the Enlightenment. Yet it is most often seen as aligned with certain reactionary developments. It defines the Enlightenment using three fundamental matters of faith: First, it believes that change is inherently good and progressive. Therefore, politics (primarily on the left) always seeks the power to destroy the old order and construct a new one. In the end, the new order is always built on its own self-interest. Second, it believes that egalitarianism, from which democracy follows, is good. This belief contaminates the decision-making process and makes the state into the sole bestower of rights. And third, it believes that the first two are universal.

On the other hand, NRx is committed to order, stability and security, and hierarchy and authority. Interestingly, these are defined not in political or social terms (as in previous reactionary conservatisms) but in formalist terms: Freedom and independence over democracy and emancipation, pre-Enlightenment western civilization over equality and difference, tolerance as being left alone over tolerance as the right to be heard. NRx is also anti-populist, viewing "the masses" as an ignorant rabble, a "howling irrational mob."

While it sometimes advocates for a version of white nationalism, NRx refuses white supremacism and the call for a race war. Rather, in the very effort to empower difference, Enlightenment modernity will bring about its own self-destruction. Democracy will destroy the very population it purports to emancipate. The result will be the inevitable "existential civilizational cataclysm," a "comprehensive crisis and disintegration" of the existing order.

Yet NRx does not advocate simply waiting for the inevitable. It embraces a paradoxical temporality, reminiscent of the 1960s countercultures. It combines a faith in the inevitability of change and a sense of responsibility to bring about that change. On the one hand, you simply have to await the arrival of the future and welcome it. Let time unfold since the future was already becoming what it was destined to be. (In the 1960s, this was the Age of Aquarius.) On the other hand, history needs a helping hand, a little push or pull. You have to prepare the way for what is destined to be. It is a politics of the presentness of the future and the futurity of the present. It seeks to bring about what is already given. There is an affective obligation to act as a condition of the inevitability of change. The present becomes the condition of its own inevitable disappearance into and replacement by an unknown and yet (known to be) radically different future.

What follows will be a new communitarianism in which the nation is reconstructed as a political community by a new elite. Its status will be based on their knowledge of the "common good," and their work will be accomplished using technological tools.[7] This communitarianism will not simply recreate political governance. It will oppose the very practice of politics and the existence of the state. Communitarianism entails an anti-political governance committed to a "techno-commercial nationalism." All governance will function as a corporation. In fact, in some versions, there will only be mini-states. A return to feudalism but each will literally be a corporation, whether in the modern or pre-modern sense. They will be connected, but they will also compete. Not surprisingly, NRx rejects both the authoritarianism and the populist insurgency commonly associated with other reactionary politics.

NRx bears some striking similarities with the anti-political techno-utopianism and libertarianism usually associated with Silicon Valley, which is often seen as being rooted in the 1960s countercultures. Increasingly, this position is propounded by ultra-wealthy oligarchs between tech and finance. These oligarchs agree with NRx and reject the social and political values of the Enlightenment, including liberalism, democracy, equality, etc. And both seem to hold onto the values of reason and science. They differ over a fundamental contradiction. While NRx is communitarian, these techno-wealthy are radically individualist. Like NRx, they are confident the world is doomed. For them, however, the only possibility for survival is to exit and establish new places. Images of such imagined future places abound: Dispersed nations connected online, escaping "the tyranny of place," adventure capitalism with its frontiers and grand risks, network states linking digital nomads, post-human spaces (e.g., outer space, the under-spaces, or technological spaces). The exception is those who valorize the sovereign individual. While their positions on social justice vary widely, they generally share a vision of an authoritarian utopia ruled by cognitive elites, who will, by virtue of their intelligence and willingness to take risks, inevitably be wealthy. Both NRx and Silicon Valley might be seen as a distortion of Plato's Republic, where wisdom is replaced by technocratic and economic savvy.

### The Modern versus the Other

The third expression of the ST locates the essence of the modern in its politics, offering what might be called an ontology of the oppressed. Modernity always creates a population that is seen as inferior and lacks the defining capacities of the modern subject. This other is excluded from the valued spaces and privileges of modern relations. And yet, the modern world needs—it even demands—its presence. It needs its difference, its otherness, its infra- or non-humanness, in order to define itself and its boundaries. (Remember that identity is negative.) The other is, simultaneously, excluded and included. This position can be and has been occupied by numerous populations in different times and places (e.g., indigenous or black bodies). At the moment, the most compelling stories start with the colonized subject. They see the essence of the modern in coloniality (and racisms and ethno-hatreds as derivative). The fundamental assumption is that coloniality (leaving open its relation to capitalism) is constitutive of the modern; it defines its essence. There is no modernity without coloniality.[8]

Coloniality is more than the political reality of conquering, subjugating, and exploiting a population, land, and resources, sometimes to the point of destroying them. In these stories, coloniality is a very powerful character. Coloniality simultaneously defines reason and difference and the logic of space and time. These functions saturate every aspect and location of modernity. Everything important about modernity—capitalism, the nation-state, its cultures, its organizations of social differences—is an expression of coloniality.

One current version of this expression of the ST is the "decolonization" project. It begins by dismantling modernity's universalizing and essentializing of hierarchies of difference, which have been inscribed everywhere. We have to deconstruct coloniality by systematically erasing the traces of modernity or, at least, the ways it has established its total domination of the nation and its cultures. If you recall, I suggested that critique (and this is another version) requires some sort of double consciousness, a second position from which to question and challenge the first. In the decolonizing project, this is identified with the history and experience of the colonial subject, in the very extremity and inescapability of its violent subordination.

Who or what exactly is this colonial subject? Does it depend on imagining some pre-modern (indigenous) populations who have not been contaminated by or seduced into the modern? Then we can measure the effects of their colonization or, better, the reconstruction of their reality under coloniality. Or is it a re-animation of memories of a past never completely forgotten and not totally erased? The most promising stories see the colonial subject as more than just the colonized subject. The colonial subject lives on the border at the limits of modernity. Remember that the colonial subject is the excluded included other. The colonized as colonized only exists as the necessary other of the modern/colonial. The colonial subject, existing on the border, is never outside of the modern, nor completely inside. It is always hybrid. At the border, where the colonial subject exists, you cannot separate a prior indigenous subject from a wounded, conquered subject. The border is where difference (otherness, alterity) itself is constructed. And that border, that difference, is itself the result of coloniality. Perhaps this constructed hybridity points to a way beyond coloniality?

As you might expect, I am uncomfortable with the reduction of modernity to the single logic of coloniality. Why is there no modernity without coloniality? Why is there no coloniality that is not modern? I am even more uncomfortable with the abstractness, almost to the point of universalization, of coloniality. If it is always the same across centuries and geographies of modernity, what is it? Is coloniality a singular thing and, if not, do the different manifestations matter? Is it another term for the production of the sufferings of inequalities of negative differences of power? If it is expressed in the entirety of social reality, it must have a kind of ontological existence. Are we seeking another modernity or a non-modern way of being human in the world?

The decolonization project is deeply, affectively rooted in the past. It reaches back into the past (often located elsewhere) to claim a future past and a past future. As an expression of the ST, it is formally parallel to two other political expressions of the ST, which are also built on evocations of the past. After Trump's victory in 2016, the Claremont Institute began reconsidering the significance of the new populism for conservatism, calling its project MAGA.[9] MAGA argued that the American present and foreseeable future, dominated by the liberal-left, were incompatible with human nature. MAGA was confident that liberalism would inevitably undermine itself. It rejected the new right as already compromised. And it imagined itself to be a "re-founding" of a uniquely American conservatism, which rejected all the political norms and pieties of establishment elites. In their place, it offered two distinct and apparently contradictory commitments: First, it was committed to the self-evident truths of the Declaration of Independence and the Constitution. These provided "a universal standard" of equality and justice, and the rights that follow from these. Second, it was committed to the idea that these documents were only offered "on behalf of one people in one place."

MAGA acknowledged that the resulting combination of nationalism and popular sovereignty would require a bit of tyranny—"more control and less freedom." Nationalism demands that politics be defined by what is good for the nation. It is concerned with what preserves the American way of life and its body politic and enables them to flourish. This would only be possible if it were tied to a specific form of populism as the necessary, contemporary form of political sovereignty. This form of popular sovereignty is the true American founding principle. And this would lead the nation to its rightful state of "American greatness," but only by the "virtuous action of the sovereign people." It is not a matter for experts or elites.

Who are the sovereign people? Despite the occasional appeal to a white Christian nation, MAGA's most common answer is affective: It all comes down to a matter of priorities: American first, before and above any other identification. Xenophobia is redefined: Do you want to be an American before all else? If you come to be an American, great. If you come to be an XXX-American, not so great! This appeals to an almost pre-modern sense of national identity. It is not defined by a pre-existing ethnic homogeneity but by an affective unity, constituting a new national populist sovereignty.

More recently, this notion of popular sovereignty has become increasingly militarized. Continuing MAGA's secular discourse, some writers have called for a counter-revolution against the majority of Americans who are not Americans "in any meaningful sense" and are, at best, "citizen-aliens" participating in a "tyranny against democracy." For example, in the New Apostolic Reformation, Christian doctrine has been rewritten to simultaneously democratize prophesy and declare a holy war against non-believers. As frightening as these developments are, there is a certain irony to them: They are not racist. Anyone can find Christ and join the army of the NAR.

I do not think that expressions of the ST are, by themselves, evidence of an emerging fascism. The term is thrown around a lot these days, although it is rarely defined. For some, it refers to a vague sense of an authoritarian state deploying forces of hatred. For others, it reveals detailed parallels between the present and the rise of the fascisms and Nazism our grandparents and great grandparents defeated in the Second World War. Those forces were hardly opposed to the state; in fact, they sought to make the administrative state more efficient through its relations to corporate capitalism and technology. Moreover, while their plans were visible, they relied to a large extent on their invisibility and the unpreparedness of large sectors of the public. And if, like all political struggles, they deployed affective relations, they operated in a very different habitable landscape and a very different international context. If there are elements that warrant the description of fascism today, they demand careful analysis.

If there is a way to ground fascism in the ST, it might be found in a very different version of "Traditionalism" than what I described earlier, for example, in the work of the Italian fascist turned Nazi Julius Evola and the French Islamic metaphysician René Guenon. Their political philosophies were built on highly esoteric understandings of the nature and place of religion in politics. Rejecting the secularism of both Renaissance humanism and the Enlightenment as dangerous lies, Evola, for example, described modernity as a disaster that could not be forestalled, undermined, or even escaped. Everything had to be "blown up" in the cause of a spiritual politics based in (pre- or non-modern) "primordial faiths." So it was, so it will be. Long live the future past.

## Notes

1  It is most eloquently defended by Arturo Escobar, 2020.
2  Dugin, 2021, 2023.
3  While this seems increasingly unlikely given Russia's diminishing power, it may explain its growing hostilities toward Europe, and the odd relation between Putin and Trump. This doctrine may also shed light on what seems to be Trump's attempt to resurrect something like the Monroe Doctrine.
4  This can be traced back to the philosophy of Immanuel Kant.
5  Deleuze and Guattari, 1977, 1987.
6  Land, n.d.; Goldbug, n.d.
7  While their love of technology might seem to contradict their anti-Enlightenment stance, they do not attack Enlightenment concepts of reason and science.
8  There are many versions of decolonization theory, depending in part on the particular regional experience of colonization. One of the most powerful expressions, from Latin America, is by Walter Mignolo. See Mignolo and Walsh, 2018.
9  Here MAGA has to be distinguished from the more general. populist movement. It initially appeared online (https://amgreatness.com) and subsequently in print (*Claremont Review of Books, American Mind*). It was sometimes described as the "west coast Straussians," and led by Harry Jaffa, referring to one of two competing interpretations of the great Spinozist political theorist and scholar of classical and early modern thought, Leo Strauss. (The east coast Straussians, led by Harry Mansfield and Allan Bloom, were aligned with the more cosmopolitan version of the new right, emphasizing the need for moral and political order and the benefits of education modeled on the Great Books. It defined the early years of *American Affairs*.)

## References

Deleuze, Gilles, and Félix Guattari. *Anti-Oedipus*. New York: Viking, 1977.
Deleuze, Gilles, and Félix Guattari. *A Thousand Plateaus*. Minneapolis: University of Minnesota Press, 1987.

Dugin, Alexander (Aleksandr). *The Theory of a Multipolar World*. Budapest: Arktos Media Ltd., 2021.

Dugin, Alexander (Aleksandr). *Talking to the Wolf*. Budapest: Arktos Media Ltd., 2023.

Escobar, Arturo. *Pluriversal Politics: The Real and the Possible*. Durham: Duke University Press, 2020.

Land, Nick. *The Dark Enlightenment*, n.d. https://keithanyan.github.io/TheDarkEn lightenment.epub/TheDarkEnlightenment.pdf

Mignolo, Walter, and Catherine E. Walsh. *On Decoloniality*. Durham: Duke University Press, 2018.

Moldbug, Mencius. (Curtis Yarvin). *Unqualified Reservations*. n.d. www.unqualified-reservations.org

# 13

# WE STAND FOR WHAT'S RIGHT

## The Pseudo-Revolutionary Tendency

If the ST imagines overturning the abstract logics of modernity, the PRT attacks the concrete working principles, institutions, and practices of modernity. It has, over the past decades, become the dominant, if not the defining, tendency of the third conjunctural moment. In what will likely be my most controversial claim, it has infiltrated and inflected both the right and the left, albeit in different ways and with different successes. The PRT right has largely conquered and united the institutional and movement rights (or at least marginalized competing possibilities). With its electoral victory in 2024, it is enacting a strategic plan to destroy modernity with chaos (although it has apparently attached it to a second oligarchic project). Whatever devastation this causes, it is not clear that the PRT has changed the political culture sufficiently for most Americans, and mainstream culture, to abandon their commitment to at least a weak sense of fairness and equality. The PRT left has retreated somewhat in the face of this challenge, but its effects on the broader left, the ways it has re-articulated the progressive project, remain. As the left panics before the onslaught of the Trump regime, we need to recall that politics is downstream from culture. I will repeat, one last time, that my description of a shared formal affective logic does not make the substantive differences between the PRT right and left any less stark or important.

I start by reducing—in the culinary sense—the PRT to its two core affective commitments. It starts at the same place as the new right. Culture is the primary ground—both the weapon and the stake—in the political battle for America's soul, but it immediately begins to separate itself. Culture is understood in wildly diverse ways (e.g., identity, selective readings of sacred texts, moral norms, attention-getting, disruptions of everyday life,

DOI: 10.4324/9781003662587-16

apocalyptic or catastrophic threats, etc.). The most effective uses of culture are stories that assume the world is ruled by conspiracies, which can be found everywhere.[1]

Second, the politics of reform and compromise are simply more fruitless gestures of the modern; they are traps set by the existing system of power to keep itself in power. As paleo-conservative Barry Goldwater put it, "Extremism in the defense of liberty is no vice, moderation in the pursuit of justice is no virtue." Or as Roy Cohen, the powerful New York conservative attorney, preached (to Donald Trump, among others): Never admit you're wrong, never back down. And when you are attacked, double down on your position and attack those who dare to criticize you. Above all, stand your ground.

Modernity has gone as far as it can. Everyone can see that the cost has been too high. There is little or nothing worth saving. There is no point considering how it has addressed various social functions, how well they have performed, or where they have faltered. There is no point proposing alternatives because they end up having to compromise their efforts to meet already valued ends; they end up merely reproducing modern power. Consider radical ideas like defunding the police or abolishing prisons. Both were meant to solve certain problems, and have certain benefits, which made their costs acceptable. If the costs become too high, and the benefits shrink, perhaps the experiment is over. Defund the Police is immediately confronted with stories about how various communities depend on policing, in multiple ways, for some limited if flawed sense of security. It becomes a proposal to move certain functions (and funds) outside the responsibilities of policing and to identify and support other possibilities of accomplishing them. (The first story expresses the PRT. The second, more pragmatic, story is less clear for the moment.)

The PRT commonly operates with a temporality in which the present trumps history, both the past and the future. The PRT is all about the present. Previous tendencies still understood or at least vaguely recalled that social transformation and political change take time—time to identify and construct problems and solutions, time to offer other stories, time to coax people to your positions and recruit them into your struggle, time to forge the bonds of compassion, empathy, and affiliation that enable movements, and time to build the institutions that can sustain these movements and the changes they seek to produce. Social protests, even movements, are not and do not necessarily arrive at political formations that produce sustainable changes. And many operated with some, often weak, sense of a common future, even a utopian one.

The PRT is all about urgency and immediacy. The intensity of the present overwhelms all other enactments of time. Tactics erase strategy. Attacks erase contexts, making each an easy mark for hyper-inflation. This is a temporality inherited and re-articulated from the 1960s: We want the world, and we want it now. It is a demand for all or nothing NOW.

While the actions determined by previous tendencies often had a short life-span because of the media, actions defined by the PRT, like the 1960s Yippies, embrace the media's norms. Their stories seem pre-made to emerge dramatically and shine for only a moment. They disappear just as quickly, but like the media, they leave their traces behind (e.g., as slogans, memes, yard-signs), fading moments to be nostalgically revisited. (On the left, consider, e.g., Black Lives Matter or Occupy.) At their best, their presence brings a specific problem into the light, but they are too easily co-opted by the next shining moment or old taken-for-granted stories (e.g., All Lives Matter). The right creates a crisis over there; it disappears, then reappears again, or reappears in a different form somewhere else.

There is something almost Nietzschean in the PRT: Modernity (as liberal modernity) has ended up in crises of commensuration (relativism). This is largely a matter of affect (will). The result is close to what Nietzsche called passive nihilism: There is no god, no truth, no value. The PRT offers two non-exclusive responses. The first is a very non-Nietzschean moral absolutism, a polarized fanaticism of certainty and rage. The second follows Nietzsche, for whom the only true response to passive nihilism is to turn it into active nihilism. Active nihilism pushes the crises of commensuration even further, tearing down everything and producing chaos. For Nietzsche, this opened the way for the coming of the Übermensch, the fully creative individual who claims the right to produce their own truth and value. There are moments when the PRT, both the right and the left, does seem to offer its own version of a new locus of moral and political virtue and authority.

## Politics as Fanaticism

The PRT most commonly presents itself as a form of affective fanaticism. (Please remember that I am using this as a description of a particular affective relation and not as an immediate condemnation.) It is the assertion of absolute certainty. Politics is equated with morality. Political judgment has to adhere to a specific morality and logic of moral calculation. The result is an increased need for moral policing.

Political struggle becomes a quasi-religious battle between the righteous and the immoral. Politics is not a matter of winners and losers but of saints and sinners. The sinners have silenced the saints—their sainthood evidenced by their suffering—long enough. It is time the saints stepped up to the pulpit and silenced the sinners. To be politically on the wrong side is a sin. Even falling short of whatever the saints think, say, and do is a sin. As a sinner, you have to start by admitting you are a sinner (e.g., a racist, privileged, elitist, cosmopolitan, liberal). If you refuse to repent, you remain condemned as a sinner, and you may not enter the temple.

In the particular temporality of the PRT, there is a strange notion of confession and retroactive guilt. You can be guilty of something that is a sin today even though it was not a sin when you committed it. While it may appear as if they are absolute and timeless, they really only exist in the immediacy of the present. There is a further paradox at work here: Before the sinner can be changed, they must change the structures of oppression that have made them a sinner. But before they will be willing to change those structures, they will have had to change themselves.

Morality demands absolute fealty and adherence, complete subservience to the cause. The sinner is banished to somewhere outside the temple. Renouncing your sins involves leaving the temple that you have held by acts of manipulation and power. You must surrender the pulpit to the oppressed (or to those whom you have oppressed). Having unjustly occupied the temple, the sinner has no right to the sacrament or sacred texts of the saints who now rightfully dwell within the temple. They cannot quote or use these voices, because such appropriations would, as it were, allow their sins to contaminate the voices of the saints. When I was once told that I had no right to "appropriate" the voice of Stuart Hall (I assume they meant quoting his words), it was clearly because he was black, as was my confessor in waiting, and I was not. Anything deeper—that Stuart had been my teacher, mentor, and close friend for almost 50 years, and godfather to my son—was not transparently visible and, therefore, not relevant. Apparently, what you see is what you get as far as sin is concerned.

Each side claims the right to police everyday life and language because the stakes are more than political. Confess your sins—you are always sinners—knowing that confession is never enough to expiate them. At best, you might end up on the doorway of the temple, doomed never to enter but never willing to depart. Actions are not to be judged by their effectiveness but by the moral position from which they arise. The secret truth is that morality can only be an individual affective certainty. In the final calculation, all that matters is that the saint feels good because they have done the right thing. It does not matter what anyone else thinks or if anyone else knows why it is the right choice. Hence, what others see as failures may well be experienced as a sign of glorious success because you have remained true to your moral self-righteousness. But the other side of this secret is that individuals are little more than cyphers of collective positions in the relations of power, either victimage or privilege.

On the other hand, once a sin, always a sin. For example, if something's origins make it a sin, nothing is likely to change that. The sin cannot be exorcised. And whatever it is, it cannot be used in the righteous struggles, even if it might offer the opportunity to transform a den of iniquity into a new temple. This moral certitude forbids either camp from risking its own soul, thus guaranteeing that the den of iniquity will remain a home for sinners.

Let me tell you a story, a rather personal example. The University of North Carolina at Chapel Hill has, for decades, been under considerable pressure, from select donors and politicians, to establish an institutional site for conservative thought (supposedly to balance the liberal bias of the faculty). In the early 21st century, the Catholic Chancellor asked a Senior Associate Dean (also a proud and, I must add, brilliant conservative thinker and astro-physicist) to investigate the options. Along with a number of faculty and administrators, he visited various programs at peer institutions. They decided that this was not something that UNC should pursue. Instead, the SAD took this as an opportunity to address a crisis of U.S. political culture that many commentators and scholars, across the political spectrum, were identifying: The declining space for public disagreement and productive arguments.

He invited me (and another colleague, an expert on argumentation and debate) to join a focused conversation. During these efforts, we consulted with many different people, including both Robert George (the Princeton conservative legal scholar) and Cornel West (at the time, at Harvard). To be honest, we were more interested in their efforts to stage intelligent conversations together than in their political views.

We ended up proposing the Program for Public Discourse (PPD). It would have three functions: First, it would stage exemplary public events. This would likely mean bringing conservative thinkers willing to defend their views to campus. Second, it would offer those teaching classes resources and guidance in how to foster the skills for productive arguments. And third, it would teach classes that provided the material and skills necessary to develop such a culture on campus and in the wider community. Instantly, the most visible and vocal elements of the faculty (PRT) left opposed it on the grounds that it was "clearly" a Trojan horse for a conservative think tank. They could not get past the paranoid belief that it could only ever be what it was originally intended to be, decades earlier, by the right-wing legislature and Board of Trustees. I was called a traitor and worse. Despite their strong opposition, the faculty voted to support the program. Unfortunately, an unimaginative Dean turned it into not a conservative think tank but just another boring university program. It was and remains my firm belief that it might have been an exciting and innovative program had the left not boycotted it and advised their students to avoid it.

Turn the clock ahead a few years. The faculty approves a new curriculum. (It happens every time a new dean needs this for their CV.) This one requires all students to have a class on oral communication. Meanwhile, the various conservative forces in the state revive their call for a larger conservative presence on campus in the form of civic education, and they passed a significant budget for a School of Civic Life and Leadership. The new Provost had been the SAD who had previously proposed the Program for Public Discourse. He envisioned the new school combining the functions of the PPD and the new oral communication requirement. Perhaps you won't be surprised to learn that the same elements of the left accused the new school of being a puppet of the right. They boycotted it and urged students to do the same.

By refusing to participate at every stage, the PRT left's accusation became a self-fulfilling prophesy. What could have been a robust intellectual experiment and an extraordinary opportunity—given the diminishing funds for the liberal arts—was given over to conservatives partly because the PRT left, in their paranoid moralism, defined it that way, even before it began. They continue to tell the same story, a story in which they conveniently ignore their own role, so that they can speak as the self-righteous truth-sayers who knew all along that origins are destiny. So, now the School is torn apart by two opposing visions, both clashing with strongly institutionalized norms. Is this any way to make a future?

The demand for purity also means that any possibility of error could lead to sin. Every provocation or threat from sinners (i.e., the institutions of oppression), even if it has no chance of actually happening, has to be met first with panic and, then, with the full expression of moral outrage. But how would you know whether the threats are real or just meant to scare, unless you stopped and asked questions? And that is not allowed. Conversely, every offering that comes from saints has to be supported and celebrated (including, sometimes, violence from a position of oppression).

The most common expression of this moral fanaticism is so-called cancel or call-out cultures of individuated but public humiliation, shaming, and, sometimes, threats. Instead of calling out the sin, you call out the sinner, reducing someone to that singular moment or aspect of their lives. This new articulation and increasingly intensive resurgence of what was unfortunately called "political correctness" involves a set of struggles over the effort to "govern" the psychic space of political culture. Although, thanks to the efforts of the right and the media, this is usually identified with the politics of the PRT left, it is at least as common on the PRT right (although rarely reported in such terms). Ironically, while political correctness was originally an ironic term for members of the left to use to criticize others who took their beliefs too far, today the practice of calling out individuals is a renunciation of those who do not practice the right moral politics. In the older version of PC, you would be criticized for what was not in your work, although it rarely had serious consequences. Everyone knew completeness was impossible and it was a matter of a judgment of pertinence. In the new expression, incompleteness is more than an error; it is a sin, making it a failure of redemption and the perpetrator a sinner, or at least complicitous with the blasphemers and sinners.

Judgment is immediate; everyone can be reduced to a single moment, and in the case of the sinner, usually their worst moment. To disagree about anything is likely to get you cast out. To try to step back from and question your habits and assumptions—unless they are keeping you from the truth—is itself a sin. And if you refuse to be judged, if you refuse to be spoken to by stories of moral polarization, you will be condemning yourself to a no-person's land of … complexity, which is a sin anyway. Few dare to speak out for fear of being called out as infidels.

In this absolutist universe, polarization dictates that there are only two camps, two stories, two truth claims, and two recognizable moral positions. There is only absolute innocence and absolute guilt, devoid of history and context. Those who feel they may not belong to either camp—the apathetic, passionless, middle-of-the-road, or whatever—cannot exist in this universe. Each camp negates every possibility beyond itself. It is not merely rejecting the value or legitimacy of the other; the other becomes disposable, something that can be exterminated. One of the great "mysteries" of the contemporary world is the extraordinary rise of everyday violence, even of the most horrific kinds. Even "genocide" itself seems to have become more ordinary, a possible reconstitution of relations among neighbors.

These two competing affective spaces of political morality battle over American identity. Starting in the late 1960s and 1970s, the existence of an imagined national identification, which happily co-existed alongside all sorts of hybrid identities (Jewish-American, Irish-American, etc.), was shattered. The left and the right responded differently, although both expressed the same affective absolutism, with an almost religious fervor.

The left imagined America primarily as a gathering together of differences (black, white, men, women, Asian, gay, trans, etc.). The many different identities become more important than and precede any commitment to an imagined American unity. As numerous identities demanded to be recognized in their own right, the result was a proliferation of identities (e.g., thinking only about sex/gender identities, LGBTQIA+). Today, the answer to the question "who am I" is inevitably a long list of identities. The right prioritized national unity, reaching for a single, uniquely "American" identity. And when it could not ignore the left's challenge, it appropriated a distorted version of the left's identity politics and drew upon a long history that equated American identity with whiteness and excluded all others.

For each camp, these competing logics depend upon an almost sacred political morality. For the left, under the sign of justice (equality, freedom), identity is measured in terms of victimage and privilege, suffering and oppression. Identities are the creations of power, and justice demands that power be overturned. It is the experience and feelings of the oppressed groups that have to be valorized and privileged against the power of modernity. Consequently, it is those already recognized as the suffering oppressed who have the authority to say which identities matter. The right sought to convince people that the left did not care about their suffering. The right operated under the sign of liberty as the founding relation between the sovereign individual and the community (often in the form of the church). However, crucially, this foundational relation has been suppressed by the power of liberal modernity, making the majority of Americans, the true Americans (white, working class, rural, small-town, Christian, etc.), into the victims of urban, cosmopolitan elites and their favorite minorities (empowered through their control of the cultural institutions of authority, including the media, the academy, the sciences, and even popular culture).

## Overturning Truth

The PRT asserts that truth as we know it, as well as the institutions and tools for its production and protection, speak from and for the dominant power structures. They belong to the "master," the powerful, the privileged. But the PRT does not abandon truth. On the contrary, the very concept of truth itself has to be seized and overturned. It begins with truth as a matter of perspective, but this is not your mother's old perspectivism, which ends in relativism. This new perspectivism makes its own absolute claim on truth as certainty, re-establishing Truth with a capital T as entirely affective. It is the victim, the one who has suffered and is oppressed, who has access to Truth. Victimage constitutes a new category of privilege. It becomes the fulcrum point, the sole determination of the judgment of Truth. Every other claim to Truth is the devil's work.

As I have suggested, it is not the specificity of identities that gives the individual this privilege. People may be oppressed because of their specific identity, which defines whether they will become a victim. But it is the fact of their being a victim, their experience of victimage, and the feelings that accompany it that guarantees their status as keepers of the Truth. And with a simple twist of a wand, Truth, which used to belong to the oppressor, now belongs to the oppressed. Truth is anchored, narcissistically, in the experience of the subjugated and marginalized and in their personal feelings. The more you are beaten down, the more you become a victim, the greater the miracle of your transformation, and the greater your Truth. Your victimage becomes an affective magnet around which all social relations can be organized and measured or dissolved and rejected.

There is no need for dealing with criticism, disagreement, or difference; such things elicit only immediate rage in moral judgments of evil and self-righteousness, social assumptions of cynicism and apathy, or political judgments of "old," privileged, or elitist ways of thinking. Criticism itself has been politicized, easily read as a sign of opposition or indifference, complicity, or treason. And there is no need to step outside the comfort zone of the temple's very selective readings of history, politics, political geography (do you ever wonder why one place matters while others do not), and cultural and intellectual texts. There is no need for careful analysis and rigorous thinking, or even for public discussion and debate. There is no basis, other than moral, for the choice of rhetorics and tactics, even if they have been shown to be of limited value in the past. The result is often new forms of anti-intellectualism.

The PRT assumes that its Truth does not need any justification or defense. Similar assumptions have a long history in American politics, especially in the current conjuncture. For example, the initial victories of the civil rights movements were won in court decisions and legislation. But afterward, there was apparently no need to educate those who opposed them, no need to explain why the changes were right and good for the country. There was no need to understand the opposition as anything other than guilty of the sin of racism. There was no need to find stories that would speak to them, that would move them. Fanaticism dictates that there can be no room for heterogeneous positions within a struggle, even if they appear to support the same moral values. Ultimately, disagreement is dismissed as a conspiracy of evil.

Conspiracy stories have played an important role in the present conjuncture (and going back much further in American politics). The left sees them everywhere on the right, going back at least as far as Nixon and Reagan. The right has been telling them since Kennedy, Johnson, and Clinton. But the real panics started with Obama and the emergence of the PRT. The left does not need to look very hard for the evidence because, surprisingly often, the PRT is upfront about what it is doing "behind the scenes." The right finds traces, if not solid evidence, of conspiracies all over the actions of Democrats and the progressive left. The PRT is a master of weaving conspiracy stories. I wonder why either side is the least bit surprised, given how cynical they are about state governance and public affairs. What are being constructed as stories of conspiracy could also be told as stories of the nitty-gritty workings of the state and the political economy viewed at a more concrete level of day-to-day operations. They are often surprisingly complicated stories, but perhaps not all complicated stories are better stories.

The Truth, according to the PRT, is that we face an enemy so powerful that its victory is almost complete; the enemy's plans are absolute, and its tools are insidious. People are pawns in a game in which they do not understand the rules. All our problems can be blamed on this enemy, who has been hatching this nefarious conspiracy for a long time. Maybe we were not sure who the enemy was, and maybe different sects in the temple have different ideas about the best candidate—capitalism, a political party, the State, the media, academics, consumer and entertainment cultures, technology, savage meritocracies, etc.—but it usually boils down to liberalism and the PRT left, or conservatism and the PRT right (and everybody's favorite, capitalism).

The evil is all around us, everywhere, just waiting to be made visible or, if it is already visible, waiting to be confessed. Everyone other than those already sanctified (having the right oppressed identity) is guilty, a sinner. The sin contaminates everything in our society like mold. The different degrees and manifestation of the sin do not matter. For example, every white person is a racist, from the white supremacist to the anti-racist academic. Every conservative is an ignorant racist. More sophisticated conceptualizations of the sin—e.g., racial apparatuses,[2] ontologies of blackness, the black body as death—do not change the story, except perhaps to make it even more depressing. Instead, they become mind-numbing in their repetitiveness, generality, and certainty. Just another story of the evils of ... fill in the blank ... (of course it is evil, thanks for reminding us) or of the endlessly proliferating search for the essence of racism, or capitalism, or white guilt or ....

Fortunately, apparently, the keepers of the Truth, the saints, have escaped this horrible conspiracy of power and found refuge in the temple, where they have protected the Truth. Of course, each side denies its Truth is a conspiracy theory because ... well, it is True. Each side appeals to affective hyper-inflations, calling the other side fascists and Nazis. Every hint of racism is white supremacy. Every hint of social justice is communism. Only my side has the right to claim to have suffered and to call itself a victim. Both sides have a miraculous ability to rewrite or erase history. No white people have suffered or are suffering. Black people no longer suffer. If only people knew what they (the righteous saints) and only they know, then vast numbers would join them. Everything would change, and victory would be theirs. The story would end.

But the stories continue—powerful stories reconfiguring and redirecting people's feelings of rage and fear, disappointment and resentment, hope and despair. Rather than letting truth lead our actions and passions, the PRT creates stories in which actions and passions lead truth. If it feels right, it's true. What is perhaps most interesting is how the PRT balances the contradiction between absolutism (certainty) and relativism. It is, in its own way contextualist: there is an American truth and it is not exportable to other places. Those other places have their own truths.

## A Necessary Detour

I assume it is obvious that I am not a fan of the PRT. Perhaps I am guilty of my own hyper-inflation. But I do think there is enough truth in my description to warrant serious consideration—and serious criticism. I think it demands that we be willing to stand against the PRT as an inadequate and even dangerous response to the failures and possibilities of modernity. I will raise two questions: The first challenges the over-valuing of victimage. The second challenges the under-valuing of those outside the temple, so to speak.

Before addressing these, let me be as clear as possible because to be misunderstood could be dangerous. All sorts of differences have become irrational hatreds, deeply embedded in different forms and in different degrees of oppression and subjugation, in so many interactions and institutions. There can be no doubt about that. And the suffering this causes, the toll it takes—physically, cognitively, emotionally—is enormous, often unbearable, and sometimes unforgivable. These histories and experiences need to be heard and, to whatever extent possible, shared, collectively felt, and collectively challenged and undone in every way possible. The people marked by these experiences and the suffering they cause may have unique insights into the realities of the powers and hatreds with which they have been and are being confronted. These insights are crucial elements in our efforts to construct the stories of the conjuncture (and its longer histories and its conditions of possibility).

But why assume that such suffering guarantees privileged insight into the full and complicated nature of the conjuncture, the organic crises, or the many conjunctural struggles? Why assume that power can be understood by equating its only consequential effects with the experiences and feelings of victimage? Or by any single group or experience? (I am not suggesting, in its stead, some spurious claim to objectivity as given by pseudo-scientific statistical measures or socio-cognitive science.) Why assume that stories of polarization are the best way to capture the complicated distributions of victimhood and privilege? Isn't it possible, even likely, that people are privileged in some ways or in some places, and are victims in other ways or places? How do we decide which differences, which experiences, which sufferings are included in the pantheon of the oppressed? Do we understand the inequalities of inequalities? Are we so confident that we can judge them? Are we implicitly working with a comparative measure of suffering and privilege? How far are we willing to go in abandoning old social norms or accepting new ones in the name of ameliorating suffering or ending privilege?

There is probably no clearer example of these questions from the past decades (and especially since the Hamas attack in Gaza on October 7, 2023, and Israel's near-genocidal retaliation) than the status of Jews in such a moral politics. Anti-Semitism is probably the oldest surviving form of hatred and persecution in the west (although its expressions have changed). Why is the assumption that it no longer exists fundamentally different than the assumption that black racism no longer exists? There is a long history of anti-Semitism on the left (despite the key roles Jews often played), but an even longer and stronger history on the right. (Why has the media been allowed to focus all the attention on the left?) Is there any other case in which the actions of a state, even a religiously identified one, have been used to justify (pre-existing) prejudices against an entire diasporic people? Does Modi condemn all Hindus? Do the actions of Islamic state leaders condemn all Muslims? But perhaps it is less diabolical and more crass: The right condemns anti-Semitism not for the benefit of the Jewish people, but for their own purposes. (Some pro-Palestinians use anti-Semitism to very different ends.)

Jews are now commonly seen as white and privileged, until they are not. I grew up in Brooklyn, New York, in the 1950s, with a significant Jewish population, and yet I was not infrequently on the receiving end of anti-Semitic abuse (and even violence). And although I was too young to realize it, there were certainly circumstances in which I was merely tolerated. It has followed me my whole life, although compared to many other Jews, I have been quite fortunate. When I moved to Illinois, I was warned by a colleague not to try to "jew" down the rent of my house, and in Indiana, when swastikas defaced an exhibition of Torahs, the university dismissed it as a prank.

As a people, Jews, despite their successes and privileges, have continued to be made victims and continue to suffer. (I am not saying that this in any way justifies Israel's long history of violence in the occupied territories or its extreme actions beginning in 2024. I do think there are explanations, but not justifications.) Why is Jewish suffering treated differently? Has it been sufficiently mitigated by Jewish successes? Do we know the costs—in experience and feeling—of those victories? Who decides which histories matter? Why do people complain that Jews play the Holocaust card too much? (I am even sympathetic to the argument.) But no one complains about the ways the Middle Passage and slavery are used. Do we assume that the latter are more palpably present? Maybe—actually—Jews live their suffering differently.

Let me offer a personal example, perhaps strange because of its insignificance. I am sometimes criticized for my aggressively passionate and critical tone, no doubt a somewhat accurate description of my argumentative style. Without meaning to be too defensive, I grew up in a culture—New York Jewish immigrant culture—that was filled with extraordinarily generous and loving people. But you would not have known it if you listened to them in public. Every culture has its own affective expressiveness. In my culture, generosity was assumed and rarely explicit. A mitzvah (a good deed) is not quite as good if it is publicly announced. I have assumed, obviously mistakenly, that people understand this. I have assumed that people begin by accepting the reality of cultural differences. Apparently, mine are not worthy of being acknowledged. Instead, they are read as signs of authoritarian privilege (and not of the generosity with which they would be received in my culture). I recognize, admire, and even sometimes marvel at my friends' ability to perform generosity more colloquially, to offer criticism as gifts, in more generally recognizable ways. I have always assumed I am doing the same thing, but in very different cultural forms. Perhaps I should have learned from my friends and that is on me. But the judgment that ignores cultural differences certainly cannot be right, and I often end up thinking that what people ascribe to my privilege—for example, as an old white professor—was partly a judgment of cultures they did not understand. Or even worse, as I walked away angry or depressed, a backhanded form of anti-Semitism (i.e., I become the hated, stereotypical New York Jew).

The second challenge speaks to an old problem in political struggles, especially among those who assume they are right, but the PRT's affective absolutism has significantly intensified it. A revolution may begin with a bang, but it ends, neither with utopia nor with a whimper, but with the collective stories of the ordinary people who initially sit on the sidelines watching the action until they decide what to do. They decide the fate of revolutions. Both the left and right versions of the PRT have to face these people. The PRT begins by dismissing (perhaps too quickly) those who consent to evil, or disagree with sacred Truth, or refuse to join the camp of the righteous. The PRT can offer many explanations, but they all boil down to the judgment that those outside the temple are sinners who cannot see the righteousness of the holy keepers of Truth.

Yet the reality of political culture dictates that the PRT, like most affective tendencies, still has to face numerous constituencies. First, "the base" identifies those who are deeply and intensely committed to the PRT's politics. They are the devout believers, the saints inside the temple. Second, there are the people—perhaps a majority of either side—who are committed to a particular politics and follow the temple's activities but remain largely on the sidelines. They are the Sundays and holidays-only church-goers. Some might dismiss them as saints in name only. Third, there are the people stuck in the middle—the undecideds, those uncertain about their political positions, and those who struggle against being pulled into the temple of absolute certainty. The last are often the people who, for any number of reasons, choose to remain uninvolved. They often do not bother voting. They do not seem to care enough. For decades, the left has been screaming at them: Where's the outrage? Where's the empathy? We do not really know how many there are in each of these constituencies.

Political struggle normally demands that you consider the effects your actions and discourses might have, which requires taking account of how these different audiences might perceive and understand them. How your actions are seen by others partly determines what sorts of effects they can and will have. But recall that the PRT emphasizes intentions over effects. Consequently, it often seems largely unconcerned with how it is perceived, not only by the broader formations of its possible allies, but also in the broad spaces of popular opinion and feeling. It is concerned mostly with its base, although it may pay some attention to the second constituency, trying to mobilize their passion and commitment. The PRT right does a better job here, but it does this largely by constantly turning a distorted mirror on the left, highlighting its supposed hypocrisy. Until recently, both the PRT left and right have largely ignored the third constituency, but, recently, it has become more important as a result of the right's increasing power. The PRT right has been able to mobilize this third constituency against the failings of existing modernity (which it can blame on the left). The PRT left, however, needs to construct a monstrous foe. As horrible as it may sound, thank god for Trump, Inc.

The PRT calls for a different kind of politics, built around another contradiction: chaos and order. Modern thought and politics depend upon the possibility, desirability, and even necessity of organising the chaos. The world is chaotic. Power is the struggle over how to construct an order on chaos. The PRT writes the equation differently. Rather than either/or, its politics are defined by the necessary conjunction of the production of chaos and the assertion of absolute order. This would be impossible in modernist terms; it defines a new politics.

I should add that, in smaller doses, chaos in vital (and one might say that slow thinking starts by producing its own chaos). Chaos blows apart our assumptions, the things we are least likely to question. It wipes the table clean for a moment, throws all the pieces of the puzzle on the table at the same time. We have to start over. Maybe those aren't the only solutions? Maybe that is not the problem? Who knows? Chaos cannot be rendered predictable. (Once again, I think the right is much more adept at using, even managing the chaos than the left.)

### Politics as Chaos

The PRT—directly on the part of the right, indirectly and often unconsciously on the part of the left—seeks to bring modernity down just as modernity brought down the ancient regime.[3] The days of liberal modernity are already past. Or, at least, its failures have been revealed to be the deeper failures of modernity; the PRT right rejects the very assumptions and institutions of modernity itself (with the exception of capitalist greed). It constructs the second organic crisis as a radical rejection of anything that can be identified with the old regime, the old way of doing things, with modernity. Modernity has not only lost its legitimacy, it is actually over. It just hasn't realized it. The only legitimate action is to declare its death and burn its remains.

Chaos is the necessary condition for doing away with the old order. Everything, including the old truths, values, and norms (even, for some on the right, capitalism), must go. Only wealth, power, and culture remain. The PRT will leave nothing of the old order behind but its chaotic ruins. It denies the very possibility or necessity of a balance in the field of forces. It makes chaos into a new principle of governance (a new affective fundamentalism?), setting loose a free-floating sense of abandonment and rage, fear and uncertainty, anxiety and depression, and frenzy and terror on the affective landscape. Chaos becomes its own crisis and its only solution.

At times, chaos may look like an impossible version of anarchy or a world given over to insanity, but it is neither. This is a different kind of politics, a more radically anti-political politics, a politics aimed against all politics. It leaves only the spontaneous acts of power that produce nothing but chaos itself. Its actions are meant only to interrupt and disrupt what we take to be normal over there, leaving other places of normality alone, but leaving us to worry that their safety is only temporary. And it can certainly feel like the PRT is out to drive people crazy, make them ever more paranoid and unsure about what is going on, and create panic and, above all, more chaos. It does not so much change the rules of the game as operate as if without rules.

And after you tear down the orders of modernity, what you are left with is not so much a space of transition but a chaos of ruins. The PRT does not drain the swamp; it expands and deepens it. It shreds modernity's playbook. It makes the chaos into the new normal. Thus, Steve Bannon could state: "The Democrats don't matter. The real opposition is the media. And the way to deal with them is to flood the zone with shit." (And in 2025, the media apparently have to report every outlandish action of the Trump regime, regardless of their actual chances of being realized.) In other words, throw lots of shit against the wall and see what sticks.

The PRT does not offer solutions to the crises we face. It does not attempt to find order in the chaos or to re-configure it. And it does not seek possible ways out of the chaos. It offers little hint of what comes next or where we are supposed to go. These questions are too modern: There can be no itinerary, no structure, and no strategy. (Hence, the politics of chaos seems to end, or bring to an end, the long strategic plans of the right.) You might think that the moral politics of fanaticism is what fills the empty space of order, but the relation between chaos and fanaticism keeps changing. Sometimes fanaticism appears under the cover of chaos, or as a bulwark against chaos, or, most commonly, as simply adjacent to the chaos. The PRT seeks only to foment and further chaos. Chaos becomes productive, even as it provides cover for an unknowable future. (In 2025, an oligarchy?) A politics of chaos and chaos as politics? Let chaos reign!

### The PRT Right

I want to take a moment to look back on the PRT right, before its current (2025) regime, starting with its hijacking of the infrastructures and successes of the new right. This included a significant part of an already available constituency but also tools for further recruiting, and a widespread and dense network of activist groups, institutions, and think tanks. In some ways, the PRT right continued the new right's hegemonic strategies, fighting a war of positions, but always in the background. It reshuffled temporary alliances among some of the same set of fractured groups, re-articulated into the PRT's stories. It also moved to the front many of the groups that the new right had excluded. Consequently, it was able to continue the struggles of political culture and the effort to take the reins of the Republican Party and many of its affiliated institutions. It effectively defeated, or at least silenced or relegated to the margins, more recognizable forms of conservatism (including those which were, in their own times, thought to be rather extremist).

Despite the way it is often represented, the PRT right is highly fractured—perhaps even contradictory—along various dimensions: There are significant demographic differences, including spatial (wilderness, rural, suburban, and even urban), ethnic, gender, and class. There are numerous hatreds, including misogyny, racism, nativism, anti-Semitism (toward both Jews and Muslims), homophobia (and recently transphobia), and xenophobia. Different groups offer different justifying grounds, ranging from the Constitution to the Bible, from liberty (and individualism) to prosperity, from American exceptionalism to the Second Coming. Different groups emphasize different (non-exclusive) styles and practices, including cultism and conspiracy theories, media disturbance (hactivism and trolling), strategic politics (occupy the government to destroy it), survivalism, violence (insurrectionism, domestic terrorism, revolutionary militia), corruption, and what I can only describe as outright sleaze and greed. And there are numerous ideologies moving in these spaces, such as paleoconservatisms, traditionalisms, white nationalisms and supremacisms, fascisms and Nazisms, technological utopianisms, post-libertarianisms, various secular and religious salvationists, etc.

Throw all these (and more) into the mix, with potentially different strengths and commitments, and you have a unity-in-difference always on the verge of chaos. Attempting to manage the chaos becomes a crucial aspect of the PRT right's efforts. The PRT right operates with an impure politics. The impurities, which may seem important to its opponents, largely do not matter inside the movement. But acknowledging and even taking advantage of the differences rather than ignoring them may provide openings for those who oppose it.

There are two other crucial things the PRT right inherited: First, despite appearances, the PRT right has practiced its own kind of strategic politics. It has allowed different groups to have their own plans, strategies, and tactics. At the same time, it establishes forms of communication and oversight. Second, it has focused most of its attention on the political culture, and further strengthened the primacy of the culture wars. And despite what many on the left assume, this has included a continuing investment in serious intellectual work.

But the PRT right also declared independence from the new right. It simultaneously rejects the hegemonic tendency and a hegemonic politics and wages a war of maneuver, investing completely in stories of polarization. It's not about policies or even its more extreme (and mean-spirited) re-articulations of the new right uses of, for example, various hatreds, anti-elitism and anti-science, repeated lies, highly emotionally charged images, erasing unfulfilled promises and predictions, projecting its responsibility onto others, populist identifications, etc.

What is most important is the way the PRT strategically sets about recomposing the affective landscape, working with and re-articulating its structures of feeling. It does so precisely in its powerful affective stories of polarization, victimage, abandonment, and systemic crises. Those stories provide a context in which it can, paradoxically, systematically use chaos to take down the old order. The stories affectively prefigure a scorched earth policy, "burning down the house," or, at least, it is constantly threatening to do so, all of which creates chaos. The result is an anti-politics.

The modern—going back to an as-yet unspecified point—has to be overturned. And the PRT right does so with impunity, even using a variety of forms of intimidation and manipulation, often simply ignoring or changing the rules and laws in mid-stream. The PRT right does not seem to care about the law; it rarely cares about changing the law. This change of tactics is significant. The reactionary right is not focused on deregulation but on what it takes to be the second element of modern governance: A commitment to expertise, knowledge, and competence. Postwar liberalism instituted this in the civil service (the deep state). People are flabbergasted by the lack of competence of Trump's appointees, but competence is part of the old order. They do not understand his attacks on education, science, etc. It's not about the ideologies of those in charge of the relevant institutions (though those provide useful images) but about the affective faith in knowledge production and its consequences for what sorts of constraints on their behavior people are willing to accept.

Values traditionally associated with American modernity like decency, fairness, competence, and empathy disappear, although, to be fair, we do not know how various supporters of the PRT right feel about such tactics. We are frightened by Trump's new geopolitical realignments with friends and enemies; it is difficult to foresee the outcome, but he is announcing the end of the old world order. We are horrified by the lack of any recognizable ethics … the old order. We are terrified by the brazen disregard for every norm of behavior, including the law … the old order. The irony is that the PRT right reclaims the modern state to use it as the site for bringing down the modern. What makes it acceptable is that the PRT's identity is only defined by its opposition to everything modern.

The PRT right does not seem to worry much about what a non-modern version of America would be. They do not agree about whether to worry about it, and when they do, they rarely agree about what it might look like.

Their future is defined in largely negative terms. The future is a radical break with the present. Insofar as there is a future written in the present, it seems to go back to pre-modern forms affiliation and power (e.g., an imagined Judeo-Christian tradition, or pre-industrial tribes). Perhaps we are already caught up in postmodern forms of affiliation and power. Trump's attack on the state is a kind of imagination that you can have a nation without a state. Can we imagine sovereign individuals without society? Can we return to premodern forms of authority and truth in the service of "the people"? The PRT right seems to be projecting what I might call an anti-modern but technological neo-feudalism, often with a good dose of mercantilism (given the need for rare minerals, etc.). It is often assumed to be some as-yet unimagined synthesis of authoritarianism and communalism and corporatism and technology, under the competing signs of violence and entertainment. It is a new America, so that the concern for national identity become crucial, and trumps all others.

Let's talk about Trump. The left too quickly and easily dismisses Trump as stupid or ignorant, evil or mentally unstable, or a fascist. Should it matter that it thought previous Republican presidents in the conjuncture were ignorant or crazy or fascists? It did not get the left very far, either in understanding what was going on or in developing effective strategies of opposition and progressive transformation.

Trump is rather the perfect ringmaster of the devastating circus of an anti-politics of anti-modernity. His claim to lead this Movement—not as the strategist in chief but as the leading role—is that he is able to hold the contradiction between chaos and order in his hands, to make it so visible that everyone ignores it. His great political talent is the ability to produce chaos and embrace the ensuing panic, while publicly supporting the fanaticism of the moral and patriotic right (in his deeds if not his life). He sees politics as a refusal to organize, to be consistent, and to follow through. The fact that Trump contradicts himself all the time, that he lies, or that he does not do what he says he is going do, it just doesn't matter. Instead, he orchestrates a grand proliferation and celebration of chaos itself. Chaos appears to be both the means and the apparent end. And the fact that he seems so comfortable living in the chaos is a crucial part of his charisma.

There is strategy in his madness. He uses a wrecking ball to destroy agencies; he drains the swamp of money and labor. But most of all, he keeps starting fires and fanning the flames. A thousand points of light. There are alarms going off all the time, everywhere. Emergencies come and go and then come back. Inconsistencies, contradictions, lies, broken promises, kept promises, hypocrisies, none of it seems to matter. Chaos reigns, and it is almost impossible to focus; our attention is constantly divided amongst a thousand brush fires of all sizes. It is a pyromaniac's plan for building an unstoppable conflagration. It is as if general anxiety disorder meets ADHD. This is chaos as anti-politics. It appears, simultaneously, feudal and postmodern. And yet, at the same time, Trump's appeal depends on his willingness to impose, almost arbitrarily or out of blatant greed, his own will. He asserts what I can only call a kind of sovereignty.

The successes of the PRT are deeply bound up with the possibilities of media, including the old but still clinging to existence, media, and the newer social media, not only as conduits and forms of communication, but as an affective logic of a "reality politics" program, in which the lines between entertainment (including horror), profit, and power all merge into a single affective landscape. Trump seems to live in the contradiction as if he were living in a mediascape and expertly using the power of the popular media to produce the greatest reality TV show ever imagined. Reality TV does not simply blur the line between fiction and reality, nor is it some postmodern simulacrum. It works in a world of conditionals and counterfactuals: For example, if something could be, then it is; if something is, then it must be, etc. This is a reality of possible worlds, a more sophisticated form of affective constructionism than is understood or credited. The most bedazzling reality TV show has become the scene of politics. The PTR right has marketized and weaponized chaos, turning the given, unsettling complexities of the modern into a resource and a tool against the modern.[4]

This closes the circle that connects the new right, and, even more, the PRT right, to the 1960s left/counterculture as its dark mirror image. The Movement of the 1960s—emblematized by the Yippies (Youth International Party)—constantly announced and performed its opposition to an illegible yet affectively graspable "system." That system now stands exposed and named: The modern. The PRT right's strategies—so media-bound, affective, impure, irreverent, anti-political—all echo the Yippies' anti-political politics, entertainment and politics coexisting in a common space of political culture.[5] (If there was ever a need for calm, collective thinking and strategizing ...)

**The PRT Left**

The various configurations of the left have made important—crucial—contributions to this conjunctural history. They have inaugurated numerous new political forces—new subjects, new struggles and agents, new practices, etc. Yet they could not mobilize a stable hegemonic politics in the second moment. And in the third conjunctural moment, the PRT left has not offered stories capable of constructing an alternative organic crisis. Their stories have not reshaped the affective landscape or re-articulated the political culture. While the PRT (and ST) lefts do suggest that modernity has failed or that it is corrupt to its core, they often continue to tell stories that speak in its languages and institutions. These remain both its own condition of possibility and the conditions of possibility of its stories of democratic change.

That is to say, the PRT left almost inevitably betrays its own anti-modern commitments. Since it cannot imagine the "revolutionary" event that would bring about the transformative change it desires, and since it largely refuses the long-term strategizing and institutional work within the admittedly corrupt system, it must always fall back into the very political and cultural realities it condemns. Its stories evince a strange nostalgia for the failed promises of modernity. Since its efforts at cultural politics have been largely restricted to matters of identity and difference, it continues to need to ally itself with more liberal and weakly progressive elements. Consequently, its stories sound like attempts to shore up the dams that they admit have failed to hold back the floods and flames. Its fanaticism simply reverses the terms of modernity's failure.

The PRT left has not mastered the challenges of chaos or of the affective landscape. The PRT left seems paralyzed when confronted with chaos, and with a politics that produces chaos. It seems too afraid of the chaos to confront it head on, even as it contributes, perhaps unconsciously, to its production. It has become impossible to have any sense of a common belonging that cannot be immediately challenged and fractured. As identities continue to proliferate endlessly, there is no end to the chaos in sight, except to return to a fanaticism already doomed to fail.

The PRT left makes history into a collection of tactics, resistances, and escape routes, with little sense of their outcomes. It turns power into a collection of the experiences and feelings of the oppressed. They have the necessary right to struggle by virtue of their suffering. And their struggles, their efforts and spirit, have to be celebrated. These struggles do not become lessons from which we can learn, but exhortations and judgments. There is little consideration of how such tactics may be seen by and affect people not immediately implicated—but who may become actively involved—in the struggle. Speaking metaphorically, it is as if seeing the spaces between the bars could get you out of the cage and prevent those still outside at the moment from being caged. The result is that, all too often, groups keep repeating what has been done in the past, hoping for a different outcome. Politics becomes a chaos of oppressions and resistances, which continues to fuel the chaos with even more chaos, with nihilism and despair—under the affective sign of a hyper-inflated sense of self-importance.

The PRT left has failed to take seriously the strategic nature of the right's politics. Just as importantly, it has failed to construct its own strategic politics. It can only respond defensively to an immediate threat or attack. The result is that, at any instant, people on the left are freaking out over something, whether real or imagined. People panic and declare their hatred for the latest treachery. Everything is hyper-inflated. It does not matter if we knew that what happened was going to happen, that it was entirely predictable. Universities have known for 50 years that the PRT right, given the opportunity, would come after them. They knew that one point of attack would be affirmative action (or DEI, once it was bureaucratized). They even knew many of the tactics and rhetorics. But when the PRT right gained full power, and the attacks came, the response was surprise, panic, and moral outrage—and more chaos. When did panic become the default mode?

If the PRT is constantly augmenting chaos by ramping up anxiety, fear, and depression (among other affects), then escaping the chaos might require that the left stop panicking. It may have to stop telling stories of the PRT right as foretelling the coming end of the world, as evil incarnate. It may have to stop producing even more anxiety. And that might mean questioning the PRT left itself and preparing for the challenges to come.

## Conclusion

I don't know if there is a strategic politics capable of holding back the reactionary moral authoritarianism of MAGA and the technological totalitarianism and pseudo-libertarianism of the new oligarchs. I don't know if there is a strategic politics capable of challenging the chaos, of finding a way out of the chaos, or of finding other ways of producing order from the chaos. I think it will demand that the left take the right more seriously, not only as a threat and source of panic, but as a strategic project to be understood and systematically—strategically—countered. I think it will demand that the left examine its own place in the stories being told and its role in the construction of the affective landscape.

Is it really so hard to understand how people could be led into following Trump? People are angry and, to some extent, hopeless, even desperate. Such feelings can be transformed into resentment against a system that failed them and those who defend it. (Has the left never had similar feelings? Don't many of its stories do similar work?) Is it really so hard to understand how they could be drawn into stories that took their feelings seriously, that promised to make their lives better, that foretold the end of the system keeping them down? Or maybe they were drawn in by stories that told them the country has been and continues to be headed in the wrong direction and promised to radically change that. What did the left do? It said that Trump was lying, and it had the truth. But the right's stories were ready for that. Of course, the left would say that because it was defending its own interests in the existing system. So, what does the left do then? It calls them stupid or racists or worse. Is it really so obvious that everyone who follows Trump embraces the whole package? Might he simply be the (despicable) lesser of two evils, the worse evil being the Democratic Party and the woke left? At least he stands against the liberal state, against the arrogance of the liberal elite, and allies himself with those who abhor the absence of a moral compass. Might it simply be that the stories of the PRT right actually do a better job of speaking to some people where they are on the affective landscape and then moving them by recomposing the very structures of feeling? Is it really so hard to understand why people would simply give up on politics, and any sense of their own civic responsibilities?

Because the PRT left does not have better stories, it has retreated into a compromised position and partly backed off from its fanaticism. It refuses to embrace the fact that it shares many of the right's attacks on liberalism and modernity (e.g., on the liberal state and the postwar world order, on the existing institutions of authority, including science, on the wastefulness of government bureaucracies, on media biases, on judicial corruption, and on unwarranted elitisms). Instead of standing by these criticisms, it retreats into stories that imagine new ways of tinkering with the modern world, imagining a better version of the failed reality. And when challenged to tell better stories than the right, it retreats back into fanaticism and chaos.

There is an irony in the current moment, in the entire story I have been telling. Large parts of the left, in fact, I would say most of the left, has been skeptical about the importance of culture. It has actively relegated matters of feeling, etc. to the spaces of the irrational and, hence, the undesirable. It has associated them with lesser versions of humanity (i.e., women and children) and even the non-human. It has had a long-standing mistrust of popular media, and it has been relatively blind to the increasingly affective power of popular stories. It tends to refuse the kinds of impure politics and relationships that characterize the affective landscape and the popular culture. These proclivities have been strengthened, for the most part, in the PRT left. Consequently, it seems unable to tell stories that might turn elements of the affective landscape to its own advantage. It seems unable to offer compelling popular stories that reimagine the national crisis and reshape the possibilities of political struggle. And insofar as the PRT affectively dominates the left, perhaps that is why, to a large extent, it is losing the culture wars.

The PRT left constantly complains that it is misrepresented in the media and popular imagination. It always finds someone to blame for this. Part of the explanation lies with the left itself. To put it bluntly, the left is generally lousy at controlling its image because it is generally lousy at communicating with what I described earlier as the second and third constituencies, the majority of the people in the country. It is lousy at advertising itself and lousy at controlling its own public relations. Many will say, that is not politics, that is polluting the sanctity of politics, that is playing their game. But that is where politics is being fought out, and where power is being won. The irony is that the left is blessed with many intellectuals who do know something about culture and the media. And it is equally blessed with many cultural workers who know a great deal about how popular stories are constructed and can be affectively and effectively communicated. It seems that no one wants to listen to them.

There are many stories that can be told about the struggles to shape America's future. I have begun to tell one that begins in the 1950s and 1960s, focusing on political culture. For the moment, moral absolutism clashes with chaos as competing expressions of the PRT. The PRT right has constructed stories that work, if only temporarily, to call people into their lived—affective—realities. And they have enabled a range of destructive actions that are producing further suffering and misery. But in its stories, they may well be the sugar that helps the medicine go down. The PTR left, on the other hand, seems paralyzed to do much of anything. It can surrender, retreat to safety, scream, give in to hatred, or just continue doing the same things, knowing that they have not worked before but hoping that this time will be different. We protest, wondering how many people have to be on the streets before someone notices. We file lawsuits, hoping that he who would be king listens this time. (Does anyone try to convince capitalists that the dominant story is not actually going to work for them?) But the story continues. The possibility of better stories always seems just out of reach. But that is exactly what the left needs. It needs to find and nurture other affective tendencies and better stories if it is to have any hope of repairing the world. At the very least, it will need a politics for what will come next.

## Notes

1  It may be that Trump has abandoned this idea. His politics may have moved upstream of the culture. The contradictions on the affective landscape are playing out in the political culture.

2  An apparatus refers to a composition that includes a discursive formation but also specific tactics, behavioral prescriptions, structures of governances, etc.

3  The PRT right's anchor in religion can be traced back to 1864, when Pope Pius IX outraged European and American opinion by condemning the notion that "The Roman Pontiff can, and ought to, reconcile himself, and come to terms with progress, liberalism and modern civilization." It was, of course, a thoroughly modern sentiment.

4  It is not coincidental that in this reality, while the democratic-left formations are always asking for donations, the right is always selling something. Everything can be and is monetized.

5  The Yippies could be one of the inventors of reality TV. Their politics was defined by staging media events, such as dropping one-dollar bills onto the floor of the New York Stock Exchange and filming the stockbrokers brutalizing each other as they tried to grab them. Abbie Hoffman's books included *Revolution for the Hell of It* and *Steal This Book*. The latter had to be removed from the bookshelves because so many kids took its title literally. Can you imagine Trump as some version of Hoffman in the Upside Down (from the popular TV series, *Stranger Things*), as a dark, inverted mirror image? A Yippie cabinet would have been no less ludicrous than Trump's. My favorite bumper sticker in the 1960s was "America: Fix it or fuck it." For the PRT right, fixing it may well mean fucking it.

**PART IV**

# We Would Build a New World if We Only Knew How

# 14

# THERE IS A CRACK IN EVERYTHING (POLITICS)

If the previous chapters were especially grumpy and angry, the following chapters will seem overly generous and naïve. I want to propose another possible affective tendency. It offers another possible configuration of the balance in the field of forces, responding to the challenges of the third conjunctural moment. And while my discussion will seem focused on the left, I am attempting to find something on the other side of the PRT.

The Popular Tendency (PT) embraces the open-endedness and uncertainty of history. It knows that reality never stands still long enough to be fully captured, and that the future is never guaranteed. It can be seen as an attempt to develop a constructionist politics and political culture. It offers a naïvely pragmatic politics that reflects on what it is doing and on the effects of its own efforts. The PT attempts, hesitatingly at best, to find a new politics, one that avoids reproducing the mistakes of modern politics. Those mistakes seem to always land us in an irreconcilable difference between political values and practices, with only temporary moments of respite. And they have done so once again, but without the promise of any respite whatsoever. Whether the present maelstrom is a moment of transition, with its morbid symptoms, or the first moment beyond the transition makes no difference. We need another politics.

## A Popular Politics

It is embodied in an impure, imperfect, and incomplete politics. No political action can solve every problem or even solve any problem completely. Any action may have positive effects over here, but it may also have no effects or even slightly deleterious effects over there. These are the practical negotiations

DOI: 10.4324/9781003662587-18

that make change difficult. And they demand sophisticated thinking and practice. They demand to be spoken with a good dose of humility (and even humor when possible).

A popular politics accepts the uniqueness of human life. It recognizes that human beings play a unique role in constructing their realities, but it does not assume that they are in control or that they are the only agents involved in such processes of construction. It does not assume that there is a universal essence to humanity but, instead, considers how it is constructed and how new relations and commonalities might be articulated in the conjuncture. It seeks to repair humanity, making it capable of repairing the world it has made.

It does not imagine eradicating power, or abandoning the need to govern people. Instead, it affirms the desire to be governed—perhaps less, but certainly differently. It does not seek the immediacy of revolution but the substance of a long revolution to change the face of the habitable landscape. The PT is not a logic of tolerance, acceptance (to each his or her own), or compromise (in some illusory happy middle). While it sees the value in a war of positions, in configuring the political culture as a distribution of temporary alliances, it does not seek consensus or even consent. While it is committed to starting where people are, it is not satisfied to leave them there. The point is to move them somewhere else. The point is to forge larger affective unities-in-difference capable of reconfiguring the political culture and, ultimately, the conjuncture.

Freedom can only flourish amidst differences in new forms of belonging and sociality. I remember watching various communal dances—e.g., country line dancing, Cajun dancing, mosh pits, Jewish celebrations. I was awed by their ability to synchronize people's actions without any further demands. And I delighted in the glimmer of another world that they manifested. Sometimes, you can see possibilities in the smallest of details.

Change does not arrive in some spectacular revolution, but by advancing, whether by steps or leaps, along the many interconnected relations of power. A popular politics is strategic; it understands the different temporalities of change but is more concerned with their implications for political practice: What it can do in the short term, what it aims to do in the long term, and what it struggles to do in between. For example, it does not expect to overthrow capitalism in the near future, but it does not settle for capitalism with a friendly face. It refuses to abandon the challenge of justice by simply reversing the calculus of privilege and suffering. It cannot erase the violence inherent in so many aspects of American life, but it can force the country to face its own darkness. I could go on, as I am sure you can as well.

Forcing people to change their habits or their thoughts is bad strategy. Too often, all that accomplishes is hardening the line between public and private lives. You have to win people (hearts and mind) over or at least coax them to think and live otherwise. You have to engage them, and not merely call out their micro-habits of thought and muscle memory or accuse them of being ideologically unacceptable. A popular politics refuses to abandon the challenge of democracy by allowing it to refer only to those who are already happy to go along with our politics. It has to be capable of addressing and winning over other constituencies: Those who are not already committed; those who agree with some things but not everything; those who are not yet willing to politicize their feelings and values and take action; those who are only willing to fight the small battles they are confident of winning; those who have lost faith in the possibility of actually producing change; etc.

Every political project has to find ways of calling people to action. It has to find ways of inviting people into its spaces and offering them a variety of ways of inhabiting them. At its best, it would make its practices meaningful, mattering, and even enjoyable. Otherwise, it is likely doomed to fail. And a politics that is not willing to risk itself in the face of the challenges that others pose to it, that is not willing to accept that it may have to change in ways it had not foreseen, has not understood the nature of democratic change. After all, it is the very concept of articulation: Articulating new relations requires that both terms will be reconstituted.

Too many projects are willing to abandon those who refuse to enter its spaces or oppose the project itself. A popular politics will not abandon people. It will not throw up its hands in frustration. It will not surrender to its inability to understand how people can believe the things they do. It refuses to judge others—perhaps even those it opposes—before trying to gain a better understanding of them. It refuses to assume that it knows and understands what they believe and feel. People may be powerfully divided on some issues and in agreement—for different reasons—on others.

A popular politics refuses to assume that it knows the problems in advance. Before you can try to talk to people about a problem and its possible solution, you have to reach some agreement that it is a problem, what the problem is, and what a solution might look like. People may disagree about whether some state of affairs is actually a problem, even if they often assume that whether something is a problem is immediately and viscerally obvious. But it actually takes both intellectual and political work to make something a problem and to make it visible as a problem (or to deny that it is a problem and render it invisible).

Even if people agree that something is a problem, they are often complicated in their own right and made even more complicated by their relations with other problems. Sometimes, the feeling that there are simply too many problems, and that it is all too confusing, seems unavoidable. Whether this is any different from previous eras—there are certainly more tools, concepts, and information available today, which in turn makes the complexity more available to experience. But they may also help us find ways of organizing problems, since people are rarely happy with a laundry list of problems.

Further, in constructing something as a problem, you also have to locate it. Conservatives sometimes refer to Pope Pius XI's 1931 doctrine of subsidiarity. Subsidiarity asserts that political matters should be dealt with by the lowest, least centralized, most competent authority, i.e., at the most immediate and local level at which they can be resolved. In less provocative terms, a problem should not be generalized (or universalized) too quickly or unnecessarily. But this is rarely obvious. It, too, takes work and passionate dispute.

### Higher Education[1]

Let me tell you a story about the current attacks on universities and DEI as it might have played out in a popular politics. What might a defense of higher education look like if it had started decades earlier? (I doubt it would work today, but I could be wrong.). Here, I want to speak as a retired faculty member of a prestigious state university, the public appeal of which rests as much or more on its sports as on its academics. We should begin by partially separating the general issue of higher education from DEI. And we should make the general issue even more general and talk about education. Education has a special place in the imagination of America. The founders conceived of a nation of educated citizens, and the access to education has, over the centuries, sometimes been thought to have replaced the gold that supposedly lined the country's streets. In any case, we might agree that education is vital to living in the contemporary world. My own university even refers to itself as "the people's university."

Can we explain what we mean by education? Let me throw the first pitch. (Even I have succumbed to UNC's powerful sports culture.) I doubt that everyone is born with equal and infinite talents or capacities (as one ad claims), that people can actually be anything they want to be. Becoming an individual involves selectively nurturing some capacities and not others. Some capacities are generally thought to be necessary for survival in any society, some, in a particular society. For example, besides physical and biological capacities, people might need certain forms of literacy.

Sometimes the choice is not a choice. It is the result of environments, relations, institutions, and norms into which you are thrown and even imprisoned. Sometimes the choices are real, whether a matter of practical concerns or passionate devotions. I choose to develop my mechanical skills because my father needs me to work in his garage, or because I believe there is money to be made in the field, or because I want to be a mechanic in the Air Force, or because I love figuring out how machines work and inventing new ones, or just because I like fiddling around on the side. I may have the desire but not the capacity. I always wanted to be a rock and roll star, but unfortunately, I have no musical talent. Someone else may have the capacity but no opportunity or access to the resources that would let them develop their talent.

Education has at least two purposes: First, it allows us to explore our capacities, which will have already begun to take shape by the time formal education begins. And second, it gives us the resources and instruction necessary to develop the capacities we choose to develop, whether by necessity or passion. This is rarely a single line, although there are always prodigies who, voluntarily or not, increasingly devote their lives to one talent. For most of us, we commit ourselves to several talents, although we prioritize them depending on the purposes we assume they can serve. Moreover, the capacities we are interested in developing will likely change over time, coming and going, and sometimes coming back. This process of development can go on as long as you let it.. Therefore, generally speaking, the best education would be both deep and broad, critical and generous, challenging and inspiring. An educated person would be willing to admit their mistakes as soon as they realize it, even if their decisions were made with the best resources available at the time. They would admit up front their fallibility. (Consider the responses to Covid-19.)

In order to develop your capacities, you need two things: Skills and the material (content) on which to use those skills. The skills enable you to change the material, to make something different. You can change a lake into an irrigation system, an empty field into a bountiful harvest, and a bountiful harvest into delicious meals. You can change parts into a telescope, and a telescope into an experiment. You change words into poems, and poems can change people's minds. Of course, these are rather advanced skills. But at the beginning, the skills and materials you acquire are likely to be much simpler, fitted to your abilities, and based on the skills you have already acquired. And as your skills grow, what you are offered will advance. They will advance as much as you are willing to let them (or as much as the institutions demand of you). The idea behind the American system of graduated education is that after 12 years, individuals should have developed capacities that enable them to make a living, to find some enjoyment and meaning in their lives, and to feel valued as a citizen. Obviously, this is not working, but we cannot discuss higher education without discussing the inadequacies of K-12 education. If people have lost faith in education, then the problems begin here.

I am not going to discuss the question of what it would mean and what it would take for public education to work as well as it should. It is beyond my competence. I will say that I am not sure it ever has, because that would take serious funds, but it has worked better than it is working now. If it did, then higher education would serve any and all students whose passion (or sense of economic possibility) leads them to think they need to further develop their skills and their familiarity with materials. The individual who says, I am a great plumber but I want to be able to find solutions to the problems we can't solve. The person whose passion drives them to understand how farming can evolve to address the world's hunger crisis, or even just to make the family farm better. The student who is so fascinated by a subject, be it history or astronomy, that they have to become part of more focused conversations. The person who is dedicated to helping people who are ill or in distress. The young adult who knows they can be a great writer or artist. Or perhaps, someone decides that they simply love learning, that they love the conversations, the exposure to new and different ideas. Is higher education their only option? No, but it is certainly one option and, in many ways, an attractive one.

The painful truth is that the current system of higher education has come about partly as a result of the failures of public education and that, often, it reproduces those very failures. But again, let's start by looking at higher education itself. We know that the media have constructed (and increasingly attacked, often with good cause) a particular image of higher education. But this image is both distorted (but not entirely false) and based on the small set of Research-1 universities. That network of universities, as centers of research and knowledge production, has been seen around the world as one of America's crowning achievements. It is what has made America the leader in science and technology and, as a result, in many business enterprises. But its influence has been felt in the humanities and social sciences as well.

The arrogance of the R1 university comes from knowing that they are what most Americans think of when they imagine the university. It comes from their large research budgets and, often, large endowments. And it comes from knowing that America's universities are the envy of the world largely because of their research. (I wonder how many scholars, outside the practical sciences, could defend the significance of their research.) But that arrogance often ignores the fact that America's universities are so widely admired as much because of the education they offer to so many students as because of the research. (They do not ignore it entirely. Their reputations allow them to charge high tuition fees.)

When we consider post-secondary teaching, a very different picture emerges. There are fewer than 200 R1 schools, but almost 4000 accredited degree-granting and almost 2000 non-degree-granting, post-secondary institutions. Most people know that there are many public and private universities as well as liberal arts colleges, but are less aware that many of these are R2 and R3 universities, smaller and regional state university campuses, historically black colleges, vocational schools, and (over 1000) community colleges (the last serve 6.7 million students). This is a higher education system devoted to teaching, to helping students develop their capacities and skills. Much of what goes on at (especially elite) R1 universities is foreign to the cultures of higher education's other institutional types (and to the people who work and learn there).

Perhaps those teaching at R1 campuses should be a little less arrogant, especially since there are many reasons to question what has been happening to their research mission. In my appendix, I suggest that it is being increasingly shaped by the demands of accounting and law, politics, and the media, which has never understood or presented the real nature of scholarship and research, as an ongoing experimentation and conversation.

Teaching is perhaps the most misunderstood and misrepresented aspect of higher education, again, no thanks to the media. It probably doesn't help that most college teachers are never taught to teach; they learn by observation and, if they are lucky, apprenticeship. Many become teachers because they love it, and they spend their energy developing their skills. A surprising number end up being exciting and rigorous teachers, devoted to both what they teach and the students they teach. Like many capacities, when you reach a certain level of skill, it becomes as much an art as it is a skill. It is the art of thinking, thinking about .... Thinking has nothing to do with indoctrination. Teachers leave that to politicians, preachers, and the media. Teachers do not tell students what to think or how to think. They engage them in conversation (even if sometimes that conversation is embedded in a lecture). They teach them how to gather together as many of the different things that have been said about that skill or that material as possible, and then they teach them how to make their own conversations. Even learning skills involves a conversation; you have to look at whatever you are trying to do in different ways. There is not one way to use a hammer or a plough, or to remove a tumor, or to write a poem, or to .... It depends on ... let's talk about it.

Teachers teach students that thinking takes work, that you have to wrestle with other people's thoughts. Not indoctrination but skepticism, but not skepticism as an end in itself but a way station on the road to better talents and better answers. In a world increasingly defined by affective certainties and valorizations of experience and common sense, maybe thinking is a kind of indoctrination—an indoctrination into the values of self-reflection. Thinking means questioning, pushing your capacities further, beyond what you can see at the moment. I am not claiming that this is true of all teaching in higher universities, only that this is what good teaching does. And that there is a lot of it.

When critics argue that higher education is a bastion of liberal and left politics, often using only R1 universities as their examples, I wonder if this sense of questioning, curiosity, and uncertainty is what really frightens them. I am often embarrassed by the responses: Liberals and leftists are just smarter, more intellectual, or more open-minded than conservatives. Or to reverse the logic, intelligent and open-minded people are more likely to embrace the left. Bull! Smartness and dumbness, open- and closed-mindedness, are equally distributed between the right and the left. People come to teach or do research because they believe that ideas, knowledge, and thinking matter. Higher education is supposed to be a refuge for artists, intellectuals, and scholars—all of whom are teachers.

While the attacks often intentionally misconstrue what (elite) universities do and the problems they face, they are not entirely wrong—and many have been becoming truer over the past few decades. Nor can we deny that some of these problems have appeared in other forms of higher educational institutions. We cannot respond by simply calling the critics out as liars or anti-education, even if some are. At the very least, we have to understand why so many people are so easily caught up in and spoken by such stories. We have to locate the attacks in their context and consider that education itself, and higher education in particular, is being perceived as either a failure, a threat, or an elitist scam, in this third conjunctural moment. But we can find ways of responding that re-animate education as the engine that has always pushed America to seek out new frontiers and new successes.

Finally, let's turn to the attacks on DEI. Affirmative action was proposed in the 1960s as a band aid on and not a solution to a very serious problem. Certain socially identifiable populations were being denied access to resources in higher education and elsewhere. To some extent, the problem was internal to universities and colleges, but it was also the result of the historical and systemic failures of the K-12 system and, ultimately, of larger social histories. For higher education, affirmative action was an immediate remedy, perhaps the best that could be won at the time. I doubt that anyone thought it would solve the problem and outlive its purpose. Even before it began to be challenged in the 1970s, some discussions in higher education recognized that the programs were flawed, but that was to be expected. It could have been taken as a temporary beginning, seriously criticized, and developed into more nuanced and sophisticated alternative efforts, but by then it was already being bureaucratized and professionalized as DEI.

The more such programs were attacked, and the more the new right and, ultimately, the PRT right reassembled the affective landscape, the more DEI became a liberal conspiracy and a powerful site around which to mobilize resentment. The response was all too predictable: Its defenders circled the wagons around a flawed solution to a profound problem and continued to expand its reach. Its principles even spread into curricular and research agendas, and the privilege given to the victims of oppression and suffering in matters of truth and value was extended and further institutionalized. The under-represented demanded representation in the production of knowledge and the educational mission of the university. This is a reasonable demand and, in a small way, I participated in it. Such programs had and continue to have many positive benefits, not only for the individuals involved but for the larger university community. But they have not come close to solving the problems. Perhaps the various institutions of higher education should have found better ways, over time, to change themselves and their communities. But it is clear that many of the choices they made and defended—selective hiring practices and admissions, the creation of semi-autonomous units, the imposition of diversity requirements in the curriculum, etc.—gave the PRT right fuel for their fire of resentment and the accusations of indoctrination. The current (2025) attacks do not even have to bother to specify the programs and ignore the Supreme Court's rulings that have largely stopped affirmative action in admissions. It has become an affective attitude to be attacked, further stripped of any content like its association with charges of anti-Semitism.

Regardless of whether the resentment is legitimate, the feelings are real, and they need to be addressed rather than dismissed. Are all the people who oppose affirmative action (DEI) or who think it has gone too far racists? Certainly not all of them feel like racists. Do we even consider the possibility that while the attacks may be partly about racism, even mostly for some, they may not be only that. Those who support affirmative action never did the work of educating people on its costs and benefits. They never explained the calculations—largely about moral reparations—by which a drop in the bucket, under certain circumstance, is a reasonable step forward. The attacks have been around for 50 years, and still the defenders are unprepared.

I should add that I do not have an alternative solution waiting behind the curtains. We are dealing with institutions riddled through with the intricate histories of racisms and other forms of inequality, already affecting what capacities can be identified, actualized, or repressed. Changing it will take an enormous investment of resources (including money) and an equally enormous change in our culture. I will leave that for others to figure out, but please take the time to think.

## The Popular

A popular politics operates in the domain of the popular. The "popular" is not to be confused, at least not entirely, with popular culture. The popular describes the forms and practices that people use to live on and navigate the affective landscape—the languages, logics, and structures swirling around in and constantly reconfiguring it. These include the full range of already commercialized (and increasingly monetized), mainstream popular cultures, as well as those folk and "underground" popular musics that exist on the edges of commercial culture. They also draw from the fractured and contradictory wisdom of traditions and common sense, and the often illogical logics that people use to make decisions and judgments—right from wrong, true from false, good from bad. The popular appears largely inconsistent to an outsider and largely coherent to those living it. It is the primary locus of the affective stories we live in, the stories that speak us, the stories that speak to us and for us, and the stories that we tell to ourselves and others.

How can you expect to move people, if you reject the popular and those who inhabit it as stupid, debased, evil, ignorant, etc.? Whether people are, for example, ignorant or stupid, or duped into false consciousness, can only be sorted out by engaging with the popular. Unfortunately, all too often, the left (including the PRT left) demonstrates little more than contempt for the popular, especially when it can debunk its revolutionary politics or condemn its oppressive ideology. It does not know how to speak about or within the popular, except down to the lowest common denominator.

Having flunked Media 101, the left seems sure that popular media texts are racist, sexist, capitalist, right-wing, etc., even when they are trying not to be. They co-opt resistance and trivialize or exaggerate it. But this is not how culture, including popular culture, works. Popular culture, especially as it functions on the affective landscape, always resonates with many meanings, and its politics is usually full of contradictions. Mainstream media often present a largely urban, multicultural society, populated with differences but also fears. It may be politically conservative on many issues (e.g., patriotism, police, environmental politics, and the corruption and incompetence of state bureaucracies, although the left would probably agree with the last). But it will be politically liberal on others (e.g., increasingly, on issues of compassion, anti-hate, and social justice). And it will struggle politically or end up in ambiguity on still others (e.g., on matters of equality and stereotypes). It tends to be overwhelmingly pro-capitalist, but cracks have begun to appear. I am not suggesting the media, either legacy or cable, are now left-wing; they will do and say anything for profit. But they can be read in many different ways by different audiences. You can understand how some people can think the media are basically right-wing, while others, raised in different cultures, think that they are controlled by liberal elites. The difference might also be understood generationally: For people who began watching films and television in the 1950s and 1960s, we have come a long way (and in some instances, perhaps we have gone too far); for people who began more recently, they might reasonably think that this is not yet where we should be. The one thing the media have always done is make us afraid of the world.

The PT demands that we think about the popular in more complex and contextual ways and that we learn to speak to and in the popular, something which the right has done very successfully. A popular politics seeks ways to address the effective gaps between people's fears and desires, and between their sense of being stuck and their sense of possibility. It attempts to re-articulate the popular itself, away from its commercial determination to a sense of the many ways people express their own conditions of life and possibility. A popular politics needs to understand how the popular is formed from folk traditions, family habits, popular culture, the media, etc. And it acknowledges that it itself is embedded in and shaped by the popular. It is already implicated in the world it is trying to repair.

## A Movement of movements

Politics involves work. Those who struggled to found unions understood that they could only arise from three converging paths: Educate, Agitate, Organize. The relations among these—which lead and which have to follow—depend upon the conjuncture, although I believe there is some intention behind the order that is more than poetic.

I want to talk about organization. "A thousand points of light" made for a good campaign slogan. A thousand struggles and the political practices that accompany them are unlikely to make for an effective politics. Consider the information environment. The right has Fox News and Breitbart, and if you want to go down the rabbit hole, X; the left has the endless proliferation of Substack and its own rabbit hole, Bluesky. The left is very good at organizing and not so good at organization and what Gramsci called the long march through the institutions.

I assume that political change is more likely to happen and sustain itself if groups and movements can come together in forms of unity committed to cooperation, collaboration, and solidarity. Opting out may end up being a form of surrender to other forces. At its extreme, it may simply join with the chaos. It seems clear that the right, even when operating as expressions of the ST and PRT, has grasped the need for both formal and informal organizations. Sometimes, the left sees these efforts as conspiracies and reacts as if there were something inherently fascistic about them. That is a mistake; organizing and institutionalizing are at the heart of politics.

There are good reasons to be suspicious of existing institutions and the common forms of organizational unity. Such efforts often end up rather dismally, with the energy of struggle commandeered for other ends, often just sustaining the institutions themselves. And the struggles themselves are usually co-opted and disarmed or, at the very least, weakened to make them more palatable to greater numbers of people. The struggle is often left as a shadow of what might have been. Of course, the left should be suspicious of any such efforts. We have failed and will continue to fail if we approach them in the same ways as we have in the past, rather than reimagining the possibilities of organizations and institutions.

It might be objected that I am overstating the case. It is probably not fair to say that the left does not support organizations. On the contrary, it loves organizations. It keeps creating them. They are everywhere. I know this will get me in trouble (again) but there are too many of them, so many that they end up competing against each other, competing for people's attention and commitment in time, energy, and support. In a way, they abdicate doing the work of organizing a movement, pushing the choices onto their potential supporters, who now face almost impossible decisions.

The left is organizing all the time, everywhere. It has been most successful at community organizing, when it limits itself to local matters or specific struggles. The resurgence of union organizing was, for a while, a light shining through the darkness, due, in part, to its successful adaptation of the strategic (corporate) organizing practice of identifying vulnerabilities—either weak points or points that matter—that then can serve as the point of attack. The left has successfully organized networks of affiliation such as Indivisible and Move-on, and it is continuously constructing vaguely defined, national movements like Occupy, MeToo, and BLM. Unfortunately, these often have their 15 minutes of fame and disappear. And while their effects may linger and spread, they can too easily be challenged and undone, precisely because they lack any enduring structures capable of standing up to the forces arrayed against them.

Has the refusal to organize itself, to organize its own organizing, enabled the left to be more successful? Has it prevented it from being co-opted? No, it is going on all the time, right in front of us. Protest is reduced to symbolic commodities. Occupy has become a meme for sale. BLM has become a yard sign—also for sale. MeToo has been appropriated by the new puritanisms. Does the left have any better strategy to sustain itself? Has the refusal to organize given the left any greater control over how it is constructed and perceived?

Unfortunately, for many on the left, especially in the third conjunctural moment, such questions of organization have largely been taken off the agenda or, more accurately, they are excoriated, relegated to the failed past and the demand of unwanted power. The refusal of totality, institutions, and centralization means that the struggles and even the victories remain disconnected and isolated. Only desperation drives the left to accept the price of coordinating its efforts. Only false hope (Obama) and panic (Trump) have driven the left back into the arms of the Democratic Party. Not surprisingly, they are confronted with what they already knew: That the old forms of organized power cannot answer the conjunctural challenges and cannot accommodate the political desires and possibilities of the left.

What would a popular (PT) organized movement look like? I propose to look for guidance in the 1960s Movement of movements. This is exactly where the PRT right went for its model of a populist movement. But I need to separate the legend from the reality, at least as I experienced it and came to understand it in my research. The legend allows its critics to excoriate it for having overseen a radical redistribution of economic and political power in direct opposition to what its various elements supposedly stood for. This was one of its many unintended effects. The truth of the legend is that the Movement put forth numerous attacks on the status quo, defined an anti-establishment politics, recognized the power of culture, and was populated in large part by baby boomers, many of whom came from dominant class fractions (i.e., college students). It created many sites and forms of struggles. It challenged and changed many fundamental social relations and cultural assumptions. Whatever the participants may have thought of themselves, they were not, for the most part, revolutionaries, although many were utopians. The truth of the legend is that the U.S. has been living in the shadow of baby boomers for a long time, in both positive and negative ways.

The legend was a story the media created and, like most such stories, its truths were outweighed by its exaggerations, erasures, trivializations, and attacks, which were offered without any opportunity to think and respond. The legend was useful because it made many of the styles and practices available to be co-opted and sold, both as media events and commodities. It was easier (and more profitable) for the media to focus on college campuses and youth cultures. It was easier (and more profitable) for the media to market the irony of a rebellion within the dominant class than to sort out the many dispersed constituencies involved. The legend painted a portrait of either well-intentioned but naïve youth or spoiled and manipulated youth. The media suggested they all wanted to believe they were the heart and soul of a revolution.

The legend painted a picture of a Movement divided into two camps: Politicos and hippies, anarcho-communists and spiritualists (drop-outs and druggies). Both camps tried and failed to reconcile the contradiction between their claims to communitarianism and individualism. And both eschewed the need for structure and organization. So the legend goes. Those in the Movement were set up to romanticize and identify with the images of a failed revolution.

Unfortunately, many baby boomers were actually just naïve and parochial enough to embrace the media's legend, despite their own experience and despite the fact that, everywhere else, they were claiming that the media lied— about Vietnam, the economy, shady political dealings, and even the anti-war protests and protestors. The media (except for the Movement's alternative media) lied about what was happening around the world. They didn't tell Americans about all global uprisings, protests, and countercultures. Instead, they presented the Movement as if we were alone, divided even among ourselves, dispersed across the nation.

We need a better story. It would start by recognizing that the Movement was always messy, sometimes appearing to border on chaos (especially to outsiders). It was composed of a myriad of sites, issues, and tactics of struggles, projects and styles, lifestyles and political cultures, musics and popular cultures, informal organizations and formal institutions, leaders and those who refused leaders, constituencies, ideologies, and affective regimes, as well as a lot of social diversity. And all sorts of events, everywhere, all the time.

It created its own habitable landscape on an increasingly affective landscape. On any day, you might have: Tried to raise the Pentagon to exorcise the evil spirits, been tripping on LSD while practicing Tantric meditation before returning to your hippie commune, been trampled by mounted police at a Yippie gathering (led by Abbie Hoffman, who constantly told us he was not leading us) in Grand Central Station, watched El Teatro Campesino in support of La Raza, attended a rally for the Panthers, given out food at a shelter for the homeless, marched against the war in Vietnam, worked at the office of the Draft Resistance, listened to a free concert by the Dead while high (on freely distributed drugs) in Central Park, met with the dictatorial publisher of the underground newspaper for which you wrote a column, overseen the curriculum and finances for the alternative university, worked with the local library to organize a celebration for Earth Day, attended an SDS meeting—led by the very solemn chairperson, in jacket and tie, where the drug culture was condemned and you discussed whether to boycott the next presidential election—harvested crops on an urban commune, attended a demonstration against police brutality, attended a well-organized meeting of the Alternative Media Alliance, or attended a rally for the local congressperson. Oh, and through it all, you were probably attending classes or working at a job and, of course, partying (move your ass and your mind will follow!).

Yet, it was ordered and organized. There were all sorts of connections, interactions, and networks. It was always composed and composing itself albeit in strange ways. Because all this was taking place already on the affective landscape. Many of those ways, including the institutions, were collective paths through the affective landscape. There were also individuals' paths, logics of articulation, defined by and defining the positions you lived.

I draw three conclusions from this story: First, there were many ways an individual could participate in or live inside the Movement. Most of them involved doing lots of different things that might not seem related but were, affectively. Second, the Movement included a variety of organizations, from ill-defined collectives to mission-specific institutions. Some were hierarchical; others opposed hierarchy. Some had clear leaders; others refused leaders or simply operated without them. Some were quite formally structured, others celebrated their structurelessness. To some participants, that mattered. To others, it did not. Some had identities, others did not. Most organizations functioned as spaces open to any number (albeit limited) of ways of belonging to or identifying with the group. They encompassed many positions, practices, and stories. They existed as comfortable places to tell stories.

Finally, despite the apparent chaos, the Movement had a sense of its own unity that could be called upon when necessary. It was stable enough to mobilize and act, and unstable enough to change and adapt. It was not a unity to which every participant responded every time, but it was a unity just the same. You could experience it at protests, at concerts, on the streets, etc.

It was taken for granted because people were constantly constructing it in the ways they lived it. It defined a space that expanded and shrank as it sought to encompass all the ways people moved within the Movement. Waxing poetic, it was a space of many speeds, rhythms, and vibrations. It invited many ways of belonging and possibility but also asked for many obligations. (Do your own thing sounded better than it played out.)

It existed as a unique space of improvisation. Sometimes, it sounded like musicians playing to and around a common riff. At other times, it sounded like a freer improvisation in which there is no common riff. The players come together and move apart through the constant construction of rhythms, textures, and timbres. The riffs appear and disappear, temporary, partial, and creative. And yet the riffs, the relations, are absolutely necessary—they are what the music is all about.

The appeal to music is not coincidental, because the unity of the movement was not ideological, ethical, or even immediately political. It was an affective composition, perhaps the first attempt to realize and respond to the emergence of the affective landscape! It was always reaching to change the affective landscapes of people's lives, empowering them to renegotiate realities and repair the world. The Movement was attempting to be a way of living, aimed against an increasingly unstable, irrational, and self-destructive affective landscape.

I do not mean to romanticize nor wax nostalgic for the Movement (although I probably cannot avoid doing some of each. It was the best and the worst of times. It was a lot like the current times.) I certainly do not want to argue about its many successes and even more failures. I offer it as a potential model of a popular movement. It was an ordered chaos, a particular kind of unity-in-difference. But it existed in the first conjunctural moment, and so much has changed. Whatever is possible and necessary in the third moment will have to be very different, but it might draw some lessons from the Movement. I want only to offer some suggestions, to point toward some possibilities.

A popular Movement of movements could create imaginative ways of connecting grassroots struggles, social movements, political, intellectual, and cultural organizations and institutions, electoral parties and state apparatuses, and corporate enterprises. Think about the last two. A movement that would include key elements of the very system it opposes. It would not simply partner or compromise with, or reform, on the one hand, corporations and corporate responsibility and, on the other hand, the institutions of representative democracy. Nor would it appeal to pragmatic convenience, using them as resources when necessary. You have to imagine re-articulating them as part of a larger movement. No one said this was going to be easy or quick.

And it would have to close the enormous gap that exists quite commonly between activists and policy wonks. It would have to take the nitty-gritty practicalities of governance and economics seriously. For example, I recently had an argument about the administration's brutal treatment of an individual. When it appeared that the criminal courts would not provide any justice, my colleague happily imagined the civil settlement that would be leveled against the government. Justice would be served according to the rules of just compensation. I asked him what he knew about these rules, and where he thought the funds would come from. Not much. The money for such judgments is part of the calculation (partially through insurance) of discretionary spending. And that means something else will ultimately have less funding. Is this any way to impart justice? Or consider the common practice of petitioning particular institutional administrators to take actions and accomplish goals. My guess is that some of them would like nothing better than to do what the petitioners ask. But, in what will always sound like an excuse, they will plead that they are operating within very tight constraints. Anything they might do will likely have equally serious, unintended consequences. I had one friend call me and say, just tell me how to do this. Essentially, we pass the buck. A popular movement would build relations between the different kinds of decision-making that are involved in actually trying to change the world.

It might also forge connections across the different ways the local, the regional, and the national are organized. It could rethink the boundaries differentiating the urban, suburban, rural, and wilderness, making each more complicated and more open-ended. It may even find ways to limit the proliferation and redundancy of organizations, often the result of well-intentioned people or groups who are sure no one is doing precisely what they are. Maybe they are right, but a common result is to add to an already overpacked, competitive marketplace of resistance. It needs to be able to coordinate the actions of multiple movements and groups.

A popular  movement will be wary of imposing an agenda on the long revolution, but it probably should not define itself in purely oppositional terms. It seeks a better, more humane world. It seeks to repair the world. It doesn't have to assume complete unity and agreement around a specific sense of its shared project; it can see that project as always evolving. It is continually being shaped, and not necessarily by the loudest, most active, or most erudite voices. The project emerges out of all the efforts to organize the movement as an affective landscape.

A popular movement might create the possibility for individuals to engage, participate, and identify with different elements in different ways. People might be willing to make different kinds of commitments at different sites. Different sites might demand different levels and kinds of commitments. Both might have their own conditions on any possible relation. Rather than pre-arranged, fixed relations, these would be coalescent, sticky ways of belonging, of entering and leaving, of consenting to identifications and allegiances, and of constructing forms of stability. (Listen to the music!)

This allows it to be open enough to reach beyond itself, inviting strangers into common spaces, and generous enough to allow neighbors to follow their own paths. It would accept that people can share common goals but disagree with the analysis of where we are and the strategies being used or that they can share common strategies but not common goals. It would accept that people can agree on some issues, disagree on others, and still be part of a common unity-in-difference. It might even be open to the possibilities of reaching into what is thought to be the opposition, opening up the crack where people are living in their own contradictions, to win them into new affective possibilities. Remember, nothing is guaranteed for one and all times.

A popular movement would think strategically about and be open to a broad range of tactics[2] and forms of institutionalization. Asking what tactic or form is appropriate to a particular context or situation involves considering their potential effectiveness. That effectiveness could involve not only the immediate struggle but also the larger context. This tactic may work here but not there. It may have multiple effects, and in one context, one effect may be more significant than another. Institutions have histories and what worked at one time may not work at another. The movement has to be open enough to recognize the need for institutions when the moment demands, without granting it power beyond that required for the struggle at hand.

And it would approach problems of authority and expertise (and whatever kinds of power they require) similarly. Whether visible or not, organizations always have forms of authority and expertise. They also have processes of decision-making. The reality of political organization is that decisions have to be made, and real tasks have to be assigned and accomplished. And these work only because they are distributed across many positions with different responsibilities, including not only the expert and the authority, but the participant, the organizer, the leader, the observer, the supporter, the witness,[3] etc. That is, they work only as part of the movement itself.

A popular movement is a coming community. It is a unity-in-difference that welcomes differences. It seeks them out. It constructs them. Just as importantly, it experiments to find new differences and new capacities for living with differences. But it refuses the easy ways out offered by utopian, dogmatic, self-righteous pronouncements. Sometimes, and judging from the past, often, these differences will lead to arguments and conflicts. The affective landscape of a popular movement, as well as the spaces of the various organizations and institutions within it, are fields of convivially lived conflicts. Resolving conflicts over priorities and tactics will never be easy or fully successful, but such efforts are surely better than the fragmentation and forced obeisance that too often undermine our collective efforts. Those conflicts are part of how the movement constructs itself as something to be realized, an achievement. It is this re-articulation of present futurity that allows victories to resonate throughout, and defeats to elicit collective reflection, strengthening the whole so that it can together resist future attacks and defeats and project its own possible futures.

Not surprisingly, I do not know how this is to be accomplished in the present conjuncture. I do believe that there have been previous moments when such experimental unities-in-difference were attempted: e.g., the Popular Front, the civil rights movement, and the 1960s Movement. And they were, if only temporarily, successful. More importantly, I do not know if the affect is right. I heard about a Mexican writer who said that the anti-globalization movement was doomed to fail because it had no music. Where is the contemporary popular?

## Conclusion

Is there a way forward or does the PT become merely speculative? The answer depends upon a rather strange aspect of the Popular Tendency. It does not seek its own victory against the other conjunctural tendencies, including the PRT. That would simply augment the present chaos and possibly reconstitute a war of maneuver. It does not reject them. Nor does it seek some happy co-existence living alongside them.

Instead, the PT seeks to change the context, the political culture, in which they operate. Rather than offering its own logic for a new stable balance, apart from the other tendencies, it seeks a balance among the tendencies. It makes living on the affective landscape into a constant production of new points of balance and leverage amongst at least some of the contending tendencies.

Let me tell you a story. I am most definitely a New Yorker. Yet I lived for over two decades in Champaign-Urbana, a small college town in central Illinois. Let me just say that it was not the most exciting, interesting, or beautiful place (although it was within driving distance of Chicago). Friends would often ask why I chose to live there. Why I chose to teach there rather than in the rich, radical environs of New York. My answer? New York has many wonderful advantages, but also many unpleasant features. Champaign has other advantages. My living in Champaign-Urbana was neither a calculation nor a compromise; it was not a "trade off"—tit for tat.

It was about finding a comfort zone of livability, what astronomers call the Goldilocks or habitability zone. I found a balance point there between my desires and pressures. Or if you prefer, it was a fulcrum which enabled me to be content-satisfied-comfortable with my life and to meet my social and public obligations. It was, temporarily, a "sweet spot" (yes, I like the sexual connotations). You cannot break it down into its benefits and costs. It's more of a quality. It's a feeling that this is where I can and do belong, even if only for a while. I suppose, if pressed, I could have given reasons for feeling that this was a good place to stop and do what I wanted to do, but they would be only afterthoughts. I would not say it was a place where I was particularly happy (I think happiness is overrated in a consumerist world). It just felt like it was the right place to be for the moment. And then it wasn't.

But the very fact that it is so hard to describe in anything but cliches suggests that there is something more, especially in more collective and political ways. The sweet spot on our collective affective landscape is where enough people (yes, I know that needs work) can belong, where they can feel at home. That is what I mean by a moment of balance. That is what the PT proposes. But it is not a stable and singular notion of balance. It is a discordant unity-in-difference that is constantly being recomposed on the affective landscape. And it involves a constant re-articulation of the tendencies as they engage each other. It is an attempt to live with the ongoing construction of our reality.

Perhaps I am thinking about what comes next, after the chaos, after the third conjunctural moment. I do not even know where to begin. Perhaps a good place to start would be wherever conversations are possible; perhaps those of us convinced that American political culture has to be radically transformed, and that the left has to rethink its role, need to speak up, despite the abuse we are likely to receive. My pessimism returns. Still, given where the country seems to be heading, we can't do much worse.

## Notes

1  This section arose out of a conversation with Megan Wood.
2  Tactics might include: direct actions, demonstrations, mobilizations, petitions, occupations, performances, free spaces, alternative economies, online networks, boycotts, refusals, symbolic protests, community organizing, squatting, collective assemblies, consensus-building, spiritual and religious appeals, and prefigurative and intentional communities, but also elections, legislation (at every level), regulations, judicial battles, budgetary fights, media exposure and PR campaigns, and institution-building. I draw the line personally at violence, except under the most extraordinary circumstances.
3  Consider the case of the embedded journalist who witnessed the My Lai massacre. Where did his ethical responsibility lie? Should he have intervened to prevent the deaths, even if he assumed he would fail and might himself have been killed? Was reporting the event in the hope that the perpetrators would be punished (only one was), thus preventing future occurrences (it did not), the right thing to do?

# 15
# THAT'S HOW THE LIGHT GETS IN (STORIES)

Educate, agitate, organize. The PT understands that agitation and organization are not, by themselves, sufficient to repair the world; it requires education. It is committed to education, not in the narrow, institutional sense, but as the need to work through the popular in order to change the stories in which people live. It recognizes that people live in stories, which are always fragile, fungible, imperfect, incomplete, and bound to particular circumstances and contexts and to particular pre-conceptions and life-experiences. It recognizes that engaging with these stories demands that we enter into the spaces and speak in the languages of the popular. The PT is all about stories. It is a continuing story about the stories we tell.

It seeks to tell better stories and, thereby, to change people's experiences and feelings, to change the ways they live in the world. Better stories try to get people to think about the stories in which they are thinking, try to get them unstuck, as it were, and move them, re-configuring their paths on the affective landscape. Stories define the limits of what we can imagine, what we can conceive of as a possibility. Even if we are convinced that our story is right, better stories do not seek to replace one story with another, usually by reversing the polarities. Better stories open up the field of possibilities, allowing people to imagine beyond any single story or small set of stories. Most importantly, better stories demand understanding before both change and judgment, recognizing that this is an ongoing engagement. In other words, don't judge before you actually have reason to think you know what you are judging, and don't start changing something before you know what you are changing. But don't think of understanding as merely a first step—something like a necessary demonstration of trust—to be left behind, as if,

DOI: 10.4324/9781003662587-19

afterward, you can "rationally" dismiss everything you have understood as lies, ignorance, or irrationalities.

Better stories start where people are, not where others think they should be. They begin by asking: What is their understanding of and response to their conditions, their sense of who they are, of what is changing, and what is possible to change? What stories already speak to or for them and why? Everyone has their own stories to tell, even if many of those stories are not of their own choosing. Stories tell people what matters, but they cannot determine whether people embrace everything the story prioritizes. The stories speak the people and people use them to tell their own story. We need to understand how people inhabit stories to create the mattering maps that guide their decisions and allegiances.

Better stories begin by listening to people's stories. The PT does not accept them or tolerate them; it seeks to understand them and to understand what they do, how they enable people to feel what they do and act the ways they do. Why are they called into those stories and not others? How do they live inside those stories? What is the backstory, which may tell us something about why people allow themselves to be spoken by particular stories: perhaps there are histories and material conditions at play. Perhaps there are local struggles and social issues. Consider the complexity of people's relations to the changes that both characterize and propel modernity: They are often not so much a part of the forces of modernization or even riding them, as it were, into the future; they are just as commonly standing alongside them, judging, resisting, being crushed by them, or trying to avoid them at all costs.

Most people think that they make the choices they do for good reasons, even if their reasons are defined by matters of faith or feeling. The stories from which such choices are made don't have to seem rational or reasonable to anyone except those living inside them. And until we understand how they have come to live inside them, we cannot know how to re-articulate them and how to move the people. Of course, sometimes, someone may think that they have no choice, but presumably, they have reasons for believing they have no choice. Reasons are often not cognitively rational; they may be entirely emotional, as in "I did it because I love him" or "God told me to do it." Still, even such "irrational" reasons are reasons: I know I love him and that this is good for him; I know God's voice when I hear it. They know it because they feel it and they feel it because they are living inside stories that tell them it is true and right.

Stories tell people what to feel and how to experience their lives. Better stories have to accept that such feelings and experiences are real and apparently reasonable responses—even if they have been constructed that way in the stories—to those who live them. They may even carry some truth. The point is not to moralize the ways people feel or to condemn them out of hand. Most people, however different the stories they listen to and tell, are struggling for whatever matters to them, and the more that people feel like they have lost control over their lives, or that the world has gone mad, the more likely they are to both shrink the world they care about and reduce the larger world to a series of vague abstractions. Most people are trying to do the best they can with the resources they have. For example, a better story accepts the reality that the stories of polarization have created, but it seeks to rescue a more nuanced understanding of the ebb and flow of historical changes and refuses to end up with absolute positions of certainty capable of dividing society into opposing camps.

## Engaging with Stories

Engaging with stories means thinking with them. It means questioning them, not on their truth but on their conditions of possibility. It cannot be accomplished as a conversation, although it often takes place in conversations. When we think about conversations, it often evokes nostalgic recollections of community. And we imagine bonds of affection, such as what makes "good neighbors" or the sense of decency that arises at another's distress. Perhaps these do not begin with the affective realities of our political relations. Conversation may also evoke notions of a common ground, either at the beginning or at the end, if not both. Where do we find these? Perhaps in shared "American" values. But again, these are often precisely what the struggles are about; perhaps in some version of the American dream, such as making a better life for your children. But many Americans simply want to pass on a life that they have found to be meaningful and satisfying. It is not sufficient to recognize that these will be "difficult conversations." Such efforts, however well-intentioned, are often affectively patronizing and a sham. In most cases, they are ultimately aimed at deconstructing the other person's bad story in favor of persuading them of the truth of your own. And engaging is different than the more recent revival of "building bridges," which seems to be all about vulnerability and forgiveness. One person admits the error of their ways and asks for forgiveness. Conversation by itself cannot significantly alter the field of possibilities, and the task of telling better stories is not conversational in any literal (face-to-face) sense.

A popular politics requires an engagement between discordant bodies of stories in political culture itself. It is about finding new compositions and changing the field of cultural possibilities in the next moment, always in the face of uncertainty and the continuing likelihood of failure; but, thankfully, there is always still a next moment and a next and .... It is a question of moving people into stories, of recomposing their experiences and opening new places where they can find themselves.

Engaging is different than simply judging the comparative merits or truth of different stories. Imagine two Congressional reports. Each one claims to prove the existence of an illegal conspiracy involving public officials and government agencies, by one side of the political spectrum. Each report accuses the other of being a conspiracy to fabricate and disseminate misinformation. Each report is the proof of a conspiracy and a conspiracy of lies. Both are in the Congressional record; both have evidence, witnesses, affidavits, etc. People can argue about the relative weight of the evidence, or the objectivity of the witnesses, or the neutrality of the committee members, but still, on the surface, they both appear to have a certain claim to truth (especially since almost no one has actually read them). Putting aside whatever skepticism we may have about any government report, why is one true and the other lies? Why are we so sure of it? What do we accomplish by presenting ourselves as the privileged knowers of truth and calling out the other side as liars? Or are we now cynically condemned to accept everyone's truth at face value?

When we talk about the truth of a story, we are talking about its ability to capture people, to offer them places in the story. By entering into the story and taking up those places, people live inside the reality the story constructs. The story lets them experience the world in meaningful and comfortable ways. It organizes the inchoate feelings they bring to the story and gives them a sense of their own value and the struggles they face. Engaging with stories changes the questions we need to ask. How does a story work? How is it made to be true? How does it work alongside the other stories people occupy or don't occupy? How are different stories articulated onto the affective landscape? And, at the extreme, how do stories make people ignorant? But if you ask this, you probably have to also ask, how do your stories enable you to make such judgments? And do you know what judgments their stories make of you?

We have to recognize that people are not reducible to any single story they inhabit; they are inseparable from but not simply the sum of those stories. People speak in and from many stories, and sometimes they carry their voices with them across stories. Sometimes, the stories work together and speak with one voice. Even that unity-in-difference is tense, often held together with a rubber band, so to speak. Other times, stories will scream at each other and, sometimes, they will attempt to silence others. Even though there may be many stories speaking, there are always others trying to be heard.

At any moment, individuals are caught in a raucous—often screaming—melee among the many voices inside their head, and those outside trying to get in and be heard (or, better, to seduce them into their landscape). Many of the voices are incomplete and contradict each other. People can have more than one thought or feeling—even at the same time. They can experience something differently, and respond to it differently, both at different moments and, sometimes, at the same moment. Someone could be a racist in one story and opposed to racism in another. "Ordinary, decent people" may also be racist. Rarely is any voice ever alone, or ever totally consistent. Perhaps some voices demand to be the only one speaking, but they will likely fail or, at least, succeed only temporarily. Double consciousness? This is the hell of a consciousness always struggling to get a hold of itself. The distribution and organization of our many voices is a crucial aspect of power often carried out by the stories being told and those in our head.

I wonder if that means we should hesitate before blaming individuals for their positions, their values, and even their dreams, however bad we may judge them to be. We do not know—and will probably never know—what the conditions were that brought the individual into those stories. That does not mean we stop making judgments. But we are judging the stories and the affective spaces they produce. And we are trying to understand how such stories have become acceptable, reasonable, and even commonsensical. Changing the stories requires knowing how and why people feel included in some stories and excluded from others. That entails taking the measure of the already available stories and the affective landscape. Then we might think about offering new stories in which people can find themselves, stories that establish new relations and new ways of living their conditions.

We may find that we even share some of their feelings and some of their judgments, if not their stories. You can respect people and accept their experiences without condoning their stories. You can see how their truths are being viscerally shaped by stories of polarization and identity. You can see how these stories direct them to lay blame—over there, on those people or institutions. And often, you can feel how easy the stories make it to find solutions in acts of hatred, aggression, and violence. If the dominant (liberal-modern) institutions have failed them, why should they continue to support them? Why not just tear them down or, at the very least, constantly call out their defenders for what they are—liars and hypocrites, greedy and arrogant people who think they have all the answers, even when reality proves them wrong.

But you have to be careful, self-conscious, and self-critical. You want to make some stories uncomfortable enough that people might be open to hearing other stories, however slight the differences. You cannot do that by simply substituting your own story, as if you know it is correct. A better story is harder to produce than that. For example, if any felt resentment toward affirmative action is always and already incurably racist, there is not a lot of space for moving people into a better story. This doesn't mean you cannot offer your own stories, experiences, and feelings as part of the engagement. It does mean that you cannot assume they are the best stories before you have even begun. It is better to remember that nobody's "what's right" is everybody's "what's right."

Engagement doesn't mean that you start by knowing where you want to end up. You may feel confident that your own stories are better. But you will have to give up some of the comfort you feel in your own habitual stories, your (political and intellectual) common sense. And you will have to give up the self-righteousness we all feel in the safety of our moral codes. Any attempt to construct better stories in a popular politics asks you to put yourself at risk. After all, a better story for another is also likely to be a better story about yourself as well. Engagement asks you to be willing to be changed by the effort to change others. And it asks that you be open to being surprised by where you seem to be heading. After all, we are all constantly organizing the cacophony of voices. We are all spoken by stories not entirely of our making or choosing. But we cannot let ourselves (or others) entirely off the hook. People have some responsibility for the stories and tendencies they inhabit since they are never completely imprisoned within them.

## Everyday Stories

As long as I have been writing, I have been told that people want simple stories. Sometimes I have been told that they are only capable of understanding simple stories. At the very least, they don't like complicated stories. So, do what the media do: Speak to the lowest common denominator. Speak in ways that are always and already understandable to everyone. This is a ruse! Better stories are about expanding the possibilities of stories. The best stories need not be the most complicated. But they must embrace the complexity.

Sometimes people are put off because a story starts by assuming that it knows more than the people it is addressing. People, on the contrary, may assume that they already know something (or think they know something) about the topic. For example, when I travel abroad, nothing irritates me as much as people telling me about what's going on in America. They often talk as if they know more than I do. Maybe they do, but I am going to start out being suspicious. But people are also put off when they cannot find or feel themselves in the imagery, the vocabulary, the characters, etc. We need stories that are complex enough to capture a broad range of relations, experiences, and feelings, not merely of those telling the stories but of those we are trying to reach, although no story can speak to everyone.

It is easy to assume that people's stories come from the outside, from the church, politicians, schools, and, most especially, the media. Do we understand how people live in the disparate and changing relations that are assumed to exist between entertainment and fiction (popular culture) on the one hand, and "reality" and experience on the other hand? Have we familiarized ourselves with the massive body of research, flaws and all, on the subject? We criticize the media and popular culture for not doing what it is not supposed to do, i.e., present a true picture of the world, without understanding what it is doing. We make it into an all-powerful monster that is producing our world for us, all by itself. Popular culture does not immediately imprint itself upon people's minds as truth. But it certainly plays a major role in defining people's expectations and fears, especially when they have no other experiences or trusted sources. Unfortunately, the owners of the media institutions care mostly about what sells—simplicity sells, intense emotions like fear and sentimentality sell, and the things we think we already know about the world (in part because we have been watching the same damn stories for years) sell.

Consider some of the stories the media repeatedly tells. Aside from assuring us that every problem can be solved by some act of consumption, the media have, for some time, largely told a second kind of story, which has evolved from melodrama to thriller to horror, the point of which is to make us afraid of the world. Media scholars have demonstrated this since the 1960s. The media not only exaggerate the dangers (e.g., crime), they have, especially in recent decades, expanded on the possible threats to our lives and well-being. To a large extent, this has fallen on representations of social diversity: Not merely who is included (if they are in fact included at all) but where, how often, and how they are included (in the dark shadows or in the thoroughfares of everyday life). Today, no doubt responding to public pressure, diversity and multiculturalism have marched out of the shadows and the closets and become highly visible.

But we need to ask: Whose reality is this? Whether it is stories of absence, threat, or liberal multiculturalism, some people will feel alienated. It is not their world. How are they supposed to respond? Is it really so hard to have some sense of why various people might feel that their needs are being ignored, that they are being treated unfairly, and that they are not being included in the stories the media tells the nation and the nation tells itself? They may feel that the America on the screen is not the country they live in every day. Am I talking about people of color? The poor? Gay communities? Various mistreated and oppressed groups? Of course, but also rural and post-industrial working class constituencies, especially outside the northern coastal areas. These latter groups might feel that the media have, in recent decades, increasingly included certain minorities[1] but not their lives and problems, at least not without blatantly stereotyping and ridiculing them. Such groups are likely to feel that someone else is determining their fate; they certainly do not feel particularly privileged.

Have we forgotten that for many, the most powerful sources of stories are traditions, local cultures, and intimate relations? Those conversations continue to exist, despite our continued fears about the technological colonization of face-to-face interactions and despite our fears that they merely reproduce the worst possible stories. What about the unremembered stories, the stories they were raised on, and that their parents were raised on, and that their parents' parents were raised on? What about the stories told in churches and on playgrounds, stories that filled the air and flavored the food and set the moods of their everyday lives growing up? However polarized we may think we are, we need to realize just how many stories there are. There was a TV show called *The Naked City*; it opened with the line: "There are 8 million stories in the naked city." Maybe we don't need to tell every individual's stories, but we do need to realize that there are many more stories—whether of rural poverty or of rural race relations, for example—than we assume. What would a politics look like that took that diversity into account?

The call to understand before judging, and to be willing to hear the truth in other people's stories, is not easy. It can become extremely difficult at times, for example, when confronted with stories of hatred, oppression, and violence. How can we engage with stories we find repugnant or even worse? How can we take on the task of understanding, for example, the stories of racism? We have to constantly remind ourselves that understanding does not offer absolution, forgiveness, justification, or even, necessarily, explanation. But understanding might identify the cracks that could disrupt stories just enough so that we might begin to change them. And then we might begin to move at least some people into more open and generous stories. I haven't seen any better options.

Perhaps we can start slowly. Many of the PRT right's criticisms of the current moment are not all that different from those on the left. Many of the experiences and feelings expressed on both sides bear at least formal similarities, although each side has its own ways of framing, blaming, and solving them. I understand, even share, the feeling that society has lost its moral compass, given the rampant commercialization and celebration of sex, violence, and greed, given the selfishness and the lack of goodwill and charity, given how we treat our children, non-human life, and the planet, given the content of the media, etc. I share the sense that liberalism and modernity have failed to live up to their promises (even as the world has made very real progress). Perhaps it is more accurate to say that liberalism and modernity seem to have gone as far as they can and that the costs outweigh the benefits. But I admit that I do not understand how the PRT right's stories end up where they do, or how to reach into their story to find the possibility for different endings. I suppose this book is my better story.

For example, when I try to engage with contemporary stories of racism, I know, in my head, that there is a long history at work here. I know, in my head and my gut, that these have been and continue to be present in my life, and part of the water in which perhaps all of us have been swimming for our entire lives. But I also know that they are always accompanied by many other stories, some even older, some more powerful. I can accept that such stories are among the voices in my head. I would like to think that I cannot hear them or, at least, that if there are any voices of hatred in my head, they are quickly drowned out by the other stories and voices. Are there moments when I feel fear and anger toward someone based on identity? Perhaps, but again, I hope they are only fleeting, overwhelmed by other voices and stories, other memories and affections.

I do not yet understand how people find so much truth in such stories that they can overwhelm other more generous (e.g., Christian) stories. Sometimes, I think I can catch a glimmer (as a Jew, a scholar, and an activist) of the experiences and traditions out of which they have arisen. I can grasp something of the work they have done and are doing to sustain themselves and provide affective succor. I have come to understand it just a little better since moving to the rural South.

30 years ago, my wife and I moved into a landscape filled with stories, a land soaked in blood and sweat and tradition, but also food and love and friendship. It is a land that has birthed so many stories, and a landscape that has been made by the telling of those stories. There are stories loudly repeated every day, stories that are only whispered in secure places, and stories that are mostly unheard and unrecognized. There are unremembered stories and the stories in the back of people's minds. There are the stories they were raised on and, repeating myself, stories told in church and on playgrounds, stories that fill the air and flavor the food. There are stories that have been repeated for decades, repeating old differences. For many of the people I have spoken to, there are stories they did not ask for and, often, stories for which there were no comfortable alternatives. There are stories that were forcibly suppressed and later re-animated in new contexts. There are stories so quiet they are available only as part of the profound ways the spatial landscapes condition their lives, and the possibilities, necessities, and likelihoods of certain relations and ways of relating.

I could hear stories about isolation, abandonment, failure, betrayal, and a loss of dignity and purpose. I could hear fear and anger in the face of the unknown, in the face of changes they do not understand. (But then, truthfully, neither do I, and I have many of the same feelings but perhaps different stories.) I could hear stories of hope, care, and generosity, of conviviality and concern, of their celebration of lives lived as well as they could be, of the desire to continue that life, and the acceptance of its end. I could hear stories of apathy, of resignation, of resilience, and of having accepted their lot in life (because that is what good people do, or what God gave them, or …). And there were always more stories. (I am aware that this could sound too romanticizing.)

But I could also begin to understand why stories about the interventionist state having destroyed their way of life speak to and for them. Why stories about how those with economic or cultural power, those who occupy the very social hierarchies championed by the liberal-left, disrespect and disadvantage them. This is all magnified by the PRT right's ability to personalize the stories and construct their experiences into feelings of resentment and hopelessness.[2]

And I could also begin to understand why they might take up stories of blame, and how blame can become hatred. But I am far from understanding exactly how the stories work. In the PRT right's stories, they recompose the concrete hatred captured in the long history of racist stories (primarily anti-black, but also anti-Jewish, anti-Catholic, etc.) to identify a new, abstract black subject. That abstract subject can encompass almost any stranger as an object of hatred.[3] In the stories, the more abstract the hated other, the better. At the same time, the stories move from the abstract black subject to the concreteness of everyday hatred and the possibilities of violence. The result is that the stories start where many racist stories start. They distinguish between the known and unknown black subjects. We do not hate the black man across the road but black people on welfare in the city, or the bad ones we see on TV. We do not hate the "good" immigrant who owns the restaurant in town but the immigrants flooding the border and taking white people's jobs. But then, the hatred and violence return home, making all others into potential strangers and targets of hatred and violence. Hatred becomes banal and predictable in new ways. How do people live such contradictions? (Remember, we all live our own contradictions.) After 30 years, I am just beginning to feel the accumulation of stories and just scratching the surface of the land we inhabit. These efforts are also part of the story I am telling in this book.

I am beginning to find a way to understand their stories. I am even beginning to find ways to understand the PRT's stories of absolute certainty. These are stories to which people are so powerfully attached, so absolutely certain of the Truth of their judgments and the horrific consequences of their failures, that they simply cannot listen to other stories. They are convinced it would mean instant death. When I was little, I went with my best friend to a mass at his Greek Orthodox church. But I was terrified of leaving because I believed that I would be struck by lightning for my transgression. I was not, and I moved on. But I have limits. I have not yet figured out how to deal with stories that justify violence, at least for the moment. I cannot find the compassion. I have not yet figured out how to deal with stories that have transmogrified religions of love into hatred. I cannot comprehend the rationalities. These stories are, at least for me, beyond the pale.

I have to admit that I am troubled by the last sentence, not least because it can too easily be read back into the problem of the limits of tolerance. How can you know which people living in which stories can be usefully addressed and which cannot? Part of our task must be to learn how to tell the difference: To know where and when it is possible to change the stories, to change people, and to change ourselves. There may well be stories we will never be able to understand well enough to find the cracks through which we might begin to let in the light and to prise apart the contradictions. But can we ever know this in advance?

## Understanding

I have repeatedly said that understanding has to precede judgment. It begins by locating a story and figuring out the work that the particular story does. Let me remind you of my general description of such work. Stories give us a place to inhabit, and ways to live at that place; they define what a problem is and shape our inchoate feelings into manageable affective responses. They give us directions for moving, telling us where and how we can stop, care, and belong. They define both the inside and the limits of a habitable landscape, as well as the places where we can be open to other possibilities. They define where change is necessary and where it is forbidden; where truth and lies, good and evil, are to be found and how to recognize them. As such, they are not texts to be interpreted but maps of the affective landscape that lead people into and through the conjuncture. The issue is less about the content than the specificities of the paths and the places they constitute.

Stories—whether a narrative, a character, a relation of colors, or a sound-image—call people into their space-times, rhythms, and possibilities. And they are always trying to get themselves (or bits of themselves) "inside" your head or, better, to get your head inside the story; they invite you to find yourself already in the story, by offering a place—a voice—in which you think you can hear yourself. Stories, if they are to work, have to speak to and from or at least intersect with the stories that are already inside your head and the voices that already speak you.

Stories have their own histories. Sometimes, some of the stories people inhabit begin to fray at the edges or even fail to deliver on their promise. Then people will listen for other stories. People will tend toward stories that they sense will help them navigate their increasingly inchoate emotions, their silenced experiences, and their disorganized transits through the affective landscape. They listen for a story that offers them a viable or even attractive place, even if it is in tension with their other stories. They may even accept a story that puts them into a still somewhat marginal and uncomfortable place if that is the only option. The alternative, if they can't hear a story that has a place for them, is to accept finding themselves silenced, with no place. Better to enter into a habitable story even if it stands them against other stories, including the very stories they are leaving behind.

Understanding is an attempt to tell a better story about stories. It does not end there. It assumes that if you understand what a story is doing, you can perhaps re-articulate it, move those living in its spaces into different (and better) stories. It engages with people's stories in order to recompose them into better stories. It seeks to re-articulate them so that they will be able to transform the complicated realities of the political culture. To do this, they have to operate on the popular, to be able to pull people into their spaces. It does not champion whatever solution is on the table but opens up possibilities for as yet unseen solutions.

To accomplish this, understanding has to be more than description. It has to involve more than simply listening to people's stories. It has to involve more than interacting with people or observing their everyday lives. It is a form of intellectual analysis. It often requires availing yourself of the available, disparate research—ethnographic, materialist, quantitative, and phenomenological. Most importantly, it demands a commitment to making the complications visible. Understanding recognizes that the processes by which people enter into or find themselves spoken by particular stories are more complicated than we assume. It recognizes that there are many stories, many different ways of inhabiting them, many different positions someone can occupy, and many different ways of occupying them.

But making this useful demands that understanding look at stories contextually and conjuncturally. A better story has to know more about the context in which people live than they do. It researches the conditions of possibility of people's lives in order to find the relations between their lives and their stories. It is not a question of seeing the world through others' eyes (although would that be so terrible?), but of understanding the determinations, limits, and possibilities within which people's choices make sense, even seem reasonable. We have to listen to people's stories and pay careful attention to their lives, without assigning them some final privilege. They provide the questions, not the answers. They are not the keys to unlock the secrets of the conjuncture, but they are vital pieces that will help lead us to better conjunctural stories.

There need be nothing insulting in this. I am not accusing people of a deficiency nor suggesting that understanding finds some secret truth that explains everything about some population or context. I am not suggesting that people do not know what they are doing but they are doing it anyway (which may be true sometimes). I am suggesting that people do not always know what they do, does.

## The Pragmatics of Climate Change Stories

I want to conclude with an example that is either banal or will get me tarred and feathered: Struggles over climate change and the coming environmental disasters. These struggles are difficult to identify with a single political position, although they have rather stark relations within the PRT. They also raise important challenges to our understandings of time, juxtaposing the epochal evolution of capitalism and the long durée of climate change with both a strategic sense of conjunctural crisis and the immediacy and urgency of impending disaster. It is an epochal story that is being foretold as a coming event. It poses unique questions about our responsibility for the sins of the past (whether centuries or millennia) and our responsibility for an unknowable future. It is not an ideological challenge, but one that threatens many forms of life, including our own. And yet, at the same time, it is entangled in both organic crises and further inflected by the peculiarities of our affective landscape.

What is immediately striking about this potentially life-or-death struggle is how little it seems to matter to many people. They will admit that something bad is happening; they may even admit that it is likely to have catastrophic effects in their children's or grandchildren's lifetime. But what then? It is difficult is to imagine a world in which our children and their children (they don't have to be our own) don't exist. It is difficult to imagine a world without a future, or without humans. The parable of the burning house seems less resonant, less capable of capturing the necessary passions. Perhaps because it is not only the house that is on fire, but the entire town; perhaps even the world itself. What if there is nowhere to run to?

We might start by asking what the problem is or, better, how climate change has been made into a problem. First, it is usually an either/or choice: Real or not real. There are rarely degrees. Second, it is a story about knowledge. It presumes that climate change is a "fact," in fact, a scientific fact. There is lots of evidence—or at least copious representations of data as evidence, whether of the coming catastrophe or of a conspiracy. A neighbor once accused the left of controlling the weather to make climate change look real. I responded that if it were true, the left would be in control of the world, to which he responded, it already is.

How many of us understand the data or know its limits? Or understand the mathematics well enough to question the methodology and the analysis? How many of us bother to read the criticisms and seek out the alternative interpretations? And how many would be capable of adjudicating among competing data and stories? People seem to overestimate their knowledge and understanding; they underestimate the expertise and work required. In the end, they appeal to authority. It's a matter of science. In this story, we either trust or do not trust science. It is a question of faith. For most of us, our faith in science is just that: A matter of faith, and that is only magnified on the affective landscape. Okay, then thank god for the U.N., our last and best ally in this matter.

But let's back up. What kind of a problem is climate change? Is it a crisis, a disruption, a catastrophe? Is it natural or man-made? A problem of the earth? Life? The economy? Civilization as it has existed for millennia? In other words, what sorts of stories are being told and how do people find a place in them? My (educated?) guess is that many people cannot find a livable place inside most climate change stories, so they live outside of them. They have normalized climate change by retelling a story in which climate change is lived out as ever-worsening weather. In this story, climate change has no discernible implications for the future beyond the consequences of bad weather, which can be very bad, as we all know.

No matter how many times we are told that changes in the weather are not direct signs of climate change, most people still appeal to increasingly extreme weather events as proof, while those who do not believe in climate change simply point to a folk history of bad weather. A sage patriarch on a popular TV series recently quipped, "We used to call days like this a gift; today we call it global warming." Mother nature will have her way. Or, like my students, people fall back on inevitability: If you're sailing on the Titanic, go first class.

But the leading story told by the climate change movement—again, I know there are others, probably more to my liking—is a story about thresholds or tipping points. Crossing them is inevitably catastrophic. You enter another reality in which everything changes, and you can never go back. And the only way to avoid the cataclysm is not to cross the line, which is already here, or just around the corner. This is a story all about urgency and immediacy, aimed against the slow-time of liberals and centrists (and some climatologists). It could be a wonderful expression of affective anxiety and hyper-inflation, especially the tendency to rush to the worst-case scenario (to awfulize). Yet it is told in a voice of scientific certainty, political absolutism, and cultural panic. A new world is coming whether we like it or not. This is revolutionary time.

I do not mean to underestimate the challenges we face or the possibilities of horrific consequences. But I am concerned with political change. The house may be on fire, but apparently not enough people are willing to do much about it. The story is not working. Why? Why might they buy into the catastrophe but refuse to follow the story to the necessarily radical, even revolutionary, changes it demands? Perhaps we need to better understand how and why different constituencies inhabit the stories they do and refuse others. Perhaps they have lived through too many end-of-the-world stories in their own lifetimes. When the great northeast blackout of November 9, 1965, happened, I was a student at the University of Rochester. When we realized the magnitude of the event, with no explanation forthcoming, the response was not to seek answers or a solution, but to organize an end of the world party. Such stories are neither particularly rational nor politically efficacious, but they are part of our affective landscape. Such apocalyptic stories seem strangely unable to reach people, to change their mattering maps, or to mobilize change.

Might the struggle to ameliorate climate change have more political effect if we could invite people into a different, better story? This is not a matter of persuasion (as if science persuades people; no, the status of science does). You have to move them with popular stories. There are other stories already out there, but they remain rather invisible and silenced by the affective absolutism of the threshold story. Eliot was partly right. The world may end in a whimper, but change does not arrive with a bang.

The most visible alternative is a pragmatic story in which change is not only necessary but doable. You want to eliminate carbon-based fuels (and nuclear power?) and turn to sustainable energy sources. Do you have them or know where they are? How are you going to pay for rebuilding the entire energy infrastructure? How are you going to help the many people employed— directly or indirectly—in these industries and services? Aha! You're going to invest in education and social welfare. How? Don't tell me about the burning house. Somewhere in people's calculation is always going to be: What will happen to me and my family? How will we live? This is a liberal story of slow incremental change that protects the basic infrastructures of capitalism and nationalism, while unnecessarily (and, to some extent, unintentionally) sacrificing human lives and wellness. Such stories are not frightening enough; as if we can just go on living our lives with some minor adjustments, a few more regulations, without actually addressing how new burdens will be distributed, etc.

Another story that becomes more visible is that we start by thinking about zero growth, which is often understood in purely economic terms, as if climate change is all about capitalism. But what does zero growth mean (and is it really any clearer how to get there)? Isn't growth natural? Doesn't anything die if it doesn't grow? Maybe we have to distinguish growth from change. We have to find a story that admits that something dies if it doesn't change, if it doesn't adapt. Growth is only one view of change, one perhaps partly dictated by the economy and economists, but also by many religions, principles of education, etc. Or perhaps we need to suggest that there are many ways of growing. How do we open up possibilities for relating to change, without reducing it to economics, or ontology, or geopolitics, or identity? Is the key to be found in our relation to the non-human, or is it a more spiritual exercise? This too is a story told in a voice of certainty, of revolutionary time. We want—need, demand—a new world NOW! These stories are often lovingly speculative, rarely touching down into the reality of people's lives with anything other than vague appeals to utopian possibilities and little sense of how they can be accomplished.

I am taken with stories that begin by assuming that the "problem" cannot be defined in scientific or economic terms alone. Could the material effects of climate change be catastrophic? Yes. What are the probabilities? That is uncertain. Perhaps the catastrophe is already here and it is not the one we are thinking about. Rather, it is an epistemological crisis, because the more data we have, the more variables are accounted for, the greater the uncertainties. The problem is not that we have a good idea about what's going to happen; the problem is that we don't know what's going to happen. We face the terrifying chaos of not knowing the future. But hasn't that always been our common predicament? We face uncertainty and act in the face of uncertainty throughout history and, for that matter, for most of our lives. How is this different? It is no doubt more frightening because it is more extreme, but we have faced that before as well. It is a story we are more accustomed to.

This story does not have a conclusion yet, and like all stories, it cannot have a conclusion because it is not yet written. The story does not tell us what we should do, but it does perhaps change the place of climate change on our affective landscape. How much are we willing to gamble—for that is what it now appears to be—on the future? Where is our comfort zone? Given better analyses of the conjuncture as the precondition for possibilities, what capacities might stories of uncertainty have? Might they enable us to build forms of cooperation, if not solidarity? Might they enable us to accept that the future is never simply all or nothing? The truth is, I do not know. The future is never guaranteed.

Maybe the most ethical position for this third conjunctural moment is the uncertainty. Maybe uncertainty is the only possibility for the moment between chaos and absolutism, the only place where we can rest for a while. Maybe it will enable us to measure the difference between better and worse stories. Maybe it will allow us to arm ourselves with a moral compass, while acknowledging its fallibility. Maybe it will help us avoid the slippery slope of selectivity, manipulation, and even deception as we attempt to move different constituencies by telling stories in which they can find themselves.

Maybe that's not a bad way to live and think for the moment.

## Notes

1 An informal bit of research on cable channels suggested that biracial couples and families, and gay people and couples, are significantly more commonly represented than their number in "real life" would suggest.

2 And I understand something about how some of those stories enter into the middle classes, who are constantly facing what they see as arbitrary limits on their access to resources and benefits. Why do the wealthy (and, they believe, the poor) escape their obligations when they feel honor-bound to fulfill them?

3 The reversal of the Bible's instructions on how to treat the stranger. "You shall not wrong nor oppress the stranger, for you were strangers in the Land of Egypt" (Exodus 22:20).

# 16

## I WISH THERE WAS A TREATY WE COULD SIGN (DIFFERENCE AND BELONGING)

Struggles over immigration have a long history in America. They have often been constructed as a problem that speaks to America's unique identity. People have fought, sometimes quite literally, over these questions. With the exception of the various indigenous peoples, everyone else has been immigrants. The only question is when you or your ancestors arrived. Different waves came from different geographic regions and classes, but each has faced its own challenges, including the resentment, if not hatred, of previous waves. Every wave came to escape something and to seek something. And almost every wave was accused of stealing jobs, refusing to assimilate, and bringing strange, uncivilized, and often illegal behaviors. Each wave brought good people and bad people, just like those who were already here. Each wave brought its own stories. Many of those stories eventually changed, as people came to see themselves not as immigrants but as Americans. Many people continued to maintain cultural and familial ties to the old country. And the stories of the different waves were added to the repertoire of American stories.

Current waves, whatever their differences, might have ended up following the same patterns (and they still might). But they have been caught up in other battles and stories, only indirectly about immigration and the immigrant. They have been made into emblematic affective figures: On the one hand, they have become one of the sites around which the two organic crises of modernity have been constructed. To what extent is America's modernity bound up with its being a nation of immigrants? On the other hand, they have been too easily and neatly slotted into the stories of polarization and identity. These stories have created an identity category that erases the extraordinary differences among the immigrants. Whatever their origins, their identities

DOI: 10.4324/9781003662587-20

before arriving, and the stories they bring with them, they become raced and made to stand in for either a single, terrifying threat to the sanctity of American sovereignty, or the oppressed.

Stories of the immigrant as an absolute threat push the reasonable demand for regulating immigration into a desire for an end to immigration, to close the borders at any cost, to erase the frontier. It has produced the image of building a wall that could isolate the country from any and all outside others (i.e., possible threats). Stories of the immigrant as the new icon of oppressed populations do not depend on their identity prior to their migration. Instead, they depend upon their existence as immigrants. Questions about whether or why they were oppressed where they started or whether they might be oppressed once they arrive here are not central. They are assumed to have had good, perhaps even necessary, reasons for leaving. Their status as oppressed is defined by their treatment at the border and by their identity being reduced to that of an immigrant. The choice seems to be to refuse all immigration or to refuse all attempts to limit and regulate immigration. The fact is that immigration—and the movement of people—has always presented serious challenges, from the administrative to the governmental to the ethical. Those challenges have only become more complicated given the state of the world, and they demand serious and complicated solutions.

Finding the cracks that make other stories possible has motivated and produced a lot of serious intellectual and political work, shining a light on other possibilities of living with others. Such work has offered up numerous alternative (and often better) stories of identities, differences, and ways of belonging together. At different times, some of these stories have entered into and even impacted academic, activist, and popular stories. And then they have disappeared. They may leave traces, often in the form of misunderstood phrases. The PRT and polarization stories have effectively erased most of them.

The PT does not ignore the reality of existing constructions of identities. It does not deny the reality of how we live them. It does not pretend that identities do not matter or that, in the current context, they do not matter in very particular and important ways. But it does argue that this particular construction of identity is just that, a construction of relations and stories. It undercuts its claim to being natural and necessary, the one and only truth of identity.

I want to retell—revive—two of the stories: The first deconstructs the negative binary stories that have dominated the conjuncture and been absolutized by the PRT. It offers a more complicated understanding of the ways people are located in relations to others. The second asks how the present reality of identity has been constructed and naturalized. Treating it as a contingent historical construct, it proposes the possibility of a world without such an organization of differences. I will offer a brief glimpse of each, recognizing the enormity of the literatures and the diversity of positions.[1]

Both stories are better stories than those that continue to dominate political struggles around identity and otherness. Both offer ways of embracing the complexity of differences, and both open up the possibilities for living with differences. That being said, there are no guarantees as to how such stories will be realized in any particular context. While either story may function as a progressive possibility at one moment, it might be taken up and articulated to very different political ends at another. Or more likely, at any moment, the political implications of these stories will be fought out on the terrain of political culture. Still, in the current conjunctural moment, they offer the best possibility for moving beyond the PRT and stories of polarization.

## A Story of Differences

We can think of identities as ways of organizing, living with, and struggling over differences. We can problematize and make visible the complexity and contextuality of differences on either side of the binary (although I will focus on only one). Let me begin with a not so metaphorical metaphor: Differences (and the identities that come out of them) exist in time and space. Differences exist in time. They have histories. More than that, they are changing all the time. Stories often assign them a fixedness or stability, but that is a construction that is always contested. Differences are more fluid than any story can allow.

Now we can turn to the spatial complexities of differences. We can begin by multiplying the categories of otherness—race, ethnicity, gender—and we add sexuality, age, ability ... and there are more. Struggles over identity are, at this level, attempts to find the sweet spot between compassion and chaos. Then we can acknowledge that each category is itself a complicated articulated unity. And we can unpack it, but in doing so, we are actually breaking it up and reassembling it anew. "Black" doesn't tell us what it includes and how its components are related. Rather, the stories of race and racism compete to compose the category. At times, within particular American racial regimes, black referred to African Americans but less so to Africans. At times, it has included Jews, Irish, Italians, Muslims, etc. At different times, it has referenced physical attributes, cultural habits, assumptions about genetics, etc. And those who inhabit positions marked as black often construct their own differences within the category. After all, differences do make a difference,[2] and being black in America is a complicated thing.

It is still more complicated. The categories are inseparable; they never exist in some pure, isolatable form. It would be so much easier if race was over there, gender over there, ability over there. You could study each and people could inhabit each, if only temporarily, without regard to any others. Unfortunately, that is never the case. Every claim of belonging to one category of difference already carries with it the baggage of others. There is no pure category or essence of being black or being woman. The category is always and already fragmented and multiplied by its relations with other categories. And these articulations cannot themselves be simply isolated and identified (as if at some intersection). Every category itself only exists in all its relations to the others. Every category is a composition, always impure, compromised, syncretic, and hybrid. Hybridity is all there is, always and everywhere. Hence, there are only multiple hybrid categories, multiple ways of assembling the categories, and multiple ways of inhabiting any category.[3]

What is true of the category is true of every identity. Once again, people are complicated, fragmented, and articulated. A person is a densely packed unity-in-difference of many—and many sorts of—positions of difference offered by the many stories they inhabit. Identities are the tense constructions that result from the relations among competing social, local, and more personal stories. But that is too strong. Perhaps it is better to think of these stories as offering you locations that you might occupy. But that is too weak. Stories ascribe identities to you; they attempt to put you into particular positions in the story. But they cannot guarantee that you will take them up and occupy them. And even if you do occupy a position in a particular story, the story cannot guarantee how you inhabit it or how you perform whatever actions it suggests.

That raises one final complication, which you will be glad to know I cannot pursue here. Where does the gap between what is offered and what is taken up come from? It is one of the great mysteries of philosophy and religion, sometimes cast as the problem of free will. Is it merely an illusion and we are really always fully determined by forces outside our own consciousness? Is it a matter of chance and contingency? Or is there some authentic "self" standing behind every choice? Does it have something to do with subjectivity, which defines the position from which you can and do experience the world and your own self? (And is subjectivity different from agency, which defines your capacities to perform certain actions or, at least, the capacity not to perform them?) Or is it simply that individuals are complicated and have complicated histories?

Let's get back to complicating the story. What is true of categories and individuals is true of societies as well. Societies are complicated, fragmented, and articulated; a society is a unity-in-difference composed of many—and many sorts of—relations and dimensions of difference that cannot be treated in isolation, apart from their relations. The attempt to understand, for example, questions of race and racism, or gender and patriarchy, by abstracting them from the rest of society is misguided. We need to deal with a society that is raced, a society that is gendered, etc. But any society that is raced is always and already gendered, and so on. Any specific set of struggles—e.g., against racisms or against racist policings—is inseparable from and always articulated to other stories and relations, many of which will involve matters of identity and identities. Of course, you have to start somewhere, and you seek openings that seem most pertinent to the problems being posed. But you could be wrong.

There is yet a further complication to the question of identity. The third conjunctural moment has witnessed one other significant re-articulation of the category of identity. The enlightenments separated the domains of political, economic, cultural, and social relations. Consequently, they also separated the corresponding identities. They did not understand that each domain is culturally constructed in stories and, moreover, that stories assemble them in conjuncturally specific ways to construct a society. (It is when those stories no longer work that society may face an organic crisis.) The PRT and ST have collapsed all these constructs of identity into the political. Increasingly, political identity becomes the essence of identity, overriding all others. You are your politics and, increasingly, you have to wear it on your sleeve. Perhaps it echoes certain colonial histories. The anthropologist David Scott (2004) tells us that when the great Caribbean intellectual C.L.R. James revisited the Haitian revolution of 1791, he came to a rather startling conclusion. He saw that the demand for freedom was based on Enlightenment notions of subjectivity and argued that it was, therefore, misplaced. What should have been demanded was another way of being in the world—a cultural revolution as politics.

This story of differences has important implications; let me give just one simple example. In matters of identity, we should probably stop thinking in terms of the representation of diversity, as if we only had to expand the number of voices, until we encompass ... everyone? (This probably holds true for viewpoint diversity as well.) This notion of simply adding constituencies is a failed liberal fantasy; it ignores the ways a history of stories have constructed identities against one another, making the possibility of living and working together more daunting than we imagine. It works if you assume that you only need more black voices, or more gay faces, or more conservatives. Any one will do. Not!

## A Story of Belonging

The second story I want to tell is both obvious and surprising. And its consequences are profound. It starts by asking: Why do we organize the social field into a system of differences and identities? How have the resulting identities been made into the defining essence of both individuals and communities? How have the very meaning and practice of identity changed and why? Given the above description of how complicated such notions are, why do they keep appearing as single unified categories existing in simple binary relations?

The answer turns everything upside down. Most stories begin by assuming that races, for example, exist. Then, various forms of racism result from the confrontation between them. Sometimes, stories will even acknowledge that races are constructed, but it doesn't seem to change the story. What if we took the constructionist claim seriously. We would have to start by asking how they are constructed. The answer is that racisms produce races. Or, more accurately, races, even the very category of race, are the construction of various racist formations. As the formations change and multiply, as the forms of racisms change and multiply, so do the realities of races.

There are many forms and practices of racism, even in this conjunctural moment. And the formations of race have histories, impure and hybrid, to be sure, of their own. Ignoring this can minimize or even erase differences that matter. It can too easily avoid questions about how different formations are constructed, how they function, and how they can be effectively judged and opposed. I would want to tell stories (others might tell different stories) about the many racist formations currently at work in American political culture, including: forms of (often unintentional and even unconscious) habitual and everyday racisms, implicit bias, overt discrimination, structural racisms, economic deprivation, cultural erasure and denigration, and political oppression. I am sure there are more. Many of these exist side by side and overlap with, merge with, and support each other.

In the stories that dominate the PRT, these are not only often conflated, but they are also commonly gathered together under the signs of white supremacism and white nationalism, in an anxious act of hyper-inflation. These require, in fact demand, stories of their own alongside stories of their relation to other racial formations. To clarify, I take white supremacism as the assumption of the inherent (necessary, universal) superiority of the white race. I take white nationalism as the assumption that the presence of "the other" threatens the very existence of the nation. If the former opposes egalitarianism, the latter opposes the very possibility of multi-ethnic and/or multicultural societies. Both of these often assume that they are justified (in God's name?) in using forms of racial violence, including slavery and racial cleansing (race war).

But other forms of normalized racism can also end up in accepting and even legitimating forms of violence and profoundly consequential mistreatment if they allow themselves to see the other as somehow less than or infra-human. This is partly the result of the articulation of racisms into the long history of military and police violence in the United States, which has been directed against indigenous peoples, slaves, Jews, gay populations, and people of color, but also union members, protestors, and youth, as well as the governments of other countries when it was felt to be in the nation's "interest."

According to this second story, hypothetically but not speculatively, if we could end racism, refuse the formations of racism, and eradicate the stories of racism, race as an identity (formed in a system of negation) would disappear. That does not mean that we abandon identity, but identity would become primarily a matter of belonging, of affiliation and identification, of culture. Such identities exist and they do not need an essential, pure identity; each is always impure, syncretic. They need not, and for the most part do not, define themselves in opposition to some other culture.

Nor does this story suggest that we abandon difference as a field of relations. A society flourishes when it learns to live with differences. But differences do not need to be constructed in/as negation. Here, letting a thousand flowers bloom becomes a social and cultural vision rather than a political strategy. In this story, the powerfully negative affect of anti-racist struggles is still a vital part of contemporary politics. It depends on a careful analysis of the specific conjunctural formations of difference as negation and oppression. But it is separated from the equally powerful positive celebration of the ties that bind and the differences they create. These cultural diversities may be affectively powerful, but they also need not define our very being. Both are necessary.

### Conclusion

Identity has become the cornerstone of contemporary political culture. It has become the most passionate struggle in the battle for political dominance. Is there an alternative? Is it possible to reach for a community without identity? Paul Gilroy, following Frantz Fanon, has unashamedly embraced this as the utopian thought of a planetary humanism. Personally, I do not think it is utopian. It is rather a possibility written into the very idea that reality is a contingent construction,

Whatever you might think of the status of the two stories I have told here, can we at least begin to construct a politics beyond fixed and negative identities? Maybe it would combine the stories, seeking both a politics of living with the complexity of identities and difference and a politics of belonging.

American culture has always struggled to construct a unity out of its heterogeneity—whether one that demands homogeneity, or one that refuses any unity, or one that negates some differences, or one that sets differences against one another. The creation of a nation as a *demos* (a people) depends on their capacities to forge bonds of affiliation alongside differences. Can we create better stories of unity-in-difference? Can we create stories in which different constituencies matter but don't have to matter in the same ways, or matter in ways that don't have to be measured and compared, or matter in ways that don't deny that others matter? Can we offer stories that imagine forms of unity that actually respect differences beyond any one group's own terms of acceptability? Can we create stories that embrace the many ways in which we can belong together? Can we find stories that might teach us how to live with others?

## Notes

1   The first draws upon the work of Stuart Hall (2019, 2021); the second draws upon the work of Paul Gilroy (2000). However, it has to be said that many others have contributed in significant ways to these discussions.
2   There are many ways to think about differences: In negative and positive terms; as normative or unique; as positional, conditional, or processual; as ambivalent, displacing, conjunctural, or articulated.
3   This is not a notion of intersectionality, which assumes that any individual (or specified group) is defined by the intersection of multiple categories, each of which is definable independently of the others, whether in essentialist terms or not. Every identity exists passively in isolation. The hybridity exists only at the end.

## References

Gilroy, Paul. *Against Race*. Cambridge: Harvard University Press, 2000.
Hall, Stuart. *Essential Essays vol 2. Identity and Diaspora*. Ed. David Morley. Durham: Duke University Press, 2019.
Hall, Stuart. *Selected Writings on Race and Difference*. Eds. Paul Gilroy and Ruth Wilson Gilmore. Durham: Duke University Press, 2021.
Scott, David. *Conscripts of Modernity*. Durham: Duke University Press, 2004.

# 17

# DANCE ME TO THE END OF LOVE

When I talk about the Popular Tendency, people often say, great, but you don't really think it's going to happen. (Apparently, they can't call me a dreamer anymore.) I tell them, I have no reason to be optimistic. They probably expect me to fall back on the intellectual's safe word: Communication. Everything can be solved with better communication. We need to heal or revitalize our public culture; we need to return it to reason, debate, issue-focus, and civility. I have even less reason to be optimistic about that. I doubt that we can step out of the affective landscape so easily. What about the kinds of rigorous thinking and engagements that you call for, they politely ask.

I do imagine a space of passionate dissensus and disagreement. It would be a space where people attend to and question each other's assumptions without condemnation. It would allow positions to be voiced and received generously. But it would not simply tolerate other positions. It would actively engage and even challenge them. Are we actually capable of having such convivial, agonistic encounters without antagonism? Truthfully, I can imagine what they sound and feel like. I have been there. But I cannot imagine a story that gets us there from here. I would welcome being surprised.

Then comes the final blow: Then why are you still writing? After all, given what you have said about the current state of knowledge, anything you might have to say would seem to be little more than shoveling sand on the beach. Even if you manage to build a castle, the waves will wash it away too quickly. It will just be another pile of sand among all the many other piles. (Big sigh.) I know.

DOI: 10.4324/9781003662587-21

### Communication Fail

So what's a poor boy to do? I suppose I could come up with a new theory of communication as an articulation of stories, or the forging of relations. It would be more interesting to ask why communication fails, or what we mean by that. Every act of communication produces effects. Does it fail when those effects do not comply with some expectation? Whose? The different players in the encounter? What about all those interests behind the encounter (like the media's owners)? That doesn't seem like a fruitful direction. The question of failure is really a question of roadblocks or traffic jams. Where are the places where the possibility of continuing the encounter is stopped? Where is there—or at least seems to be—an impassable gap? And if we could identify what's causing the traffic jam, how do we avoid or deconstruct it? (I know I am getting carried away with the traffic metaphor. Forgive me. I grew up in New York and live in rural Carolina. Both are crucially constituted by the flows of traffic.)

We generally assume that there are certain beliefs or commitments that cannot be proven or disproven. They present irreconcilable differences. They are the foundational principles that define our place in and responsibilities to the universe, the world, and humanity. For example, some people assume that existence is sacred, and life more uniquely sacred, and intelligent life most uniquely sacred. Others assume that the universe is a profane, relativistic quantum reality. Our foundational principles may define our place in and responsibilities to our nation and to its people, or to God.

We further tend to assume that belief systems are arranged like an upside-down pyramid. First principles support the entire structure. They cannot be challenged without bringing down the entire pyramid. I doubt that this is a good analogy. Besides, we now know that pyramids are actually much more structurally complicated than this simple picture suggests. Even so, the analogy fails us in the contemporary conjuncture. It still assumes that the traffic jams in political culture are the result of the clash of ideologies. And all ideologies lead back to irreconcilable first principles. Hence, there is no possibility of any rapprochement or even significant engagement. Polarization stories have pushed every disagreement closer and closer to first principles, as if every disagreement (potentially) threatened an entire way of life, an entire edifice of stories, an entire habitable landscape.

But if, as you are probably tired of hearing, the struggles are located on an affective landscape, the traffic jam is somewhere else. It is a question of how and how much things matter. Mattering maps are one way the affective landscape is organized. It is a prefigurative map, a set of instructions. It defines how important things—including stories—are, and in what ways they are important. Every story, in fact, anything that you might care about, refuse to care about, or not care at all about, has a place on some mattering maps. It may have a place on more than one, and it may not have a place on all of them.

And mattering maps, unlike first principles, can be questioned: Why do you care about that so much, I want to know? They can be explored. And they can be reconfigured in other stories. We need to figure out where the traffic jam is on the mattering maps. It surely matters in some ways to some people if stories speak a language of a personal God, or the sacred, or the being of Being, or the intrinsic properties of the universe. But does it matter always? Everywhere? In the same ways? Does your story assume that people are born (or are inherently) good, or evil (sinful), or just flawed and subject to external forces? Whatever evil people might commit, does it demand expiation and grace or social correction? Must we choose? How does it matter if assumptions about racial or ethnic inequalities are based on an experience (or its absence), on inherited stories, on media stories, or abstract judgments of comparative advantage? How far can the conversation go before we get stuck at another roadblock—and we start over again?

I have a close friend, an astrophysicist who builds astrophysicist-type instruments. He is also a devout Catholic and a committed conservative (of the old school). We have great conversations. We hit a roadblock. He tells me that I would need to believe in God to get to where he wants to go. I ask him why, why does it matter? He tells me. I ask him if I can get there in a different way, on a different mattering map. He says, only partway. We go that far. Then we go back and take a different path. We continue to engage. In this moment, it is enough.

## Hope and Care

I want to return to the question of why I write. Some will expect me to offer my own moral mattering map or first principles. There is no reason to assume that, as analysts and story-tellers of the conjuncture, our moral capacities are more profound, our politics more rational, than those of other people. It is not my responsibility to tell people who they should be or what they should desire. There has to be some distance between intellection and scholarship, the statement of political and moral values, and the enactment of political action.

I will take a different path. Assuming this whole book to have been something of a treatise on despair, I want to tell you a parable. It is not about optimism and pessimism but hope and despair. Hope is often misunderstood, taken to be flimsy and without substance. Nick Cave (a great Aussie rocker) saw it differently: "Unlike cynicism, hopefulness is hard-earned, makes demands upon us, and can often feel like the most indefensible and lonely place on Earth. Hopefulness is not a neutral position either. It is adversarial. It is the warrior emotion that can lay waste to cynicism."[1] Hope is not about optimism; it is not contradicted by pessimism. Hope is an act of will directed toward possibility. It is a future attempting to bring itself into existence just beyond the present. It is a prayer screamed out to the unknown. Above all, it is an act. Seamus Heaney understood it: "Walk on air against your better judgement." Hope is the capacity to act while accepting uncertainty and your own fallibility.

My parable takes place at the crossroads, where the relation of despair and hope is magically transformed. (There is, after all, magic at the crossroads. If you don't believe me, just listen to Robert Johnson's "Crossroads Blues.") I witness a gathering of prophets. I can see MiLoFo, the Maitreya Buddha, ruler of the next age, who humbles himself in recognition of the suffering of this world and then continues down the road, teaching and laughing. I see the Baal Shem Tov (the keeper of the good name), founder of the Chassid, healers of the broken and celebrants of the joy of creation. I see Miguel de Cervantes, who created a literary form to capture the emerging modern world. And Baruch Spinoza, dissident Jewish thinker who envisioned the need to bring about an already existing unity as the common effort of humanity. And Sojourner Truth, abolitionist and women's rights advocate. And Martin Luther King, Jr., dreamer. I see Diane Arbus, photographer of the social fringes. And Nadine Gordimer, chronicler of the everyday life of oppression. And Frantz Fanon, Caribbean exile, harbinger of violence and herald of a planetary humanism. And I hear Robert Johnson, still singing the blues. There are probably others I cannot see or hear.

I am trying to hear what they are saying. They are talking about humanity and the world. Both are always broken, never perfect. The result is that people suffer. A good life must embrace the suffering. But it does not embrace a nihilism that sees only suffering forever. Rather, a good life begins with accepting that we all have the capacity to suffer and that, however great the differences, we all suffer. This creates an obligation to repair the world, to leave it a better place than we found it.

They all agree that you must intervene. You can try to stop the suffering, or you can, for the sake of the future, witness and record the suffering. You can curse those responsible for the suffering or forgive them; you can offer redemption to the sufferer. You can bond and empathize with the sufferer, though you may not have suffered in the same way, with the same intensities, for the same durations. You can struggle to change the world so as to ameliorate as much suffering as possible.

But ultimately, they all agree that suffering defines an obligation. That obligation is always to the stranger. A stranger may be unknown but they are always knowable, because we are all strangers, even to ourselves, somewhere, sometime. The stranger is always both absent and present everywhere, both undefined and real. Sharing the suffering of the other, they conclude, demands sacrificing, if only for a moment, your own well-being (or lack of suffering). And in that sacrifice, suffering reveals the possibility of something else; something joyful and positive, a belonging together with the other, what feminists call 'care,' what Jesus called charity, and what the poets have always called love. Suffering opens the door for love. Humanity is life caught in this paradoxical alchemy. And then they sang the blues.

### You Don't Need a Secret Chord to Love Music

But I have yet to share why this meeting took place at the crossroads. There is a magic there, even in the present conjuncture.[2] And its most powerful magic can always be heard in music. The crossroads transmogrifies suffering in music, from the blues to upbeat celebrations of pleasure and fun. The song is a composition always reaching for the next harmony, built on the hope that arises from accepting that the next step, the path to be followed, is never given in advance. The song builds itself by finding ways to hold many voices, each with its own affect, together. Each prophet brings their voice, their stories, their mattering maps, and their habitable landscapes to the crossroads, and a new song is born, a new path is open, if only for a moment. That is the magic of the crossroads.

At the crossroads, people can listen to what they cannot hear, see what they are blind to, and open up to what they do not understand. At the crossroads, other stories are possible because other landscapes enter into the light. And when you leave the crossroads, you might begin to tell different—maybe better—stories about what's going on, how we got here, and, if you are lucky enough, how we might get outta this place. You might hear new stories of who we are, where we are, how we are living, what we are feeling, and how all this came to be. If you listen to the music … but where is the music today?

Isn't it ironic that after 50 years of trying to find a way out of this place, I have ended up with hope and a song? Pretty much where I began in the 60s. But I can't stop myself from thinking that there are no more songs to sing us from the suffering of the present into the joy of an unknown future. Where are the songs we can sing together, songs that bring hope into our contemporary world, songs that transmute despair and rage into joy and love?

I have tried to tell the best story I can. It is probably too nostalgic, naïve, mundane, compromised, utopian, …. But then, as I have said, the world is no longer my world. It is no longer a world I am comfortable in. It is no longer a world I will ever fully understand. I have tried to give it a full measure of slow thinking, but such thinking has to be part of larger experiments. Such experiments will seek more robust ways of sharing the gifts—the always limited and unequal capacities, talents, and knowledges—we all bring to our attempts to live together. Do I hope such work will be done? Yes. Am I optimistic that such work will be done? Not at all. But I continue to hope that we can find the music and repair the world.

## Notes

1 The Red Hand Files www.theredhandfiles.com. Issue #190. (April 2022.
2 Maybe the parable should be recast for the current moment: Not the crossroads but the screen; not the blues but the horrific; not suffering but the suffering of anxiety. But I have no idea who the iconic figures might be—and they seem to me to change so quickly. Perhaps anxiety is the contemporary path by which the dark landscape of suffering is transformed into more empathic, more creative expressions of community and, hence, possibilities of hope. Perhaps it is not coincidental that thinkers have, for a long time, linked something like anxiety (explained as the confrontation with death, with non-presence, with the void) to the call to more fundamental ways of being.

# APPENDIX

## The Academy and the Crises of Knowledge

Institutions have histories. They emerge in response to perceived needs and opportunities in their contexts, and they change in response to changes in those contexts, to both internal and external forces and pressures. Universities are no different. The United States has a complicated array of higher education institutions; its oldest include private, often church-affiliated, colleges and state-chartered universities, which often date back to the 18th century. Land-grant colleges, both public and private, appeared in the second half of the 19th century. The modern research university, organized by distinct disciplines, was brought to the U.S. in the late 19th century and rapidly became both the dominant model for many universities but also the most important and visible (but not the only) institution of scholarship and research in the country.

The entire higher education system was significantly redesigned and expanded in the 1950s and 1960s to meet the demand of returning vets and the coming baby boomers. Very quickly, a college degree became the necessary prerequisite for upward mobility and the required ticket for entrance into the new middle classes. Changing political and economic conditions resulted in increasing government funding for scientific and technological research, the effects of which resonated throughout the entire university.

In the past decades, it has once again gone through extraordinary changes as a result of economic rationalization, technologization, politicization, and decreasing state support. The most visible and arguably important changes have been in the institutional organization and the political economy of the academy, some of which began in the 1960s, but most of which have taken place since the 1980s. They have reshaped the academy, often behind the backs and, when visible, against the will of many faculty (and some students). Under a variety of pressures, universities have come under many of the same managerial and corporatist strategies that have redefined both governmental social service programs and private enterprises, including new demands for efficiency and accountability, often trumping more traditional values that are not amenable to quantification.

These changes have imposed new and increasing constraints on the kinds of labor that are solicited, rewarded, and even allowed in universities; they have redefined the relations of the practical and pure sciences and those between the sciences and the liberal arts; they have altered the balance of research and education; and they have meant that the sources of income and support have had to adjust to the changing political debates, policies, and pressures of the various "stake-holders." As state funding for education (which is increasingly denied as a public good) and basic research has diminished, universities have turned to investments and grants from commercial enterprises and private donors, as well as increased tuition. Universities are being driven by others' demands, while students are encouraged to think of education as a down payment on a career and themselves as consumers of a service.

Anyone who has worked in universities for more than 25 years has directly experienced these changes, including: The centralization of decision-making; the increasing demands of legal and financial accountability; the growth of administrative bureaucracies; standardization; the transfer of teaching responsibility from the professoriate to precarious labor; the increasing micro-management of smaller units—colleges and departments; increasing demands for fund-raising and self-funding; etc. How these changes are implemented may vary, but they have resulted, at the very least, in a sense of disempowerment, increased pressure, and exhaustion, an individualization and professionalization of academic careers (with a correlative diminishing of institutional loyalty and the willingness to take on unrewarded service activities), and an increasing division between research and teaching.

Simultaneously, the academy—and higher education itself—has come under attack from both the left and the right. Academics have not yet taken this challenge seriously. "Knowledge for knowledge's sake" is unlikely to carry the day when public benefit is increasingly measured in economic terms.

In fact, arguably, these changes have challenged the university's ability to fulfill its mission or, at least, to adapt its mission to its ever-changing conditions. It can feel like its core mission has been buried under the weight of the infrastructures meant to serve it. It can feel like the university itself is being held together with Scotch tape and bubble gum.

I have lived inside the academy through all these changes. I attended a private "wannabe ivy league" university (the University of Rochester) in the mid-1960s, intending to study biochemistry and genetics but ending up in philosophy and history. I did post-graduate work in cultural studies at an English red-brick university (Birmingham University) in the late 1960s. I briefly taught at an inner-city teachers' college (Bank Street College) in the early 1970s, but then decided to enroll in a doctoral program in communication research at a Midwest state university (University of Illinois). My first job was at another Midwest state university (Purdue), which lasted only one year, after which I returned to a different department in a different college at Illinois (at the time, it was called Speech Communication, in the College of Arts and Sciences). After almost 20 years, I took up my final post as a distinguished professor at a highly regarded Southern state university (University of North Carolina at Chapel Hill), until I retired in 2022 and began writing this book.

I look back and ahead. I am transfixed and depressed as I consider not only what has become of the research university (and higher education more generally) but also, just as importantly, the role that academics themselves have played, however unintentionally, in producing the crises of knowledge. In fact, the academy may provide some of the best evidence for the failures of knowledge and expertise as their work-product has increasingly become fragments without a story, utterances without a conversation. Academics have failed to explain how rigorous research works, why disagreements are necessary, and how they are adjudicated. Let me be very clear: I want to describe trends and tendencies that are, I fear, becoming increasingly prevalent and powerful. They do not describe everything, perhaps not even the majority, of what is going on in the academy. So once again, forgive me if I paint an overly bleak picture.

Academics have done a poor job of policing themselves and, surprisingly, this is most blatant in the sciences. They rarely address the scandalous failures and behaviors that frequently appear—and rapidly disappear—in the life/medical sciences and the supposedly scientific social and psychological sciences. Reports have documented serious corruption resulting from close financial ties to government and corporate interests. They have found that a significant amount of published research, including many of the most influential landmark studies in the life sciences, cannot be replicated (the linchpin of scientific claims to authority), and that data has been falsified or manipulated and its significance misrepresented. Additionally, there are numerous accusations of plagiarism, although such accusations have recently been weaponized in the service of political agendas. Where then is the rigor and transparency the sciences claim? Universities, with the cooperation of government and corporate sponsors and the media, go to great lengths to suppress such stories, because scientists and university administrators are well aware that public attention would not only undermine whatever authority they still have but also their funding. But they are failing anyway.

Such practices are no doubt partly the result of personal greed and pride, but they are also the product of the increasing emphasis on commodified measures of reputations and rankings, which demands an ever-rising bar of grant funding and numbers of publications across the entire university. The result is that academics are producing the very explosion of knowledge claims that is overwhelming them. There is too much to read and consider—too many positions, arguments, evidence, etc.—and new digital technologies have made it all accessible. It has become almost impossible to read everything you should read, everything necessary to legitimate, even in traditional terms, the claim of academic expertise or scholarship. When I wrote my dissertation, I could read everything (mostly in English) written by and about two major intellectual figures. Today that would be beyond any imagined capability. Younger scholars cannot possibly keep up, looking to an ever-expanding available past and an ever more rapidly expanding present of scholarship. I cannot imagine what my journey would have been like had such technologies been available to me. Of course, these technologies have benefited many aspects of research and pedagogical practices, but at what costs?

At the same time, knowledge production has literally been hijacked by the business of knowledge distribution. As commercial publishers increasingly own and control the dissemination of academic knowledge on a for-profit basis, the need to fill their journals and book lists with free material that they can sell back to academics and libraries becomes paramount. If you think about it, academic publishing is a nearly perfect capitalist machine. Publishers get the raw academic material for free; they package it into journals (and books, handbooks, etc.) and the journals into larger bundles so that if a library wants particular journals, they have to buy bundles that include journals they may not actually need. Libraries have little choice but to buy these bundles, because they are the ongoing record of current research and knowledge. As a journal becomes successful, publishers can increase the page count or the number of issues per year, increasing their demands for free work and enabling them to charge even more for the journals and the bundles. In the bench sciences, the situation is even more perfect, for the author(s) often have to pay for the right to have their work sold back to their own institutions. Brilliant, isn't it? At the same time, the Web has made it possible for anyone to start their own web-journal, opening up a competing space that can try to earn some legitimacy (and which might eventually be sold to a commercial press).

The proliferation of publishing outlets, increasingly aimed at smaller and more specialized audiences, has had deleterious effects, which is not to deny its positive effects of opening spaces for voices that might otherwise not have found an outlet. I myself had to publish in small independent journals when I began my career because the major journals would not even consider my work. On the one hand, it means that authors are less likely to be reviewed by (hopefully) sympathetic readers from somewhat different backgrounds or perspectives. And on the other hand, it changes the weight of the editorial demand for revisions, since the author can now simply take their essay to another journal, often ignoring whatever criticisms and suggestions were offered. (And as an editor for decades, and a member of dozens of editorial boards, I can attest to the fact that this is increasingly common.)

Many faculty report feeling an increased pressure to publish although the requirements for promotion (and tenure, while it still exists) have generally remained constant. But as the market has changed, with a significantly smaller number of available positions, graduate students are now pressured to publish, often before they should. When I was a graduate student, I asked my mentor James Carey whether I should be publishing. He responded that I should not presume that I had something worth adding to the conversation after only a few years of reading and research. Such advice seems impossible if not naive today. (Could I really propose that graduate students not be encouraged to publish?)

But the number of publications has to be put alongside measures of "impact" and visibility—whether they are newsworthy or create marketable discoveries (including patents and cures) or are significantly influential (groundbreaking?) in their own fields. Scholars are pressured (through complicated reward systems) to move into more economically and pragmatically driven research and to make ever greater claims for their work. At the same time, increased research funding in the sciences results in higher teaching loads in non-sciences.

I will focus now on how these pressures express themselves in the humanities and non-scientific (qualitative, critical) social sciences. In the past, such fields often asked—or at least began with—open-ended, important questions, which meant that scholars were necessarily involved in longer (historically) and broader (interdisciplinary) conversations. Even as your thinking came to address more specific questions within the larger context, you could never be quite sure of where you might find pertinent ideas, examples, insights, concepts, etc.; where you might find something you had not expected to find. You had to be open to unfamiliar traditions and unexplored paths of research. Who can afford the time or energy such open-ended research demands? I fear that, to a large extent, this has disappeared; it has had to disappear. There is too much to read, and so little time to go back; it's hard enough just to keep up with the most recent work. And what is true for your own field is also true as you try to reach across fields: How do you begin to know where to look? How do you choose what to look for in the past, or even in the present? How do you know where to reach across fields? What strategies enable you to construct a manageable—i.e., publishable—research project?

One strategy leads academics to define their expertise in increasingly narrow terms; hyper-specialization results in the creation of "pocket universes" and the proliferation of sub-fields, often built around a supposedly newly identified (created) set of objects. You might expect that such an approach would result in highly sophisticated and complex interdisciplinary analyses, but you would be mostly disappointed. Authors may occasionally "poach" something from the past or from another field, but they usually do so without due regard for the history, conversations, and disagreements of the other discipline. Often, they are simply rediscovering in their own pocket universe what others already know. Sometimes, the banality is covered over with new theories, vocabularies, or discipline-specific references. It can feel like intellectual history is repeating itself over and over. Yet the media just continue to celebrate such derivative work, touting its cutting-edge breakthroughs, when they even bother to notice it. Rather than locating your work within ongoing conversations, rather than being satisfied with keeping the conversation moving—offering what additions, amendments, and criticisms you can—the current academic environment encourages you to step outside the conversation.

This often goes hand in hand with a second strategy: Framing your work in highly exaggerated claims of originality (new discoveries, new theories, new solutions derived from new sources—and increasingly, new micro-disciplines) that justify the extraordinary explosion of essays, journals, and books. You can no longer be satisfied with claiming to have discovered a new piece of a complex puzzle or even an interesting redeployment of an older practice or structure, because such claims do not bring fame and glory—either to oneself or to the university. Instead, you have to have discovered something crucial: A key that unlocks something, maybe even everything. A good but relatively small idea is expanded into a metonym for the entire intellectual universe. And repetition gets called originality. Instead of complexity, uncertainty, and humility, it is better to go with elegance, hyperbole, and the ever-receding new.

Another strategy involves the appeal of theory. I am aware that many unsympathetic critics accuse contemporary scholarship of being little more than a random collection of theoretical buzz-words without meaning. While I understand such a reaction, I also want to distance myself from it, not only because it was my generation that legitimated the turn to theory, but because I believe theory serves a productive role, comparable in some ways to that of mathematics in the hard sciences. For many scholars, it is vital to their efforts to gain a better understanding of the empirical social and political worlds they engaged with in their attempts to formulate more strategic interventions. I should add that such important work continues.

But for other academics, in increasing numbers, theory has become an over-valued currency, treated as sacred and unquestionable. Theory directs the research itself—as if it could be assumed at the outset to be true. Instead of being a necessary detour, it is the magic key that continuously proves itself. The result exacerbates the already existing gap between the academy and the public on the one hand and the academy and activists/organizers on the other, to the point that, for all practical purposes, communication ceases.

Perhaps in response to a sense of its increasing irrelevance, young academics look for ways to more immediately and directly politicize their work. Politics and political allegiances become the driving force behind research and scholarship. Theory becomes a backhanded way of introducing predefined political concerns and positions or of calling to predefined audiences by serving as a public declaration of your politics. Or political sympathies, sometimes loosely tied to theoretical positions, come to define the criteria for the value and even the acceptability of intellectual work. Is this an academic version of branding? The irony is that such work increasingly moves away from the kind of rigorous knowledge production aimed at strategic social change that preceded it (and made its very existence possible), becoming ever more pessimistic and distant from the practical concerns of activists/organizers.

As much as it saddens me to say this, a significant percentage of what is published is, to put it plainly, crap—certainly not worth reading. I realize that I am speaking with a specific understanding of intellectual work, and others might disagree about what is worth reading and why. Some might accuse me of being nostalgic for a system that silenced many voices. I have no wish to resurrect the past. It was deeply and dangerously flawed. But I believe the measure of intellectual value is whether it adds something useful, something that continues the conversation, that opens new possibilities, that produces the joy of thinking. Scholarly work is not crap because it is too theoretical, or too political, or too contemporary, but because it appears to have been written in a vacuum or, at best, a rather boring conversation among a small group of people who share the same assumptions and habits of thought and have read each other's work but not much more (unless they are going to trash it). Even more disturbing, it appears to be written to justify already formed intuitions and experiences. Theory and methods become little more than retroactive justifications of opinions already held. Confirmation bias is no longer a problem but an acceptable and even necessary practice. Disagreement is merely a question of the lack of shared experiences and, often, of power relations.

Again, let me state this clearly: I do not mean to suggest that the sorts of practices and failures I have described are universal, or even dominant in the academy. There is still a great deal of good, even wonderful research being produced across the entire university. But these practices and failures do seem to me (and many others) to have become increasingly visible and prevalent in some areas as the emerging response to the changing conditions and demands of the university and of the crises of knowledge. Perhaps it is not surprising that as the academy has had to adapt to the tempos and rhythms of business, academics get caught up in the same problems as businesses—from dishonesty, misrepresentation, and exaggeration to the endless proliferation of needless products (articles, reports, and books)—all defined by the demand for profit—both commercial and academic—in increasingly unregulated competitive environments.

I fear that the university is losing its double existence. And maybe here, I am a bit nostalgic, because I do think I have experienced moments of this. The academy has been, at times, a space for both intellectual passion (a calling) and academic careers. But increasingly, the latter is displacing the former. Academic professionals have become timid and risk-averse (not without good reasons, I might add), forgetting that risk is the unavoidable condition of the intellectual life, and that previous generations of intellectuals and scholars have had to take risks as serious as those anyone faces today. But I also think that many scholars living in these conditions are uncomfortable with the choices they feel they have to make.

The university is changing; its future is uncertain. It is even unclear whether it will survive or whether what survives will be recognizable. Personally, I am not sure whether it should survive, but I cannot yet imagine what might replace it. There are many political, economic, and popular constituencies involved, each with their own agendas, responding to their sense of the demands of the conjuncture. Significant numbers of faculty are opposed to the ways higher education is being reconfigured; many of the changes are, from the point of view of scholarship and education, headed in the wrong direction. The question is whether faculty are effectively participating in the processes by which such changes are being determined. Simply opposing changes proposed and imposed can leave them in the position of defending not the status quo (which is already corrupted) but some imagined moment just before the status quo (e.g., defending disciplines and departmental autonomy, faculty governance, etc., despite their serious problems).

Too often, changes are taken for granted. The possibility that they might be openings for other possibilities is foreclosed before the struggles even begin. The current attack on some disciplines and departments is partly a redistribution of labor and a cost-cutting measure; it is also, no doubt, a re-valuation of different kinds of knowledge. But it frequently creates new interdisciplinary programs, which might offer not only short-term opportunities but also new visions for what might become of the university. Sometimes, there is an almost paranoid unwillingness to actually fight for the future and an inability to imagine the university otherwise. (Recall my story of the Program for Public Discourse.) Too often, the response to these challenges is to simply reject them as elitist, privileged, or the servants of power, or to surrender to conceptions of education as job training or skills training for good citizenship.

Quite commonly, faculty (and students) assume they already know what the coming university should look like, with little regard for how it would work institutionally or how we might get there. For example, I am often told that it should be a democracy, empowering both faculty and students, as opposed to the sham of faculty governance. I think it is more complicated. I agree that the university must encourage more democratic conversations and that decisions should be made in a transparent environment in which all voices can be heard. But it is also the case that democracy is not a universal panacea, and that the university—at least as I understand it—has to be a meritocracy, insofar as judgments of value and truth matter. This need not describe a rigid hierarchy, closed to change and challenge, or a simplistic and absolutist understanding of truth. These are the contradictions we face, and they will not be answered by crowd-sourcing or group-think, nor solved by technology or commerce.

What would it mean to fight effectively for new possibilities, new ways of configuring the universities and re-articulating their mission to the demands of the conjunctural moment? How might we make the university a space for intellect and pedagogy for our times? What sorts of knowledge, research, and education are necessary and how might they be actualized institutionally? Might we need new institutions to meet these purposes? Partly, we need to understand the challenges we face as a society and offer better stories of the place of education and research. Whatever nostalgia-tinged recollections of the academy as a space for intellectual life I might have, I do not think we can or should return to what was. We need to jump into what might be. This will require serious thought, convivial dispute, and, as you might have guessed, better stories.

# NOT QUITE A GLOSSARY OF KEY TERMS (AND NOT QUITE A SUMMARY)[1]

**Slow thinking:** a rigorous and self-reflective process of thinking that combines analysis, synthesis, and imagination. There are different ways of doing slow thinking. Only some of them are scientific or academic. They all combine a number of specific practices of thinking and bring them to bear on particular questions, usually in a specific order or relation. My version of slow thinking brings together: Conceptual thinking, critical/theoretical thinking, critique, contextual thinking, conjunctural thinking, problematization or the construction of problem spaces, and conjunctural analysis.

**Concept:** an idea or abstraction that creates or identifies a relation among particulars. It gathers together disparate things to establish a new unity or identity. For example, despite all the peculiarities and differences among them, we have concepts of reading, red, or the left. A concept can become a new particular that gives rise to higher-order concepts, such as literacy, or color, or political position.

**Critical thinking:** a controlled skepticism in which you question your assumptions, i.e., what you take for granted and what you think you know. It requires that you stand outside yourself by, metaphorically, standing in another's shoes. This is commonly referred to as double consciousness. For some, this is not a choice. For some, this is the purpose of theory.

**Critique:** an attempt to identify the processes by which your assumptions and beliefs (including those thought of as knowledge) have been made to seem not merely acceptable and reasonable, but obvious, necessary, and even natural. How did these come to be this way, rather than others? Critique is not the simple act of criticism or rejection. Critique most commonly assumes some version of constructionism.

**Constructionism:** the claim that the world and how we experience, understand, and think about it are constructed. (Not very helpful?) Constructionism assumes that the world is composed of relations rather than independent things. Nothing exists outside of, free of, relations. Relations define what the elements within it are, and what they are capable of doing (i.e., what kinds of effects they can have). And relations always exist in larger sets of relations. Constructionism describes every reality, whether physical, emotional, or cognitive, as the composing of **compositions**, the assembling of **assemblages**, and the constant re-**articulation** of relations.

Now perhaps it makes more sense to say that constructionism asserts that both the world and our accounts of it have been constructed. They did not have to be the way they are. There is a contingency about them. In fact, everything is contingent, everywhere, all the way down. The question is, what conditions made this reality and these accounts possible. But crucially, construction does not deny the reality of the contingently constructed worlds in which we live or the truth of the accounts we believe. On the contrary, such constructions are real. The fact that something is constructed does not make it any less real. While any constructed reality or experienced world could have been otherwise, it is real and not some weird illusion, precisely because it shapes and affects our lives. It has real material effects. The question is, what conditions made this reality real, and these accounts true?

Constructionism shares a strong commitment to **anti-foundationalism** with many other ways of thinking. They all reject the dominant traditions of modern western thought, which assume there must be some universal, necessary, and sufficient ground for all truth and knowledge. For the most part, modern thought has sought this legitimation in either empirical observation or reason. Constructionism does not necessarily end up in **relativism**. Relativism asserts that all constructions are equally valid, at least in particular contexts or from particular perspectives.

**Contextual thinking:** an identification of the focus of thinking and research on a (loosely) specified organization of relations and relations of relations, a composition of compositions. The location of specific relations in a context will determine what kinds of effects it is capable of producing. As that location changes, and it enters into new compositions, its capacities will change.

**Conjuncture:** the identification of a specific kind of context. Most often, a context is identified by either its level of abstraction or its scale. **Scale** measures spatial and temporal differences. For example, a context might be a matter of days or centuries. It might encompass a neighborhood, a city, a country, or the planet. **Levels of abstraction** map a continuum from the concrete to the abstract. This is often mistaken for the simple and the complex, or the empirical and the conceptual. The concrete is always complex and conceptual. It involves abstractions. And the abstract is always also empirical. Levels of abstraction rather define the different ways the empirical and the conceptual are defined and related in a context. For example, Trump's electoral victory, the rise of the reactionary right, and capitalist modernity all demand different approaches to empirical data and conceptual invention, and to the relations between them.

A conjuncture is defined by its scale, usually lasting for decades and usually having well-defined geographical boundaries (most commonly of a nation-state). But it is also defined by its level of abstraction, somewhere between the overwhelming concreteness of an event and the overwhelming abstractness of an epoch. In the example above, it is the level of the rise of the reactionary right. It is a construction based on a wager that this level of abstraction/scale is a useful and effective way to conceive of a context, both intellectually and politically, in terms of the struggles over power and governance.

**Problem space (problematization):** the questions posed to and by a conjuncture. In constructing a conjuncture, you are recomposing an already existing organization of relations. Often, in a sense, the existing organization has to be recomposed because it is, in some sense, in crisis. It faces challenges that it cannot resolve. Even worse, it cannot even understand them. It cannot yet define the questions. Constructing a conjuncture involves re-articulating the problem spaces and specifying the questions. You might think of this as identifying the cracks in the existing organization and problematizing them, i.e., making them into problems. This is where the possibility of telling a better story about the conjuncture begins, and the possibility of moving it in a better direction opens up.

**Habitable landscape:** a livable human reality; an organization of material, social, and psychological relations and institutional and everyday organizations. It produces ways of living and offers people ways of living in them which they find comfortable, meaningful, and valued.

**Culture:** the social realm of **discourse** or **expression**. It is commonly thought of as the realm of language, but it has be expanded to encompass at least all sign-behavior. It is commonly thought to primarily involve the production of meaning, but it has to be expanded to encompass a broader range of effects, including non-cognitive, non-semantic, and non-representational effects. Discourse is best understood as those relations capable of producing effects at a distance. They do not require the material contact of two physical bodies or forces. They are always organized as **formations** or **regimes**. Culture has become an increasingly important site of political struggle since the 1950s (**political culture**).

**Affect:** a crucial type or plane of cultural effects. It is what we normally refer to as feelings. But "feelings" encompasses an enormous variety of qualities and intensities, including emotions, passions, attention, moods, outlooks, sentiments, desires, longings, concerns or what matters, belongings or identifications, states of energy (such as panic and calm), etc.

Affect is one of the glues, the stickiness, that binds relations together. (Stories are the other glue.) Affective regimes hold the habitable landscape together by constituting a sense of unity (and, hence, of sanity). At the very least, they hold back—even tame—the chaos always lurking on the borders of the habitable landscape and the crises threatening to tear it apart. And they stitch individuals and groups into that landscape. Affective regimes define its vitality, its livedness. And consequently, they constitute the ways we are attuned to the world.

**Structures of feeling:** the most important affective regimes. They constitute the distinctive sense of unity and wholeness of a habitable landscape. They define the specificity of what it feels like to live in a particular time and place.

**Quasi-autonomy of affect:** the first problem space I identify. I argue that, starting in the 1950s, the relations between affective regimes and other cultural formations have become increasingly weak. The habitually intimate connection between affects and other cultural effects, especially the meanings and values to which they are almost always attached, has been broken, disarticulated. The affective dimension or plane of the habitable landscape has become increasingly independent or autonomous. The result is that contemporary culture has become almost entirely affective, and the contemporary habitable landscape has become an **affective landscape.**

**Modernity** (or **the modern**): sorry, but it cannot be done. At least, I can't do it. It is, however, the second problem space in my story.

**Organic crisis:** a particular and relatively rare kind of problem space. It defines a unique political struggle. In certain conjunctures, numerous crises that have already spread across large parts of society seem to intersect and strengthen each other. The entire social formation becomes uniquely unstable as a result of this accumulation and condensation of multiple, expanding, and deepening crises and struggles. This situation begins to take on a reality and density of its own, but it has not yet been specified. In fact, the problem cannot yet be defined.

The entire conjuncture becomes a problem space, calling into question a society's understanding and imagination of itself and its sense of identity and purpose. The existing stories cease to work, and new stories have yet to be found. The very terms in which people make sense of their social reality and political possibilities fail. The existing political forces struggle to problematize the crises and to propose new arrangements capable of responding to and stabilizing the social formation. Such arrangements offer new ways of balancing the field of competing forces. This is an organic crisis. It becomes the ground on which politics has to be fought.

I argue that the contemporary postwar American conjuncture, especially its (increasingly affective) political culture, has been shaped by two distinct but overlapping organic crises. Both crises arise out of significantly different attempts to problematize modernity itself, in the face of its presumed failures and crises. The first seeks better ways of being modern; the second seeks ways of being something other than modern. The first accepts the modern project; the second rejects it.

**Affective tendencies:** my idiosyncratic and intentionally impersonal way of telling a different—better?—story about the contemporary conjuncture. Most stories start with two sides. Perhaps that is, to some extent, unavoidable (and I certainly do not avoid it). But no matter how hard such stories try to complicate it, they usually end up with the same two sides, and their stories are all about judgment and blame.

I try to tell a different kind of story, an affective story. Affective tendencies are formal logics that set out the possibilities and limits of political action and struggle. They dictate the norms of political behavior. They define the nature of any acceptable response to the organic crises, operating on the affective landscape. They set up the end-game by circumscribing the formal conditions of any possible balance in the field of forces. Every tendency is manifested or expressed in various political groups and practices across competing political and ideological differences. Affective tendencies don't care about left and right, although they are likely to be taken up very differently. Unfortunately, left and right don't think about affective tendencies very much. They often practice their politics within the same affective tendency.

## Note

1 I wish I could provide easily accessible one-sentence definitions, but they wouldn't help you read this book anyway. And they would contradict the very sort of stories I think we need.

# INDEX

*Note*: Endnotes are indicated by the page number followed by 'n' and the endnote number e.g., 20n1 refers to endnote 1 on page 20.

Abraham 126
Adcock, Preston 8n7
Agnew, Spiro 107
Allen, Steve 24
Arbus, Diane 217

Badu, Erykah 121
Bal Shem Tov (Rabbi Israel ben Eliezer) 217
Blaser, Mario 136
Brecht, Bertolt 29
Breitbart 67, 181
Bretton Woods 106
Brown, Norman O. 25
Buckley, William. Jr. 107–9
Buddha, Gautama 29
Burroughs, William 104
Bush, G. W. 119, 120

Cave, Nick 216
Cervantes, Miguel de 217
Clarke, Arthur C. 104
Clinton, Bill 154
Cohen, Roy 147

Deleuze, Gilles 87n2, 137, 139, 144n5
Descartes, René 49
Dugin, Aleksandr 137, 144n2, 145

El Teatro Campesino 184
Escobar, Arturo 144n1, 145
Evola, Julius 144

Fanon, Frantz 212, 217
Foucault 44n3, 54, 55n6, 87
Fox News 110, 181
Freud, Sigmund 24, 30, 75
Fukuyama, Francis 113, 117

Garvey, Marcus 121
George, Robert 150
Gerstner, Nicholas 133n1
Gilroy, Paul 212, 213n1
Goldwater, Barry 107, 147
Gordimer, Nadine 217
Gore, Al 119
Gramsci, Antonio 87n2, 89, 93n1, 100, 181
Grateful Dead 184
Grossberg, Lawrence 19n2, 19nn5, 29n1, 30, 55, 87n2, 88
Guatttari, Félix 87n2, 137, 139, 144n5
Guénon, René 144

Hall, Stuart 149, 213n1
Hamas 156
Harry Potter 63

Heaney, Seamus 217
Hegel, Georg Wilhem Friedrich 43
Heidegger, Martin 27, 87, 137
Heinlein, Robert 123
Hoffman, Abbie 132, 168, 184
Hoggart, Richard 29n4, 30, 87n2
Humphrey, Hubert 106

Jaffa, Harry 144n9
James, C. L. R. 210
Jesus 19, 218
Johnson, Lyndon 107, 154
Johnson, Robert 217

Kant, Immanuel 42, 52, 54, 144n4
Kennedy, John F. 154
Keynes, John Maynard 77, 114
King, Martin Luther Jr. 217
King, Rodney 105
Kirk, Russell 107, 108

Laing, R. D. 25
Land, Nick 139
Latour, Bruno 50, 51, 55n4
Leary, Timothy 25
Ledbetter, Huddie 121
Limbaugh, Rush 110
Lundberg, Christian 55n3

Marcuse, Herbert 25
Marx, Karl 16, 30, 44n3, 46, 52
Mignolo, Walter 144n8, 145
MiLoFo 217
Modi, Narendra 156
Moldbug, Mencius 139, 145
Morris, Meaghan 133

Nietzsche, Friedrich 31, 43, 87n2, 148
Nixon, Richard 106, 117, 119, 154

Obama, Barack Hussein 80, 120, 121, 154, 182

Picard, Jean-Luc 45
Pope Pius XI 168n3, 174
Powell, Lewis F. Jr. 108, 110, 117n1
Proust, Marcel 40
Putin, Vladimir 137, 144

Ram Das, Baba 25
Reagan, Ronald 108, 111, 112, 154
Reich, Wilhelm 25
Ricoeur, Paul 24, 29n2, 30

Scott, David 70n2, 210, 213
Sedgwick, Eve Kosofsky 87n2
Shakespeare, William 40
Simpson, O. J. 105
Smith, Adam 52
Sousa John Phillip 35
Spector, Phil 23
Spinoza, Baruch 87, 217
Star Trek 46
Strauss, Leo 144n9
Students for a Democratic Society (SDS) 184
Suskind, Ron 44n2

Thompson, C. Bradley 67
Trump 2, 4, 12, 16, 64, 80, 122, 144n3, 146, 163, 164, 166, 168n1
Truth, Sojourner 217

Weber, Max 138
West, Cornel 150
Williams, Raymond 25, 29n3, 29n4, 30, 87n2, 102n1
Wolfe, Tom 27
Wood, Megan 189n1

Yavin. Curtis 139
Youth International Party (Yippie) 148, 164, 168, 184

For Product Safety Concerns and Information please contact our EU
representative  GPSR@taylorandfrancis.com
Taylor & Francis Verlag GmbH, Kaufingerstraße 24, 80331 München, Germany